OREGON'S
ANCIENT FORESTS

OREGON WILD

OREGON'S
ANCIENT FORESTS
A Hiking Guide

Chandra LeGue

MOUNTAINEERS
BOOKS

MOUNTAINEERS BOOKS is dedicated to the exploration, preservation, and enjoyment of outdoor and wilderness areas.

1001 SW Klickitat Way, Suite 201, Seattle, WA 98134
800-553-4453, www.mountaineersbooks.org

Printed in China
Distributed in the United Kingdom by Cordee, www.cordee.co.uk
First edition: first printing 2019, second printing 2019

Copyeditor: Eve Goodman
Design and layout: Kate Basart/Union Pageworks
Cartographer: Erik Fernandez, Oregon Wild
All photographs by the author unless credited otherwise.
Maps are based on data from ESRI, United States Forest Service, Bureau of Land Management, State of Oregon, Oregon Wild, National Park Service, Garmin, and United States Geological Survey.
Cover photographs, front, clockwise from top left: *Western big gym mushroom; Maidenhair fern; Pileated woodpecker* (Photo by Mahogany Aulenbach); *A lush forest of western hemlocks and Douglas-firs greets visitors along the upper McKenzie River Trail* (Photo by Greg Vaughn); back: *A deer explores a ponderosa pine forest near the Metolius River* (Photo by Brizz Meddings)
Frontispiece: *The ancient forest in the Bull of the Woods Wilderness offers peace and solitude for visitors.*

Library of Congress Cataloging-in-Publication Data
Names: LeGue, Chandra, author.
Title: Oregon's ancient forests : a hiking guide / Chandra LeGue.
Description: First edition. | Seattle, Washington : Mountaineers Books, [2019] | "Based on A Walking Guide to Oregon's Ancient Forests by Wendell Wood. Portland, Oregon: Oregon Natural Resources Council, 1991."—T.p. verso. | Includes bibliographical references and index.
Identifiers: LCCN 2018052224 (print) | LCCN 2018055014 (ebook) | ISBN 9781680512021 (e-book) | ISBN 9781680512014 | ISBN 9781680512014 (paperback) | ISBN 9781680512021 (ebook)
Subjects: LCSH: Walking—Oregon—Guidebooks. | Hiking—Oregon—Guidebooks. | Oregon—Guidebooks. | Forest reserves—Oregon. | Old growth forests—Oregon—Guidebooks.
Classification: LCC GV199.42.O74 (ebook) | LCC GV199.42.O74 L44 2019 (print) | DDC 796.510979795—dc23
LC record available at https://lccn.loc.gov/2018052224

Mountaineers Books titles may be purchased for corporate, educational, or other promotional sales, and our authors are available for a wide range of events. For information on special discounts or booking an author, contact our customer service at 800-553-4453 or mbooks@mountaineersbooks.org.

Printed on FSC®-certified materials

ISBN (paperback): 978-1-68051-201-4
ISBN (ebook): 978-1-68051-202-1

An independent nonprofit publisher since 1960

CONTENTS

HIKES AT A GLANCE

HIKE	DISTANCE (ROUNDTRIP)	DIFFICULTY	FOREST TYPE	FEATURES
NORTH COAST				
1. TILLAMOOK HEAD	4 miles	Moderate	Coastal fog zone and redwoods	Giant spruce trees on trail to ridgetop views
2. CAPE FALCON	4.5 miles	Moderate	Coastal fog zone and redwoods	Classic coastal forest and open headland views
3. CAPE LOOKOUT	Cape Trail: 5 miles; North Trail: 1 mile	Moderate	Coastal fog zone and redwoods	Ocean views and towering trees at a prominent landmark
4. MUNSON CREEK FALLS	0.5 mile	Easy	Coastal fog zone and redwoods	Streamside forests in a canyon and a waterfall view
CENTRAL COAST RANGE				
5. DRIFT CREEK WILDERNESS	8 miles	Difficult	Douglas-fir	A descent to Drift Creek through towering forest
6. MARYS PEAK: EAST RIDGE–TIE TRAIL LOOP	5 miles	Difficult	Douglas-fir	A unique noble fir stand on Marys Peak's forested slopes
7. CAPE PERPETUA AND GWYNN CREEK	6.4 miles	Difficult	Coastal fog zone and redwoods, Douglas-fir	Impressive and extensive coastal forest loop
8. PAWN GROVE	0.8 mile	Easy	Douglas-fir	Small ancient grove along a salmon stream
9. KENTUCKY FALLS	4.4 miles	Moderate	Douglas-fir	A descent through the forest to three towering waterfalls
SOUTH COAST AND KALMIOPSIS				
10. COQUILLE RIVER FALLS	1 mile	Easy	Douglas-fir, Siskiyou mixed conifer	Waterfall view in diverse, transition-zone forest
11. HUMBUG MOUNTAIN STATE PARK	5.3 miles	Difficult	Siskiyou mixed conifer	Steep ascent through forest with myrtle and tanoak
12. SHRADER OLD-GROWTH GROVE	1 mile	Easy	Siskiyou mixed conifer	Giant Douglas-fir and Port Orford cedars
13. LOWER ROGUE RIVER	3.4 miles	Easy	Siskiyou mixed conifer	Douglas-fir and hardwoods lining the iconic Rogue River
14. ILLINOIS RIVER TRAIL: BUZZARDS ROOST	6 miles	Moderate	Siskiyou mixed conifer	Recovering burned forest above the stunning Illinois River
15. BABYFOOT LAKE	2.5 miles	Easy	Siskiyou mixed conifer	Trail through burned area leading to stunning lake with diverse trees
16. REDWOOD NATURE TRAIL	1 mile	Easy	Siskiyou mixed conifer, coastal fog zone and redwoods	Redwood forest loop next to the Chetco River
17. OREGON REDWOODS TRAIL	2 miles	Easy	Siskiyou mixed conifer, coastal fog zone and redwoods	Giant redwoods mix with diverse forest

HIKE	DISTANCE (ROUNDTRIP)	DIFFICULTY	FOREST TYPE	FEATURES
SISKIYOU CREST				
18. OREGON CAVES NATIONAL MONUMENT	4 miles	Difficult	Siskiyou mixed conifer	"The Big Tree" highlights this diverse, hilly loop
19. SUCKER CREEK	6 miles	Difficult	Siskiyou mixed conifer	Lovely mixed forest and a climb to a meadow
20. COLLINGS MOUNTAIN	4.2 miles	Difficult	Siskiyou mixed conifer	Steep climb through dry madrone and live oak forest
21. GRIZZLY PEAK	5.3 miles	Moderate	Siskiyou mixed conifer	Ancient conifers, meadows, and a recovering burn with views over Ashland
22. PACIFIC CREST TRAIL: HYATT LAKE	8.5 miles (Hyatt Lake: 1.5 miles; Little Hyatt Lake: 7 miles)	Moderate	Ponderosa pine, Siskiyou mixed conifer	Scattered openings and giant pines along the PCT
23. PACIFIC CREST TRAIL: GREEN SPRINGS SUMMIT TO HOBART BLUFF	7.3 miles	Difficult	Siskiyou mixed conifer	A mix of forest conditions on a climb to a spectacular view
MOUNT HOOD				
24. LOST LAKE	3.2 miles	Easy	Douglas-fir	Classic mountain views along this developed, lakeside trail
25. SALMON RIVER	6.2 miles	Moderate	Douglas-fir	Easily accessible, jaw-dropping, and flat forest trail
26. BARLOW PASS	4.6 miles (Barlow Creek: 2.4 miles; Pacific Crest Trail: 2.6 miles)	Moderate	Alpine and subalpine	High elevation conifer forest on slopes of Mount Hood
27. BOULDER CREEK AND BOULDER LAKE	5 miles (Boulder Creek: 3 miles; Boulder Lake: 2 miles)	Moderate	Douglas-fir	Huge old forest surrounding a mountain lake and pristine creek
28. FIFTEENMILE CREEK	11.3 miles	Difficult	Mixed conifer, ponderosa pine, Oregon white oak	Unique, dry forest on Mount Hood's east side
CLACKAMAS-SANTIAM				
29. CLACKAMAS RIVERSIDE TRAIL	5.2 miles	Moderate	Douglas-fir	Lovely forest trail along a wild and scenic river
30. MEMALOOSE LAKE	3 miles	Moderate	Douglas-fir	Isolated old-growth grove surrounding a newt-filled lake
31. BAGBY HOT SPRINGS	3 miles	Easy	Douglas-fir	Cathedral forest leading to popular hot springs
32. OPAL CREEK	Opal Pool: 7 miles; Cedar Flat: 10 miles	Opal Pool, moderate; Cedar Flat, difficult	Douglas-fir	Iconic ancient forest in Santiam River headwaters
33. SOUTH FORK BREITENBUSH	2.8 miles	Easy	Douglas-fir	Riverside trail near popular Breitenbush Hot Springs
34. CRABTREE VALLEY	4.5 miles	Moderate	Douglas-fir	Oregon's oldest trees in unique, protected valley

HIKE	DISTANCE (ROUNDTRIP)	DIFFICULTY	FOREST TYPE	FEATURES
35. THREE PYRAMIDS	5.6 miles	Difficult	Douglas-fir, alpine and subalpine	Meadows and rocky peaks along this forest trail
36. HOUSE ROCK	1 mile	Easy	Douglas-fir	Lovely loop near the South Santiam River and Santiam Wagon Road
37. ECHO BASIN	2.3 miles	Moderate	Douglas-fir	Spectacular Alaska yellow-cedar grove and a mountain meadow

UPPER WILLAMETTE AND MCKENZIE

HIKE	DISTANCE (ROUNDTRIP)	DIFFICULTY	FOREST TYPE	FEATURES
38. BROWDER RIDGE	3 miles	Moderate	Douglas-fir	Ancient forests lead to meadows and mountain views
39. MCKENZIE RIVER TRAIL: FISH LAKE CREEK TO GREAT SPRING	3 miles	Easy	Douglas-fir	Forest-sheltered headwaters of the McKenzie River
40. MCKENZIE RIVER TRAIL: CARMEN RESERVOIR TO TAMOLITCH FALLS	5.5 miles with car shuttle; 7 miles round-trip	Moderate	Douglas-fir	Quiet trail along sheltered, geologically unique river channel
41. TIDBITS MOUNTAIN	4.5 miles	Moderate	Douglas-fir, alpine and subalpine	Diverse forest bridging mid- and high elevations
42. LOOKOUT CREEK	6.5 miles	Difficult	Douglas-fir	Low-elevation old-growth forest in the H. J. Andrews Experimental Forest
43. DELTA OLD GROWTH NATURE TRAIL	0.6 mile	Easy	Douglas-fir	Easy loop in a floodplain forest
44. SHALE RIDGE	6 miles	Moderate	Douglas-fir	Gorgeous forest culminating in a giant cedar grove
45. GOODMAN CREEK	4 miles	Moderate	Douglas-fir	Big trees in Eugene's popular backyard wilderness
46. PATTERSON MOUNTAIN	5 miles	Moderate	Douglas-fir	Huge trees on the way to a summit viewpoint
47. LARISON CREEK	11.5 miles	Difficult	Douglas-fir	Small stream crossings and towering trees along this lovely and diverse trail
48. BLACK CANYON	8 miles	Difficult	Douglas-fir, alpine and subalpine	Gradual forest type change on climb to edge of Waldo Lake
49. ISLAND LAKES BASIN	10 miles	Difficult	Alpine and subalpine	High-elevation forested loop with small lakes south of Waldo Lake
50. ROSARY LAKES	6 miles	Moderate	Douglas-fir, alpine and subalpine	Pacific Crest Trail hike to lovely lakes basin
51. UPPER MIDDLE FORK WILLAMETTE: INDIGO SPRINGS	4.3 miles	Moderate	Douglas-fir	Forested springs near the Willamette River headwaters
52. BRICE CREEK	4.6 miles one-way with shuttle, or 8.6 miles round-trip	Moderate	Douglas-fir	Old-growth forest along easily accessible creek
53. FAIRVIEW CREEK	3.6 miles	Easy	Douglas-fir	Lovely, out-of-the-way trail along a forested stream

HIKE	DISTANCE (ROUNDTRIP)	DIFFICULTY	FOREST TYPE	FEATURES
UPPER UMPQUA				
54. WOLF CREEK FALLS	2.6 miles	Easy	Douglas-fir	Mix of low-elevation trees on the trail to Wolf Creek Falls
55. TOKATEE AND WATSON FALLS	Tokatee Falls: 0.9 mile; Watson Falls: 1 mile	Easy	Douglas-fir	Two short, popular hikes to waterfalls near the North Umpqua River
56. TWIN LAKES	5.6 miles	Moderate	Douglas-fir	Meadows, lakes, and a view add to this ancient forest
57. YELLOW JACKET GLADE	5.6 miles	Moderate	Douglas-fir	Mid-elevation loop on the ridges around Hemlock Lake
58. CRIPPLE CAMP	5.8 miles	Moderate	Douglas-fir, alpine and subalpine	Huge trees line a series of mountain meadows
59. UPPER COW CREEK	5 miles	Moderate	Douglas-fir	Little-visited, diverse, streamside forest trail
SOUTH CASCADES				
60. UPPER ROGUE RIVER TRAIL: TAKELMA AND ROGUE GORGES	Takelma Gorge: 4–5 miles; Rogue Gorge: 2.5 miles	Easy	Douglas-fir	Dramatic river gorge lined with old trees, accessed in two places
61. UNION CREEK	8.2 miles	Difficult	Douglas-fir	Ancient forest trail follows a meandering creek
62. SOUTH FORK ROGUE RIVER	4 miles	Easy	Mixed conifer	Pines mix with firs and spruce on this riverside hike
63. CHERRY CREEK	13 miles	Difficult	Mixed conifer, alpine and subalpine	Giant Shasta red fir and a mixed forest lead into the Sky Lakes Wilderness
64. BROWN MOUNTAIN	7.9 miles one-way with shuttle, or 9 miles roundtrip	Difficult	Mixed conifer	Incredibly diverse species along this trail skirting Brown Mountain
CENTRAL OREGON				
65. METOLIUS RIVER	5.5 miles	Moderate	Ponderosa pine	Springs and giant pines line this wild and scenic river
66. BENHAM FALLS	1.4 miles	Easy	Ponderosa pine	Big pines along a popular riverside trail near Bend
67. CULTUS RIVER AND BENCHMARK BUTTE	1.5 miles	Moderate	Lodgepole pine	A short hike to a headwater spring at the base of a pine-covered butte
68. MILL CREEK WILDERNESS	11.5 miles	Difficult	Ponderosa pine	Moist and dry forests line creek and lead to unique rock formations
69. LOOKOUT MOUNTAIN	7 miles	Difficult	Ponderosa pine, western juniper	Diverse forest trail through the heart of the wild Ochoco Mountains
KLAMATH-LAKEVIEW				
70. BLUE JAY SPRING	2 miles	Easy	Ponderosa pine	Small remnant of ancient pines in a research natural area
71. GEARHART MOUNTAIN WILDERNESS	9.5 miles	Difficult	Mixed conifer, ponderosa pine	Scattered ancient forest among rocky spires
72. AUGUR CREEK	2 miles	Easy	Ponderosa pine, quaking aspen, lodgepole pine	Wet meadows and forests along a meandering creek
73. COTTONWOOD MEADOW LAKE	3.5 miles	Easy	Mixed conifer, quaking aspen	Aspen, pine, and firs around a lovely mountain lake

HIKE	DISTANCE (ROUNDTRIP)	DIFFICULTY	FOREST TYPE	FEATURES
NORTHERN BLUE MOUNTAINS				
74. NORTH FORK WALLA WALLA RIVER	4.4 miles	Difficult	Mixed conifer	Moist conifer forest on the descent into a wild watershed
75. SOUTH FORK WALLA WALLA RIVER	9 miles	Moderate	Mixed conifer	A wild river trail through a mix of forest types
76. NORTH FORK UMATILLA	5.8 miles	Moderate	Mixed conifer, ponderosa pine	Diverse forests along a wilderness river canyon
77. BUCK CREEK	3 miles	Easy	Mixed conifer, ponderosa pine	Cottonwoods, pines, and yews highlight this streamside hike
78. DUTCH FLAT CREEK	5.8 miles	Moderate	Mixed conifer, ponderosa pine	Gateway hike into the Elkhorn Mountains' extensive forests
79. SOUTH FORK DESOLATION CREEK	5.4 miles	Moderate	Mixed conifer	Lodgepole pine, spruce, and larch in this unique old forest
BLUE MOUNTAINS				
80. MAGONE LAKE	3 miles (Magone Slide Trail: 1.3 miles; Magone Lake: 1.7 miles)	Easy	Mixed conifer, ponderosa pine	Easy loop around a popular lake lined with ancient pines
81. SWICK OLD GROWTH GROVE	0.7 mile	Easy	Ponderosa pine	Accessible place to experience huge pines
82. STRAWBERRY LAKE	4 miles	Moderate	Mixed conifer	A high-elevation study in diverse ancient forests
83. SHEEP CREEK	3 miles	Easy	Mixed conifer	Moist conifer forest along a neglected trail
84. NORTH FORK MALHEUR RIVER	6 miles	Moderate	Ponderosa pine	Wild and scenic river trail to Crane Creek
85. MALHEUR RIVER CANYON	4.5 miles	Moderate	Mixed conifer	Deep, forested, and wild river canyon trail
86. MYRTLE CREEK	5 miles	Moderate	Ponderosa pine	Spectacular forests, streams, and meadows
WALLOWAS				
87. HELLS CANYON NATIONAL RECREATION AREA: CORRAL CREEK	3.3 miles	Moderate	Mixed conifer, ponderosa pine	Forested corridor in the heart of Hells Canyon country
88. COUGAR RIDGE	4.3 miles	Moderate	Mixed conifer, ponderosa pine	Ridgetop hike above Trout Creek's canyon among giant pines
89. NORTH FORK CATHERINE CREEK	8.6 miles	Difficult	Mixed conifer	Beautiful meadows and forest line this entryway to the Eagle Cap Wilderness
90. IMNAHA RIVER	5 miles	Moderate	Ponderosa pine	Ancient and recovering burned forest on the way to Blue Hole
91. EAGLE CREEK	4 miles	Easy	Ponderosa pine	Boulders, pines, and wildflowers along a wild and scenic stream

FOREWORD

In 2007 I was in my first months on staff at Oregon Wild when I went with my colleague Chandra LeGue and Oregon conservation legend Andy Kerr to see Crabtree Valley—a place that the George W. Bush administration was proposing to designate for logging. Nearly lost in the maze of logging roads crisscrossing western Oregon's Bureau of Land Management forests, we pulled out a little blue book that purported to show us the way to our destination: *A Walking Guide to Oregon's Ancient Forests* by Wendell Wood.

I have to admit to feeling no small tinge of envy when Chandra told me, in 2017, of her plan to walk in Wendell's footsteps to write a new version of the guide nearly three decades from its first publication in 1991.

A veteran of forest protection efforts in Oregon, Chandra had earned the time away from her day job to take on the daunting task of finding the best old-growth forest hikes in the state. While she was out exploring, she left the rest of the Oregon Wild staff to soak in the glory that comes from tackling the tasks of a forest advocate:

Ancient Douglas-fir trees and a variety of forest understory plants line the Brice Creek Trail (Hike 52) in the Umpqua National Forest.

sifting through National Environmental Policy Act documents, enduring long meetings while attempting to decode an alphabet soup of government acronyms, trying to convince Congress to listen to science over politics, and occasionally lifting a celebratory beer with colleagues before heading back into the fray to continue the fight for our forests.

Let's face it—we'd all rather be hiking!

Of course, though sometimes tedious and without immediate reward, the work of Oregon Wild to protect our last ancient forests is as essential as it has ever been. Small actions over time add up to a significant legacy to pass on to future generations. Through the years we have helped advance protection for millions of acres of old-growth habitat through wilderness legislation and the Roadless Rule, support for policies that protect and restore forests and watersheds, and campaigns to secure permanent protection of mature and old-growth forests in the Northwest through federal legislation. We have worked with federal agencies to make the shift to forest restoration, using advances in science and a deeper understanding of ecosystems to drive policy.

Just after the original *Ancient Forests* guide was published, the landmark Northwest Forest Plan was enacted, stemming the tide of old-growth clear-cutting in Oregon. Much has changed in Oregon since then. The state's population has ballooned by over one million people, many of whom are drawn here by the outdoor beauty. But new and old residents alike and visitors of all ages may have little understanding of the sometimes precarious protections that exist for the wild places they have come to love. There is a hunger for outdoor recreation information and a need to accompany those resources with a conservation ethic. I am so happy that Chandra took on the task to fill this void.

In the forest ten years ago, Chandra, Andy, and I puzzled over the impossibly complex directions outlined in Wendell's book. But after a dozen turns, two doublebacks, and a harrowing twenty seconds along a steep ravine, the sixteen-year-old directions saved the day.

I will never forget that day in Crabtree Valley. There I saw some of the largest, most awe-inspiring trees of my life. Knowing the power that Oregon's ancient forests have to evoke wonder in those who visit, I have no doubt this book will leave you with memories you will cherish forever.

Sean Stevens
Executive Director
Oregon Wild

OPPOSITE: Wendell Wood's *A Walking Guide to Oregon's Ancient Forests*

INTRODUCTION

Hiking with Wendell Wood was not for those looking for exercise. It involved a lot of stooping every few hundred feet to look at plants and mushrooms, and it often involved silly photographs of people adorned with lichens or pine cones. Wendell was a one-of-a-kind naturalist, environmental advocate, and fun-loving nature nerd.

Though I had the privilege of hiking with Wendell many times, his *Walking Guide to Oregon's Ancient Forests*, published twelve years prior to my start at Oregon Wild in 2003, was my go-to companion when I didn't have him along to overwhelm me with information (in the best way possible) about the plants, animals, and history of an area. The guide led me to spectacular old-growth forest groves in places like McGowan Creek near my Eugene home and to sections of the Upper Middle Fork, Upper Rogue, and McKenzie River Trails that I might not otherwise have been turned on to.

Wendell's book was far more than a hiking guide, however.

When he published it in 1991, a lot was at stake. This was during the height of the "timber wars" when advocates like Wendell and organizations like Oregon Natural Resources Council (ONRC, now Oregon Wild) were using all the tools they had to fend off the rampant clear-cutting of our remaining ancient forests and to protect iconic places like Larch Mountain and Opal Creek. Factions in Congress were alternately promising to save the ancient forests

and threatening to log more of them. Temporary court injunctions had halted the massive ancient forest liquidation, but those could be lifted and the chainsaws could come roaring back at any time. Emotions ran high in the original book. Those who read it got an earful about what was wrong with forest management, and Wendell's narrative captured the frustration of many forest advocates working at the time.

When I came on the scene, a lot about forest management had changed for the better, thanks to the work of Oregon Wild and others. Forest policies and laws implemented since 1991 have partially protected many of our remaining ancient forests that were under threat back then, and the animosity between federal agencies and conservationists has given way, at times, to cooperation around restoration instead of conflict over old-growth and ancient forest logging.

Unfortunately, a surprising amount has not changed about the threats to these forests. Federal administrations more concerned with the interests of Big Timber than those of endangered species, clean water, and climate change still seek ways to erode forest protections. Powerful interests continue to spread false information about "sustainable" forestry, the causes of wildfire, and the "need" to log our public lands. Forest advocates cannot rest on the work that has been done to protect our ancient forests. With so few of them left, every acre we protect—and the vast amounts that need to be restored—is

Forest crusader Wendell Wood at the base of one of the redwood trees he worked to protect. *(Photo by Brett Cole, www.vikasproject.org)*

the modern era but still achieving, I hope, the goal of the original.

I know why I love forests, but love is difficult to explain in the abstract. If I can encourage people to visit just a few of the places featured here, the forests will speak for themselves. They will explain, without words, what is at stake, why it is so critical that they be allowed the opportunity to persist. You may never have had the experience of a walk with Wendell, but I hope this book piques your interest, fosters your curiosity, and plants the seeds of advocacy that these forests still need—and that would make Wendell proud.

This book offers context and basic information about Oregon's remaining ancient forests. It looks at the pieces of a forest that make it whole and how forests differ across the state. It helps you visit the remaining ancient forests in Oregon so that you can experience the peace, the shades of green, the moist forest floor, and the awe of being dwarfed by a giant that these forests offer. Most importantly, it aims to inspire you to take action—to help preserve these places before they disappear entirely and to help shape a future where we are all richer for having done so.

vital for wildlife, clean and plentiful water, the climate, and Oregon's future economy. And to become effective advocates for these ancient forests, people need to experience them directly. That is where this book comes in.

Wendell didn't get around to updating his ancient forest guide before he passed away, too soon, in 2015. Appreciating the book as I did and still seeing its need, I decided to give it a try. This update turned into a major overhaul, bringing the photography and pre-GPS technology into

PART 1

UNDERSTANDING OREGON'S ANCIENT FORESTS

OREGON'S ANCIENT FORESTS: FOR RICHER, FOR POORER

From a small lake on the western slope of the Cascades, where some friends and I had set up our tents beneath towering western hemlocks and redcedars the night before, we set off through the dense forest following the stream flowing from the lake. There was no trail. We were deep in the wild and in rugged country where trail building and maintenance were not prudent endeavors, and the shrubs—evergreen huckleberry, Oregon grape, devil's club—formed green walls, making forward progress difficult. Climbing up on fallen logs three to five feet thick, we followed an elevated highway, our path a giant array of pickup sticks.

Whenever we needed a short break from the strenuous route, we gazed upward in awe at the towering trees surrounding us. The world was draped in countless shades of green, stacked in lacy layers. Everything smelled fresh and dirty and old at the same time. Small openings in the forest stood out, washed in sunshine. Birds and squirrels flittered in the underbrush, heard but not seen. We continued for hours—taking it all in. We stopped for lunch—damp, warm, scratched up, but reveling in the beauty and loving every second of the experience—in a grove of some of the fattest, tallest trees I'd ever seen. It was the epitome of peace, of joy, of camaraderie with nature and each other. While my friends perched on logs to enjoy their sandwiches, I wandered away for a vantage point—looking to capture the moment with my camera. Using the thick bark

BELOW: An old timber sale marker on an old-growth tree, from a time before some of these forests were protected.

OPPOSITE: The ancient forests of Opal Creek were finally protected in 1996. *(Photo by Gary Miller)*

of a giant tree, I pulled myself up onto a down log. Leaning on the giant and steadying myself for the photo, my hand hit paper. I looked. My heart dropped. It was a marker for a timber sale.

Picture half of Oregon's landscape, or thirty million acres, covered by dynamic, diverse forests. Now reduce that landscape by 80 percent and chop it up into pieces with roads and clear-cuts. Remove all those giant trees and grind up the shrubs and soil with machines. The result is that it is a lot harder to find a place to hike for hours through a dripping rainforest. If you're a young owl, it is harder to safely disperse to a new territory and find food. If you're a salmon, it's harder to find cool, clean water filtered by forest soils and shelter under down logs.

This immense loss is not an exaggeration. The ancient forests that developed naturally for millennia without major human interference and that once blanketed Oregon (and the greater Pacific Northwest) are nearly gone. Most have been logged, victims of the clear-cutting epidemic that ravaged the region over the past century, clearing one square mile of ancient forest per week at its height. (For the record, some have also been burned in wildfires or killed by other means, but we'll get to that.) Those that remain, mostly on federal public land, provide us with some of our cleanest sources of drinking water, the best habitat for fish and wildlife, the most spectacular recreational opportunities Oregon is known for, and the richest stores of carbon on the planet.

Much of what remains is still at risk. From the Sitka spruce rainforest along the coast, through the diverse mixed conifer forests of southwest Oregon and the wide-ranging Douglas-fir forests west of the Cascades, to the arid ponderosa pine and mixed conifer forest east of the Cascades, piteously little of Oregon's remaining ancient forest is fully protected from logging and other development.

THE HUMAN HISTORY OF OUR ANCIENT FORESTS

Before Euro-American settlers came to Oregon, forests had persisted—growing old, burning, developing anew—for thousands of years. Indigenous peoples used and, to some extent, managed forests and their bounty, utilizing trees for lodging and transportation, plants for food and medicine, and wildlife for food. When the settlers moved into Oregon, they pushed aside Native people, diminishing their influence on the forests and triggering human-induced changes to the landscape on a scale not seen before, fundamentally altering ecosystem functions.

At first, settlers saw ancient forests as more of a hindrance than a resource. Throughout the mid- and late nineteenth century, they cleared forests to make way for homesteads and farming. Forests at this time were viewed as limitless, and the tools and technology to clear large areas didn't exist. In the early part of the twentieth century, however, Oregon's forests got their first look at railroads, steam engines, and chainsaws, which opened the way to commercial timber harvest.

It wasn't until after World War II, when the demand for housing and lumber skyrocketed, that the liquidation of Oregon's forests really accelerated. Thousands of miles of roads were built to access forests; large wood was cleared out of streams to facilitate log transport and, in a misguided effort, to "help" salmon; and clear-cutting large swaths of forest became the norm. Privately owned lands were some of the first to go, but from the 1950s through the 1980s clear-cut logging on our national forestlands went from small-scale and haphazard to widespread and systematic as well. The European concept of sustained yield forestry meant sustaining only wood and ignored water, salmon, wildlife, and other things forests provide. This philosophy of forest management meant that every acre of forest needed to be converted from a natural ecosystem into a tree farm in order to be considered productive.

The unsustainable pace and scale of clear-cut logging, like other types of resource extraction, perpetuated boom and bust economic cycles in many rural communities in Oregon as forests were cleared and companies moved on. Industrial logging also wreaked havoc on populations of fish and wildlife and shrank Oregon's wildlands and functional ecosystems. By the 1960s and 1970s, in the face of new awareness of the damage of logging and concern that forests might never grow back, new laws for state and private lands in Oregon provided minimal stream protection, replanting requirements, and limits to the size of

This old stump was cut long ago, and young hemlock trees are now taking the ancient tree's place.

clear-cuts. Unfortunately, these state regulations were woefully inadequate. On federal lands, new laws required planning and analysis of environmental impacts and protection of endangered species habitat.

Meanwhile, it became clear that fish and wildlife species that relied on the ancient forest ecosystem, including the Pacific Northwest's iconic salmon, were in trouble. After decades of clear-cutting of ancient forests drove the northern spotted owl, marbled murrelet, Pacific salmon, and other species to the brink of extinction, conservationists filed lawsuits to force federal agencies to halt the logging of forest habitat and to follow existing federal laws that should have protected these wildlife populations. The timber wars in western Oregon reached a fever pitch in the late 1980s and early 1990s when these species were finally listed under the Endangered Species Act.

East of the Cascades, where spotted owls seldom ranged and the national media spotlight did not shine, a handful of dedicated activists were also working to protect the iconic and imperiled ponderosa pine old-growth forests. The logging frenzy in these forests took a similar trajectory as in western Oregon but with different forest types and different species. While clear-cutting was widespread in moister forests, high grading—removing the biggest trees from the stand—was the norm in dry pine and mixed conifer forests. In combination with aggressive fire suppression and livestock grazing, this led to dramatic changes in the structure of these forests, a severe loss of old-growth trees, and serious degradation of streams. Policy changes to address this damage in central and eastern Oregon came in 1993 in the form of the Eastside Screens—restrictions on cutting trees over twenty-one inches in diameter—and the addition of some stream protections.

THE NORTHWEST FOREST PLAN

Forest management in the Pacific Northwest took a major turn in 1994 with the development of the Northwest Forest Plan (NWFP). The federal listing of endangered species that relied on ancient forest habitat led to a furious debate over how much critical old-growth habitat to set aside for these species. Scientists tasked with developing a plan to ensure long-term persistence of native wildlife began asking a deeper question: How much of the ancient forest do we need to grow back? From these questions, the NWFP was born.

The plan, a political compromise for an ecological problem, is essentially a zoning scheme for the public forestlands that are home to marbled murrelets and northern spotted owls in western Washington and Oregon and northwestern California. It designates areas of streamside reserves to protect and restore vegetation and structure that benefit salmon, other wildlife, and water quality; areas of old-growth forest reserves that include some existing ancient forests as well as young, managed forests to be restored to functioning habitat; and matrix lands that can be logged more heavily but not indiscriminately.

While the plan was an improvement over the logging of the previous century, scientists and ancient forest advocates find it to be flawed in many ways. It does not fully protect ancient forests, leaving one million acres of these remaining forests available for logging. It also fails to adequately protect roadless areas, drinking watersheds, and complex young forests that are recovering from fire; allows logging and road building in ecologically important areas; and is too dependent on underfunded, but necessary, restoration and monitoring efforts.

The NWFP has succeeded in other ways, however. It has led to restoration of forest and

Moss and oxalis, or wood sorrel, cover the base of a tree trunk along an ancient forest trail.

stream-based habitat and structure, shifted the forests in overlogged regions from carbon source to carbon sink, and built trust among the public who now widely approve of science-based restoration practices such as thinning young stands that were planted too densely after past clear-cutting.

Unfortunately, there have been many bumps along the way in implementation and attacks on the NWFP's environmental safeguards for fish, wildlife, streams, and ancient forests. Just after the plan was enacted, Congress pushed through a whole slew of old-growth forest timber sales exempted from the plan's protections and public process. A decade in, the US Forest Service and Bureau of Land Management (BLM) were found to be in violation of the plan's requirements to survey for and protect rare species that may be in the path of logging, which led to a large and disruptive court injunction until this was resolved. And rather than focus on logging in second-growth plantations to meet timber harvest goals, a push from the timber industry for increased logging of older forests, especially on BLM lands, has led to new management plans for the BLM, enacted in 2016, that replace the NWFP's strict guidelines for stream protection and its focus on restoration in favor of increased logging.

The scientists who drafted the Northwest Forest Plan recognized that fulfilling its goals would take up to two hundred years. Now, at just the quarter-century mark, the Forest Service is also seeking to revise its management plans. The agency has an opportunity to use new science about climate change, stream function, and wildlife habitat requirements as well as the changing values of the public to strengthen the NWFP—protecting all the remaining ancient forests and placing more focus on recreation, water quality, and carbon sequestration—but such an outcome will require the public's involvement and insistence on this direction.

SUSTAINABLE FORESTRY IN THE TWENTY-FIRST CENTURY?

As the dust settled and the clear-cutting frenzy subsided thanks to new laws and policies, the damage was evident. Viewed from the air, both eastern and western Oregon show the painful legacy of a century of intensive logging with a patchwork of clear-cuts and a spiderweb of logging roads. Our surviving ancient forests are often in small patches located in areas deemed too steep and inaccessible to log, some areas

deemed special or set aside for research, and places that the logging epidemic just hadn't reached yet.

There is no denying that the excesses of the timber industry in the twentieth century decimated Oregon's ancient forests. Though the exact acreage today is difficult to pinpoint because of differences in definitions, inadequate inventories, and the dynamic nature of forests, we do know that only between 10 and 25 percent of the ancient forests that once blanketed the state remain. In 2004 Andy Kerr wrote: "There is general scientific consensus that—historically, across the landscape and over time—as much as 80 percent of western Oregon forests were over 80 years old, and about two-thirds were older than 200 years, or 'old growth.' The age of tree and percentage of old growth varied, but

Clear-cuts and logging roads scar the forested landscape, fragmenting wildlife habitat and damaging soil and water quality.

that was the average. Researchers estimate that today, only 13–18 percent of the forested area of western Oregon is old growth, a reduction of over 75 percent. In eastern Oregon, the amount of old growth that existed before Euro-American invasion averaged about 90 percent for the lower elevation ponderosa pine forests, while today it is approximately 20 percent."

In the world of 1990, Wendell Wood wrote in his original ancient forest guide, "The mainstay of the northwest wood products industry has been old growth, but this will soon no longer be true." He was right, but like any addiction, this one has been hard to give up.

At its peak, the wood products sector of Oregon's economy provided 15 percent of the state's gross domestic product. Beginning in the 1970s and 1980s, changes in technology, timber mill automation, and then a recession led to a steep decline in jobs, though not in production. In the 1990s changes in federal public lands policy to protect threatened wildlife and curb overharvest led to another decline. Today, with continued advances in timber production efficiency and a shift away from older forest logging on federal public lands, most of Oregon's wood product mills use equipment and technology that process smaller-diameter trees, from thinning of plantations on federal public lands or from clear-cut plantations on private lands. And with the growth of other sectors, the timber industry is no longer a major driver of Oregon's economy.

Yet despite the drastic reduction of older forests on federal lands, modern science calling for the protection of what is left, public outcry over unsustainable management, and a shift toward restoration on federal lands since the 1990s, timber industry representatives have continued to push for logging of natural and ancient forests and in burned landscapes on public lands. As the BLM and the US Forest Service revise forest management plans and policies, they advocate for more aggressive logging methods and look for loopholes to degrade wildlife habitat. They use public fear of fire to push for more logging, such as removing fire-resistant large trees or reducing fuel in moist forests, even where this approach is not scientifically supported. And they disguise research and scientific findings unfavorable to the industry to create propaganda supporting their unsustainable practices.

At the same time, there is a need and growing call for reforms to unsustainable practices on private and state forestlands managed for timber. Marketed as sustainable forestry, modern practices are far from environmentally or socially responsible. Aerial spraying of herbicides over thousands of acres of clear-cuts and tree plantations each year inevitably impacts water and downstream residents and ecosystems. Short-rotation tree farming also continues to threaten at-risk species and dwindling pollinators, spreads invasive weeds, and emits carbon pollution into the atmosphere. Scientists have long called for stronger rules to protect streams and steep slopes and to reduce impacts from logging roads, but the Oregon Board of Forestry has been stacked with timber interests and has failed to act. Taxes on timber companies that might help repair or mitigate these damages are remarkably low, while incentives to keep logs and jobs local are lacking.

Oregon forests will most likely continue to be a source of wood products, but their production should reflect true sustainability, modern science, public values, and a changed economy. With millions of acres of previously clear-cut tree plantations across Oregon, there is no reason for wood products to come from the last remaining untouched and ancient forests.

FEDERAL LAW AND POLICY: TOOLS FOR PROTECTING ANCIENT FORESTS

The awakening of the American public to the plight of our collective home—"the environment"—in the 1960s and 1970s led to national and state efforts to reduce pollution, limit unchecked development, and in some cases try to reverse the damage we had wrought. The result included such laws as the Clean Air Act (1963), Wilderness Act (1964), Wild and Scenic Rivers Act (1968), National Environmental Policy Act (1970), Clean Water Act (1972), Endangered Species Act (1973), and the National Forest Management Act (1976), which have undoubtedly led to cleaner air and water, the recovery of some species, and protection of wildlands for future generations. But many environmental laws developed at that time weren't necessarily intended nor initially used to protect forests. As citizens, scientists, and conservationists became increasingly alarmed by the rate of logging in the Pacific Northwest, these laws began to be used as tools for those seeking protections for the rapidly disappearing ancient forests.

The Wilderness Act enables Congress to designate large areas of the most intact public lands for this highest level of protection. Initially the Wilderness Act was used to protect large high-elevation areas on Mount Hood, Mount Jefferson, and the Three Sisters. These efforts didn't meet great opposition from the logging industry because the areas are dominated by mountains above timberline and forests with little valuable timber. But as the impacts of clear-cutting Oregon's ancient forests became more obvious, activists pushed to protect forested areas as wilderness. Conservationists sought to include more ancient forests within wilderness boundaries, timber interests worked to cut them out, and politicians (many of whom were beholden to the timber industry) struggled to strike compromises. The result has been far too few protected forests but far more than there would have been without the persistence and vision of conservationists. Nearly two million acres of forests, including many ancient forests in places like Drift Creek, Cummins Creek, Opal Creek, Middle Santiam, the French Pete addition to the Three Sisters, Boulder Creek, parts of the Ochoco Mountains, and the North Fork Umatilla, are all designated as wilderness today.

Conservationists have used the National Environmental Policy Act (NEPA) to ensure environmental analyses consider the impacts logging has on ancient forests and endangered species. NEPA does not preclude federal agencies from harming the environment; rather it requires that the government be honest with itself and the public by disclosing environmental consequences, considering less harmful alternatives, and taking comment from the public before making decisions that might do so. Conservationists have successfully used NEPA and a few other management laws to stop timber sales in ancient forests.

The Endangered Species Act requires that federal agencies work to maintain or recover the population of species at risk of extinction. Conservationists have successfully applied this law to protect several species that depend on ancient forest habitat and to ensure that enough habitat is protected or prioritized for restoration so that they can survive and recover. These species in steep decline from extensive logging have become poster children (or, more accurately, poster owlets and fry) for the movement to protect ancient

OPPOSITE: Protected forests and mountain landscapes in the Three Sisters Wilderness *(Photo by Brizz Meddings)*

forest habitat—as well as for those still seeking to destroy it.

Administrative policies, rather than congressional statutes, have also been used to protect ancient forests. A classic example is the Northwest Forest Plan, but others include the Eastside Screens of 1993 and the Roadless Area Conservation Rule (or just Roadless Rule) enacted in 2001.

The Roadless Rule was the culmination of efforts to identify and protect millions of acres of undeveloped, unlogged, and unroaded areas in national forests across the country. These last large swaths of intact forest are ecologically important, and conservationists fought to stop ongoing logging and road building that was fragmenting them. These efforts met with staunch resistance from the timber industry, led to a political battle throughout the George W. Bush administration, and were finally settled in court where forest advocates won in 2012. The Roadless Rule is merely a regulation that can be changed by future administrations, however, and reevaluated at any time, potentially opening up the nearly two million acres of Oregon's inventoried unroaded forests to logging. And, unfortunately, the roadless inventory didn't include all roadless lands. Oregon Wild estimates that nearly three million acres of sizable, wild, roadless forests were left out of the Roadless Rule.

While federal law and policy guidance have been useful in protecting ancient forests, at times federal agencies have forged ahead with logging

and other development plans that would harm wildlife, water, and forest ecosystems. In these cases, forest advocates have filed suit against the government in order to hold federal agencies accountable to the laws and policies that should protect these vital forests. The federal court system has been used to challenge large-scale management plans like the BLM's plan revision in the 2000s; agency actions that fail to meet legal requirements for protecting wildlife populations; and many individual timber sales across the state.

EXTREME MEASURES: A PLACE FOR ACTIVISM IN THE TOOLBOX

In addition to making use of federal laws and policies to protect ancient forests, another important approach has been more direct advocacy and activism. When administrative options, courts, and other means fail or are not available to protect ancient forests, passionate people tend to look for other ways to do so. Many of the remaining ancient forests in Oregon featured in this book would not be standing today without the persistent efforts of activists and advocacy organizations working to raise public awareness of, and sometimes physically stop, planned logging of ancient forests. Rallying support for forest protection through media attention and appealing to state and federal lawmakers has yielded results in many cases. In others, activists utilized tactics of direct action and nonviolent resistance, where they put their lives on the line—sitting in trees or standing in front of bulldozers—to halt logging of ancient forest groves. Places in the Willamette and Mount Hood National Forests like Fall Creek, the Warner Creek fire area, and forests on the slopes of Mount June, Opal Creek, Eagle Creek, and Larch Mountain would have been logged if not for the efforts of activists using these tools.

WHERE ARE THE ANCIENT FORESTS?

Though there are so few ancient forests left and they are important for so much, there is strangely no map showing where they all are. We do know, however, quite a lot about where they can likely be found. Most of Oregon's remaining ancient forests are found on public lands managed by federal agencies. Ancient forests can also be found in state parks, although other state-owned forestlands are largely managed for timber production.

FEDERAL PUBLIC LANDS

Our modern federal public land system came largely from the efforts of politicians (and a few conservationists) in the early 1900s who designated as "public-domain" lands that had been acquired during westward expansion and the displacement of indigenous people. The purpose was to provide for "multiple use" of all sorts of natural resources including water, fish and wildlife populations, minerals, and timber. About 60 percent, or nearly 18 million acres, of Oregon's forests are on federal public lands.

Where and how many ancient forests remain on federal public lands are largely dictated by the laws and policies that govern these lands. Lands managed by the Forest Service and BLM are subject to federal policy and planning laws that require management plans, environmental analysis, protection of endangered species habitat, and public input. These plans and analyses often have provisions for protecting old forests for their important ecological values. Other federal laws and designations put lines on maps to protect wild places and ancient forests. For example, wilderness areas, designated by Congress under the authority of the 1964 Wilderness Act, are permanently protected from roads, logging, and

Large ponderosa pines were targeted for logging in central and eastern Oregon, but some giants can still be found. This one is on Lookout Mountain in the Ochoco National Forest. *(Photo by Jim Davis)*

other development. Of Oregon's 2.5 million acres of wilderness, about 84 percent is ancient forest.

Wild and scenic rivers, designated by Congress under the authority of the 1968 Wild and Scenic Rivers Act, include a corridor along free-flowing rivers and streams with special natural values, which are protected from most development and logging. Oregon has more designated wild and scenic rivers than any other state, with over 2100 stream miles (though this is less than 1 percent of Oregon's streams). They can flow through multiple land ownerships, but are primarily found on federal public lands. In many places, the protected corridor is a quarter mile on each side of the river, comprising over a half million acres of land in Oregon, much of it forested.

NATIONAL FORESTS: The ten national forests in Oregon are managed by the US Forest Service, which is part of the Department of Agriculture. They cover about sixteen million acres or about 25 percent of the state. National forests are governed by management plans (somewhat like zoning regulations) developed under federal law to meet their mandates for multiple use, clean water, and endangered species conservation. Actions on these lands require environmental analysis and public input.

Most of Oregon's remaining ancient forests are found in our national forests, primarily in designated wilderness, in the nearly two million acres of inventoried and protected roadless areas, and in additional unprotected roadless areas (blocks of undeveloped forest areas over one thousand acres in size, but not protected under the Roadless Rule). Other areas with official designations like research natural area (RNA) and designated old-growth grove also contain, and largely protect, ancient forests.

In western Oregon, the Northwest Forest Plan ensures that ancient forests that provide habitat for northern spotted owls, marbled murrelets, and native salmon runs are somewhat protected, but federal land managers are always funding new excuses to log our ancient forests—from building new roads to "reducing fuels."

In central and eastern Oregon, in recognition of the general scarcity of large trees across the landscape after decades of high-grade logging, policies are in place on national forests that generally protect trees over twenty-one inches in diameter at breast height (four to four and a half feet above the ground). This size indicates that a tree has been alive since before fire suppression began to dramatically change the forest's structure.

BUREAU OF LAND MANAGEMENT LANDS: The BLM, in the US Department of the Interior, has eight different districts in Oregon. Best known for managing arid lands across the western United States, often for grazing, mining, and energy development, the BLM manages 15.7 million acres in Oregon, much of it high desert in the eastern part of the state.

Only 16 percent of the lands managed by the BLM in Oregon are forested, but of those 3.6 million acres, 2.6 million are in western Oregon. Management of these fast-growing, largely low-elevation forests has been especially controversial, and these forests remain some of the most threatened to this day. This is largely due to conflict over interpretations of the 1937 O&C Act (relating to lands granted to the Oregon and California railroad, later revested

back to the federal government) which calls for "permanent forest production," sustainability, and watershed protection. Subsequent laws like the Endangered Species Act and new policies based on modern science have led to protections for some of the best habitat for threatened forest species on BLM land—which doesn't mesh with the interpretation that these lands should be managed for timber production and revenue. Though initially included in the Northwest Forest Plan, the BLM's forests are now subject to a new management plan. Like the NWFP, this new plan protects some older forests as reserves for wildlife habitat with limitations on logging, but its protections are not as strong in many ways.

Regardless, some of Oregon's most treasured ancient forest groves are found on BLM lands, including in designated areas of critical environmental concern (see Hike 34, Crabtree Valley). They are also ecologically important, playing a critical role connecting the landscape and linking large blocks of high-quality habitat on national forestlands. In western Oregon, BLM lands are generally lower in elevation than national forests, providing rare opportunities for protection of these now rare ancient forest groves. In eastern Oregon, the scarce BLM forests often comprise the transition lands between national forests and high desert lands, serving as an important connection for fish and wildlife habitat.

NATIONAL PARKS AND MONUMENTS: National parks and monuments are generally managed by the National Park Service in the US Department of the Interior. National parks are areas of natural wonder that are set aside for recreation and human enjoyment. National monuments, designated either by Congress or administratively, protect areas for specific reasons such as biodiversity or cultural and historical importance.

Oregon's only national park, Crater Lake, has some lovely alpine, subalpine, and lodgepole pine forests, though much of the park is either above tree line or part of a pumice desert. There is an effort under way to expand the national park beyond its current 183,244 acres and to designate additional wilderness adjacent to it to protect this special ecosystem and its ancient forests.

Of Oregon's current national monuments, the Oregon Caves and Cascade-Siskiyou, both in southwestern Oregon, contain significant ancient forests. Expanded to just over four thousand acres in 2014, the Oregon Caves National Monument and Preserve highlights unique geology and caves—all topped by a diverse ancient forest that filters the water flowing into the extensive cave system. The Cascade-Siskiyou National Monument was designated in 2000 and expanded in 2017 to protect its unique biological diversity and forests, but this designation has been embroiled in a political battle still unfolding.

Covering more than ninety-eight thousand acres, mostly not forested, national monuments designated in Oregon also include Newberry National Volcanic Monument and John Day Fossil Beds. National monuments to protect additional ancient forests could be added in the future.

STATE AND COUNTY FORESTLANDS AND PARKS

Although most of Oregon's public lands are federally managed, some public forests are in state and county ownership. Often these are parks or other special lands that have long been recognized for their unique or outstanding characteristics, including their big, old trees. County and state governments manage their forestlands for a variety of purposes—from parks and recreation to timber production—guided by local and state laws.

STATE FORESTS: The Oregon Department of Forestry (ODF) manages about 860,000 acres of forestland owned by the state, on six large state forests and some other scattered lands. These forestlands are largely managed to produce timber and to generate state revenue, and few older forests remain on these lands. One exception is Elliott State Forest, which includes nearly forty thousand acres of unlogged native forest.

STATE PARKS: More than forty-two million visitors annually make use of the campgrounds, picnic areas, and hiking trails in the Oregon state park system. The Oregon Parks and Recreation Department has an extensive system of more than 250 individual areas, many well known like Silver Falls, Smith Rock, and Cape Lookout State Parks, though most are small. Many state parks and scenic waterways include ancient trees and forests, though often in small roadside patches rather than large blocks. Even so, their accessibility and facilities make these lovely forests popular and beloved by Oregonians. Many of these lie along Oregon's coast and are some of the last remaining unlogged forests surrounded by clear-cuts on nearby private land.

COUNTY PARKS AND FORESTS: County governments in Oregon also manage about 180,000 acres of publicly owned forests. These often small parks and undeveloped properties can be easy to take for granted in the larger context of public lands, and citizens often don't know they exist. Unfortunately, this means that these local treasures are sometimes logged outside of the public eye, as citizens in Douglas County discovered in 2016 when Busenbeck County Park, an undeveloped park with old-growth trees up to five hundred years old, was clear-cut with little or no public notice or comment.

Elliott State Forest

Elliott State Forest, in the Central Oregon Coast Range just south of the Umpqua River, includes around ninety thousand acres of low-elevation Douglas-fir and hemlock forest. Nearly half, or forty thousand acres, has never been logged and provides key habitat for spawning salmon, nesting marbled murrelets, and other wildlife dependent on healthy forest structure. While most of the forest is not older than 150 years, at a relatively young age the fast-growing trees in this area develop old-growth habitat suitable for spotted owls and marbled murrelets.

Most of the Elliott is classified as "common school fund" land—land that the federal government granted to Oregon at the time of statehood, with the proceeds of timber sales designated to fund public education. Because of the pressure it faced to fund education, coupled with the logging restrictions that protect threatened and endangered species living in the Elliott, in 2014 the state seriously considered selling the forest to private timber companies to generate funds. Conservationists worked for years to ensure that this forest remained in public ownership and its natural forests intact. In 2016 the State Land Board (the governor, secretary of state, and state treasurer) voted not to sell off Elliott State Forest to private interests and instead put the lands on a path to permanent conservation for the benefit of this and future generations. Its ultimate fate remains unresolved as of this writing.

The Elliott State Forest includes some of the last unlogged forests in the Coast Range. *(Photo by Greg Vaughn)*

PRIVATE LANDS

Ancient forests are nearly nonexistent on Oregon's privately owned lands, having been logged and converted into tree plantations over a vast landscape. While many landowners in Oregon may have small groves of ancient forests or a few ancient trees, these are mainly small and scattered. The largest private landowners in Oregon are timber companies or timber investment companies—owning nearly six million acres—while smaller landowners manage four million acres more. Private forestlands are generally managed for timber production, with short-rotation clear-cutting the dominant practice.

This means that the owners have logged most forests on these lands, often more than once, never allowing them to develop into ancient forests.

LOOKING AHEAD: RESTORING AND PROTECTING OUR FORESTS

As humans we have the ability to learn from our mistakes. Destroying our ancient forests is—I hope you agree—a mistake in need of correction. While we can't put the old-growth trees we've logged back on their stumps, there are other ways to make things right.

Trees harvested from a replanted plantation forest await processing or shipment at a Coos Bay facility. *(Photo by Brizz Meddings)*

NEW APPROACHES TO RESTORATION

The tragic legacy of fragmented forests, reduced fish and wildlife populations, and degraded streams and soils left by unsustainable logging now provides forest managers and advocates with an opportunity. Particularly in western Oregon, the hundreds of thousands of previously clear-cut forests on our public lands have grown back as dense tree plantations. These plantations lack the species and structural diversity found in natural forests and fail to provide many of their functions as well.

Many conservationists, forest advocates, and scientists agree that restoration of these previously logged forests can help speed up the development of diversity, structure, and habitat so that they might function as ancient forests again someday. Restoration can mean such active management as thinning out trees in dense plantations, adding large wood in streams depleted by logging practices, removing roads, and decompacting soil. It means using logging techniques that introduce uneven spacing between trees, encourages diverse species to grow, and creates snags and down wood that play such important roles in forest ecosystems. This work could offer a responsible alternative to logging our remaining ancient forests on public lands, a commonsense vision for Oregon's forests.

In drier forests east of the Cascades and in southern Oregon, high-grade logging, fire exclusion, and livestock grazing have changed the natural dynamic of these diverse forests, leaving hundreds of thousands of acres of unnaturally dense forests with few or no remaining old-growth trees. Thousands of miles of roads have been built for logging—fragmenting habitat, polluting streams, accelerating runoff of water, allowing weeds to spread, and allowing illegal access into public forestlands. Livestock grazing has altered natural vegetation and fire regimes (different frequencies and severities of fire) and has damaged and polluted streams. In short, more than a century of intensive management has left dry forest landscapes in desperate need of restoration. Restoration here can take the form of removing livestock grazing from some areas, thinning out small trees that have grown in since natural fires last burned and now pose a threat to old-growth trees, and using prescribed burning to restore a more natural fire cycle. Watershed restoration activities like removing unneeded roads and improving streamside vegetation are also needed.

All of these restoration activities are now common on public lands, as the Forest Service and BLM have been required to mitigate the damage that was done in the era of unsustainable logging. Such projects restore a healthier environment for fish and wildlife and create a forest landscape that is better able to respond to forest fire and support more recreation.

Unfortunately, not all management of public lands is based on restoration science. With underfunded management agencies, economics plays an oversized role, and timber volume is a driving factor behind some restoration projects. Still, finding agreement around restoration is the way forward. It's an important step away from the approaches that left us with muddy streams, landscapes carved up by roads, wildlife species on the brink of extinction, and our ancient forests that stood for hundreds of years converted to dense, unhealthy plantations.

And what about restoration on the millions of acres of private forestlands that once supported their own ancient forests? Unfortunately, this is typically not a priority for their owners, and these lands will likely continue to be clear-cut on a regular basis. An economy that values wood over the functions of a natural forest ensures that these vast areas of tree plantations are cut again long before ever becoming an ancient forest. Hope for these forests comes in the form of pressure to reform Oregon's grossly inadequate forest practice rules to extend harvest rotations, better protect streams and steep slopes, and reduce pollution from poorly maintained road systems. There is also some faint hope that climate policy might someday reward forest owners for growing and storing carbon, clean water, and habitat instead of two-by-fours.

PROTECTING THE LAST ANCIENT FORESTS

Oregon's future is as linked to ancient forests as its past was. Oregonians, visitors, elected officials, and forest lovers everywhere will choose what kind of future that will be, and the choices we make will determine whether we end up further impoverished or enriched in our forest legacy.

Oregon is known as a very green state. It is recognized nationwide for its landmark recycling and land-use planning laws, its sustainability, and its public beaches. Tourism entities tout our state's natural wonders and world-class recreation, its pristine waters and beautiful coastline. But behind the magazine-cover glamour of the state's natural beauty and outdoor opportunities lies a truth many don't realize: the ancient forests that support this image are threatened.

The same forces responsible for destroying our ancient forest ecosystems, building an unsustainable road network, and driving wildlife to the brink of extinction are still operating—lining the pockets of politicians, mounting marketing campaigns to convince the public that tree farms are just as good as ancient forests, and actively working to pass or maintain laws that allow them to pollute our water and air. Logging interests and management agencies use excuses like the need to reduce fuels and recover economic value from burned forests to target ancient forests, and old trees in the way of road-building and other development still fall victim to the chainsaw. In addition to logging, mining and excessive livestock grazing on public lands continue, and new threats from energy development (think miles of clear-cuts to build gas pipelines) are all reaching into the ancient forest pot for handouts. Such a future will leave Oregon impoverished in important ways.

The path to a richer future for Oregon is indeed in forests, but not in cutting them down. As the portion of our economy based on logging necessarily shrinks, opportunities to take advantage of protected forests abound. Restoration of forests and streams means more fish for sport fishing. Investment in recreation and quality of life means more trails for outdoor enthusiasts to enjoy. Clean water and air and access to forest recreation will attract tourists, businesses, and new residents who are drawn to these natural amenities. Without healthy, functioning forests, we'll have none of this.

Ancient forests clearly benefit the people of Oregon in many ways, including filtering our drinking water, providing life-saving medicines (like Taxol, which comes from Pacific yew), and offering a solution to climate change. Unfortunately, we tend to undervalue the vital things forests provide for our economy and well-being because they don't fit neatly into a traditional economic model.

Protecting our forests is a way to protect and restore our health and well-being too. Today our ancient forests are fragmented and so is our world as a whole—politically and culturally. Perhaps as we heal our forests we can heal the divides between each other through a connection with nature. Exploring and enjoying Oregon's ancient forests isn't just a luxury—it's an experience that should be accessible to everyone.

A STEP BEYOND CARING: AN ACTION PLAN FOR SAVING OUR ANCIENT FORESTS

Unless we care a lot, Dr. Seuss warns in *The Lorax*, "nothing is going to get better. It's not." And as much as I hope you are inspired to *care* about ancient forests, I'm going to argue that that's not enough. *Action* is necessary to make change.

Do we want our forests (especially public forests) to filter clean water, to store climate-changing carbon for centuries, to sustain salmon runs, songbirds, elk, and martens, and to nurture our spirits and refresh our bodies with their beauty? If the answer is "Yes!" then we must *act* on that desire.

The forests featured in this book would not be standing today without the advocacy of countless people, organizations, and even politicians who took action. And for ancient forests to continue to exist, and perhaps even to thrive, we must be willing to step up and advocate for their protection. Not just some of them—all of them. The

A visitor is dwarfed by an ancient Douglas-fir tree in the Coast Range. *(Photo by Brizz Meddings)*

vast majority of our ancient forests are gone. The gems that remain must be protected and as much as possible should be restored. And the truth of the matter is that some of the protections ancient forests enjoy today could be gone tomorrow with a change in policy, direction from Congress, or other laws or forest plan changes.

No one should accept the continued destruction of our ancient forests, but it can be difficult to know what we can do about it, how to be a part of the solution. The good news is that whether you are a first-time hiker getting out to explore a nearby trail, a seasoned tree-hugger with history and experience in the environmental movement, or anything in between—there are opportunities to help protect ancient forests.

To keep our ancient forests standing tall, to give them a chance to thrive for centuries to come, everyone who cares about these forests needs to speak up, to get involved in some way, to be part of the vocal public support and persistence that is needed to accomplish this goal. You can:

- Get outside! Use this guide to hike in amazing and beautiful forests and gain inspiration for your advocacy. Then tell your personal story of visiting these places—to your friends, family, legislators, social media, and local media.
- Spread the word to your friends, fellow hikers, and outdoors lovers about the need to protect forests and everything they provide.
- Financially support organizations that work to protect and restore ancient forests on behalf of their members and supporters.
- Volunteer with groups that advocate for forests.

- Let your legislators in Congress know that you support protecting and restoring Oregon's ancient forests. They have the power to pass laws regulating logging on federal public land and to protect additional wildlands, forests, and rivers.

The sign I encountered that afternoon in the magnificent ancient forest grove was, fortunately, also ancient. The imminent threat to that grove, very real fifteen years earlier, had been neutralized thanks to the persistent and adamant actions of citizens who also valued that special place. As federal land managers prepared to build a road and rev up the chainsaws in that grove, forest advocates ensured it was instead protected as the Opal Creek Wilderness.

My life—and the lives of countless other people, squirrels, birds, millipedes, fungi, huckleberries, and hemlocks—has been enriched by ancient forests like the one along Opal Creek. Without these forests we are impoverished in spirit, in essential life-giving systems, in our communities, and in our economies.

The purpose of this book is not just to help people discover the amazing forests in their backyard but to spur on a brighter future—a future in which citizens are informed and engaged in protecting and restoring our ancient forests; a future in which it is easy for Oregon's citizens and visitors to experience the wonders of an ancient forest—forage for huckleberries or mushrooms for a family meal, check a few songbirds off their life list, or take delight in their child's discovery of a salamander in the moss; and a future in which Oregon is richer, not poorer, in its ancient forest legacy.

ANCIENT FOREST ECOLOGY

What is an ancient forest, anyway? Is it the same as an old-growth forest? It turns out that the answers to these questions are as complex as these fascinating and beautiful forests.

Scientists, foresters, politicians, and activists have long debated the definition of old-growth forest. The simplest definition is quantitative—using age—which has been the basis for policy and legislation over the past few decades. For example, in the Northwest Forest Plan, forests over eighty years old are considered mature or late-successional and subject to logging restrictions when located within reserve areas. Scientists often base a designation of old growth on specific structures and characteristics that the trees develop at an age of 120 to 250 years old or older. And while they might be called old growth in size and character at that age, for many Oregon tree species that's barely middle age. Without life-ending disturbance, Douglas-fir trees can live to be eight hundred to twelve hundred years old, like the King Tut tree in Crabtree Valley. Western redcedar groves in the Opal Creek Wilderness, near the upper Clackamas River, and other spots in western Oregon are six hundred to a thousand years old.

Giant hemlocks, snags, and rotting logs form the basis of the old-growth forest structure in Crabtree Valley (Hike 34).

While the age of trees is certainly one contributor to an ancient forest, age alone does not define a forest. When we define an ancient forest, we're really talking about the age of the forest as a whole, not just the age of its oldest trees or the successional stage of a particular part of the forest. This means that if a forest naturally grows and changes without major human-induced alterations like logging, it is, as a whole, an ancient forest. This quality of naturalness in a forest means that it usually contains a diversity of tree species and structures, provides homes for a diversity of wildlife species in a diversity of habitats, and generally has healthy soils and streams. An ancient forest in western Oregon might be one that is recovering from a major fire that burned a century ago, and, while on the young side, has developed naturally with large snags, down wood, a variety of tree species, dense patches, and some five-hundred-year-old trees that survived the fire. In eastern Oregon, an ancient forest might have a few large old trees that survived dozens of fires, and the understory might have reestablished many times, leading to a mixture of ages and sizes scattered widely in the forest.

The dynamic nature of Oregon's forests means that over time they change and develop, between disturbances, in a somewhat predictable way known as succession. Different structural components define a forest in different stages of succession, forming the basis for habitat and influencing how the forest changes into the future. These structures and the other component parts of a forest—the giant trees, the layers of green understory plants, the mushrooms rising from the forest floor, and the woodpeckers hammering in the distance—are all important pieces of the complex and interacting ecosystem. These connections and relationships among both the living and dead parts of a forest allow it to

function as a forest—to recycle energy, respond to disturbance, and adapt to changes in climate or the disappearance of one of its many pieces.

Despite sharing such characteristics as age, structure, development stage, and species composition, every ancient forest is unique. The trees, understory plants, waterways, and wildlife living in a certain area change constantly and develop through time depending on the site's particular history, soil and underlying rocks, springs, cold pockets, concentrations of disease, and other factors. As you explore an ancient forest, think about the circumstances that led to how it looks right now, why it looks different from an area a mile down the trail, and how it might change tomorrow.

THE STRUCTURE'S THE THING

Every forest type and each individual forest has a unique structure based on its development, tree and shrub species, and microclimate. In general, once a forest has developed naturally for about 120 to 250 years—depending on the forest type and specific stand—it has the four major ancient forest structural components. These components aren't even all alive in the usual sense: a dead tree is just a continuation of a live tree, the next stage of its life in the forest and one that can affect the surrounding forest environment and structure for centuries to come.

BIG, OLD TREES are a key part of an ancient forest. As with people, trees develop character with age. In the wet, western part of the state, old-growth Douglas-firs can be giants, ten feet thick and hundreds of feet tall. In drier, eastern and southern Oregon, an old-growth ponderosa pine may only be three feet thick, while two-hundred-year-old juniper trees may stand only twenty feet tall. These big, old trees—often with unique deformities like twisted branches, hollow trunks, and broken or forked tops—form the backbone of the forest, the basis for the rest of the forest's structure, supplying seeds for the next generation of trees and shelter for wildlife big and small.

SNAGS are standing, dead trees. They can be large or small, depending on the size of the tree when it died. They can form when a tree dies from disease or insect infestation, from competition with other trees or drought stress, or from a fire that scorches its canopy. Generally, the larger the snag, the longer it will remain standing, rotting in place. Snags are some of the best wildlife habitat in a forest: fungi and insects work from the inside to break it down; woodpeckers poke holes to feed on insects, hollowing out cavities that other birds and mammals use for nests and dens; and loosened bark creates roosts for bats. After a fire, when many trees may die, snags also provide a variety of wildlife benefits, such as providing cover for big game or shade for new sprouts and seedlings.

DOWN LOGS, or trees that have fallen to the ground, form another vital part of a forest's structure. Down logs are a storage bank for water, nutrients, and carbon, which are slowly released and returned to the forest system as the log decomposes. They help stabilize soil and snowpack on steep slopes to slow spring runoff and erosion. They remain moist when the forest around them dries out in the summer, providing an oasis for reptiles, amphibians, insects, and small plants. They also serve as a nursery for the next generation of trees when seeds and sprouts establish themselves on top of a moist, nutrient-rich log—a leg up over trees getting

established on the forest floor. Fallen trees are also essential to streams—dissipating water energy, creating pools, sorting and storing gravel, and nourishing the bottom of the aquatic food chain.

MULTILEVELED CANOPY develops in forests with a diversity of tree species and ages in addition to the dominant species of the oldest trees. These trees might be younger, getting a start decades or centuries after the biggest trees in the forest. They might be species that don't grow as tall or that grow in wetter, drier, shadier, or sunnier conditions and have been able to capitalize on changes in the forest to start growing. This variety results in a forest with multiple levels as these different trees grow over time, creating a rich, three-dimensional structure that can be essential for wildlife like northern spotted owls as well as for deer, elk, and small mammals seeking cover.

Any forest might have one or more of these structural components, but when you put them all together, you move from components to a functioning ancient forest ecosystem. The benefits of this unique structure, working together as a whole, are many, especially for supporting a variety of wildlife.

WILDLIFE IN ANCIENT FORESTS

Different forests—depending on their structure, proximity to water, and other unique qualities—are home to different wildlife. When you walk through an ancient forest in a classic old-growth state, it can seem very quiet compared to a streamside with shrubs and hardwoods or a sunny meadow with buzzing insects and singing birds. Behind the scene, though—actually, under and over the scene, in the canopy and hidden in forest soil and down logs—these forests are

Sunlight streams through the multilayered canopy of an ancient Douglas-fir and western hemlock forest along the Gate Creek Trail in the Willamette National Forest (Hike 38, Browder Ridge). Decomposing logs return nutrients to the forest floor.

teeming with life that depends on ancient forest structure.

Mature and old-growth forests in western Oregon, for example, were shown as early as the 1980s to provide primary habitat for more than a hundred species of vertebrates, including many birds, dozens of mammals, and several reptiles and amphibians. Nearly half of these depended exclusively on older forest habitat and would not occur in intensively managed, short-rotation plantations that lacked the abundant snags, broken-top trees, and fallen logs found in an ancient forest. Hundreds of species of insects, spiders, and other invertebrates also inhabit the ancient forest—in the canopy and on the ground—providing vital functions in the ecosystem.

Indicator species are wildlife that depend on a certain type of habitat that may be at risk. The presence of these wildlife species can indicate the health of the habitat and, indirectly, the health of other associated wildlife populations. Where the habitat for vulnerable wildlife species overlaps with ancient forests, they can offer some protection for these now-rare forests via laws and policies that protect this habitat.

While the northern spotted owl is probably the best known old-growth-dependent species, many other birds find their optimum habitat in ancient forests. Raptors like the goshawk, cavity-dependent Vaux's swift, songbirds like Hammond's flycatcher, Townsend's warbler, the spirited Pacific wren, varied thrush with their "train whistle" blast, and pileated woodpeckers all make their home in western Oregon's moist forests. In central and eastern Oregon's ponderosa pine and mixed conifer forests you'll find the flammulated owl, white-headed woodpecker, and pygmy nuthatch. Bald eagles, which have made such a triumphant return from the edge

Ancient Versus Managed Forests

It can be difficult to know whether a forest is a natural, unmanaged, ancient one or one that has been logged or otherwise disturbed by human hands. Many people look at the green hillsides of western Oregon or gawk at the orange-barked ponderosa pine in central and eastern Oregon and assume they are healthy, functioning forests. Upon closer inspection, this may not be the case; just because an area is covered in trees doesn't mean it's a natural forest. For example, when a once-ancient forest is clear-cut and replanted, it grows back as a dense tree plantation. These plantations lack the diversity of species and ages of trees found in forests that have not been logged; usually don't have snags and have too few rotting, down trees; and fail to provide good habitat for many kinds of fish and wildlife.

How can you tell the difference between an ancient forest and a managed forest? Look for these clues:

	NATURAL FOREST	MANAGED FOREST
TREES OF DIFFERENT SPECIES	Yes! Look for different cones, bark texture, and needles to see the differences in species.	Often not. Plantations—forests replanted after logging—are often just a single species grown for future harvest.
TREES OF DIFFERENT AGES AND SIZES	Yes! Most of the time, undisturbed forests have different sizes and ages of trees mixed in. You can see this diversity when walking through or from a distance, where the forest canopy looks uneven.	Often not. Plantations are usually planted all at once and are dense and uniform in size.
SNAGS AND DOWN WOOD	Yes! Look for large-diameter snags and nurse logs especially, often left after a natural disturbance.	Some, but usually small. Sometimes there is evidence of old dead wood from before logging, but often the old wood has been destroyed by equipment or post-logging activities like burning.
STUMPS	Usually not, unless along trails or roads where trees were a danger to the public.	Likely. If a forest has been logged, stumps are a given, including old, rotten stumps from long ago or smaller, fresher ones from more recent logging.
VEGETATION IN THE UNDERSTORY AND ON THE FOREST FLOOR	Yes! Usually there is a diversity of tree seedlings, flowers, ferns, grasses, moss, and shrubs unless there is a dense canopy. There are often small openings where these thrive.	Plantation forests are often so dense that little can grow in the understory. In drier forests, grazing can lead to a simplified understory with shorter grasses and shrubs.

OPPOSITE: This forest in the Drift Creek Wilderness illustrates a multileveled canopy, snags, down wood, and the large, old trees of an ancient forest.

of extinction, depend on large old trees for nesting, perching, and roosting. And, in the face of global climate change, studies have shown that old-growth forests may be an essential haven for songbirds.

For deer and elk, the diverse structure in ancient forests is essential for staying warm in harsh winter weather and cooler in hot, droughty summers. Other mammals like martens and fishers depend on forest structure for their dens and hunting. Flying squirrels need multiple layers in a canopy and different sized trees to successfully glide through the forest and escape predators. And certain bats need cavities, deeply furrowed bark, and decaying snags for daytime roosting.

Ancient forest structure, with its diversity, dynamic nature, and ability to moderate moisture and temperature will be even more important for wildlife as they feel the effects of global warming. In particular, having connected forests—not broken up by roads and inhospitable habitat like clear-cuts—will be more important as wildlife may need to migrate or travel more widely for food and water in a changing climate.

THE STRUCTURE OF STREAMS

Streams are much more than water, and far from a passive element of an ancient forest. Where a stream flows can determine where different trees, shrubs, and wildflowers grow. Likewise, the trees of a forest actively shape its streams, capturing and releasing the water that flows within winding banks, but also adding the physical structure that forms pools, riffles, and lazy bends.

Trees that fall into and across streams help to stabilize the streambank in swift currents, redirecting energy and redistributing rocks and other logs. Fallen trees, sometimes piling up into huge logjams, help shade and cool the water and offer shelter to young fish. They slow water to form pools that capture gravels where trout and salmon can spawn. As they decompose, they add nutrients to the water.

The pools formed by fallen trees also capture smaller forest litter—the needles, leaves, lichen, and seeds that fall from the canopy or roll down forest slopes. In a more subtle but just as important way, this smaller forest litter also shapes a stream's ecosystem. Trapped in slow-moving pools or shallow areas formed by trees, this organic material forms the basis of the stream food chain as it is shredded and eaten by tiny aquatic organisms, then insects and fish as you move up the food chain. The diverse habitat and high water quality in ancient forest streams are also essential for amphibians like the tailed frog and the Pacific giant salamander and birds like the American dipper, which gleans insects in fast-flowing forest streams.

Unfortunately, the widespread clear-cut logging that decimated ancient forests across the state also had a big impact on stream structure. Not only did logging operations remove large wood from many streams to facilitate log transport and road building, but logging also removed streamside trees that would otherwise have shaded the water, stabilized the banks, and provided the fallen tree structure so important for stream dynamics and wildlife habitat. Logging roads have also drastically impacted forest streams. Roads and their adjacent ditches accelerate runoff that can cause erosion and scour fish eggs from their nests, and where logging roads cross streams, many of the installed culverts have proven impassable to salmon and other aquatic life.

OPPOSITE: A logjam, boulders, and streamside vegetation indicate healthy stream structure, here along the Wild and Scenic Eagle Creek in northeastern Oregon.

Today, we are left with many streams that are too warm, move too quickly to capture gravel and forest litter, and don't provide hiding habitat young fish need. On public lands, federal land managers are putting wood back into streams to mitigate past damage and are protecting streamside forests so they can one day function naturally. On private lands, some landowners are also doing their part for restoration in partnership with nonprofit organizations like watershed councils, but an ongoing emphasis on maximizing timber production on a large part of the landscape means many streams are not considered for restoration.

FOREST SUCCESSION AND DISTURBANCE

As Andy Kerr wrote in 2004, "Much of the public, but few conservationists and no scientists, view a stand of trees as a picture of how it will be forever. We must look at forests broadly both across the landscape and over time. A stand of burned trees is but the beginning of the next forest; a stand of trees that has grown up nearby will help seed and replace the burned area (assuming it was not completely logged)."

A key concept about ancient forests is that they are constantly changing; succession is ongoing. At every scale, from a half-acre opening to a landscape of hundreds of acres, young trees are becoming established, weaker trees are dying, sun-loving trees are growing tall, shade-loving trees are growing slowly, limbs are breaking, and disturbance agents (such as wind, fire, and disease) are acting in a forest.

Scientists have created a model that defines successional stages (see below) that ecosystems go through—starting with a forest- or stand-replacing disturbance and continuing as if the forest grows undisturbed for several hundred years. In nature, though, change is a constant and few places are free from disturbance for long.

DISTURBANCE AND LEGACY CREATION assumes a stand-replacement event (fire, windstorm, insect outbreak) that leaves legacies behind (snags and down wood, possibly a few living trees).

OREGON'S FOREST TYPES

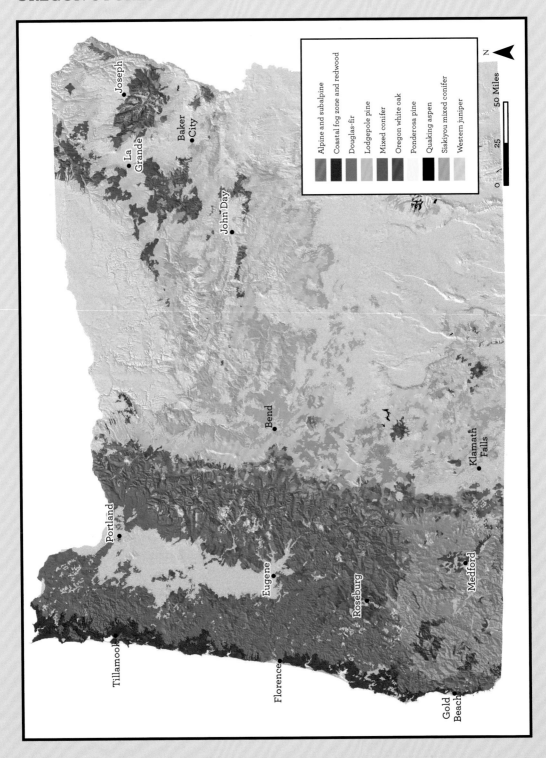

Alpine and subalpine
Coastal fog zone and redwood
Douglas-fir
Lodgepole pine
Mixed conifer
Oregon white oak
Ponderosa pine
Quaking aspen
Siskiyou mixed conifer
Western juniper

N

0   25   50 Miles

Joseph

Baker City

La Grande

John Day

Bend

Klamath Falls

Portland

Eugene

Roseburg

Medford

Tillamook

Florence

Gold Beach

Oregon's Forest Types

From the mixed conifer forests of the Blue Mountains to the Sitka spruce and hemlock rainforest in the coastal fog zone, Oregon's forests come with a lot of variety. Across the state, factors that determine general forest types include geography (such as elevation, steepness of slopes, and proximity to water), geology (soil types), and climate (for example, west or east slope of mountains, amount of rain or snow, seasonal temperatures).

Forests in any local area can still vary greatly depending on their development stage, disturbance history, and microclimate. This is especially true east of the Cascades, where drier, warmer slopes support different types of forests than moister, cooler slopes do, often near each other.

In this book we explore the major types of ancient forests in Oregon, which appear on the map. Riparian forests, found on the banks of rivers, lakes, and other natural waterways, are mixed in with all the other types and are not shown on the map. These forests are often dominated by deciduous trees like maple, alder, and cottonwood, as well as a variety of shrubs. They can be found in featured hikes in every region in this book.

ALPINE AND SUBALPINE forests are generally found at elevations above 5000 feet. Trees here are adapted to colder temperatures, a shorter growing season, and a lot of snow. Species typically not found elsewhere include Pacific silver fir, subalpine fir, noble fir, Alaska yellow-cedar, and mountain hemlock. The trees here don't grow as large as those at lower elevations, though they include such species as western hemlock, Douglas-fir, western white pine, Shasta red fir, and Engelmann spruce, which also grow in more hospitable conditions. At the highest elevations, outcrops of stunted and less common trees like whitebark pine grow in scattered pockets. These forests tend to have a few hundred years between fires, allowing for a long recovery and natural development of diverse species. Featured hikes in this forest type can be found in the Mount Hood, Upper Willamette and McKenzie, Upper Umpqua, South Cascades, Northern Blue Mountains, and Wallowas regions.

Alpine and subalpine forest

Coastal fog zone and redwood forest

COASTAL FOG ZONE AND REDWOOD

forests thrive only within a dozen miles or so of the coastline, where high humidity, from fog and rain, and mild temperatures prevail. Most of this zone is dominated by Sitka spruce, with western hemlock, western redcedar, Douglas-fir, and red alder mixed in. The forest understory is usually lush with moss, shrubs, and ferns, and young trees commonly grow on nurse logs packed with moisture and nutrients. Right along the shoreline, shore pine (a variety of lodgepole pine) can grow in dense, short forests. On the far southern coast, this forest type includes coast redwoods and evergreen hardwoods like Oregon myrtle and tanoak. Fires are few and far between, as fuels don't often dry out enough to be easily ignited. Featured hikes in this forest type can be found in the North Coast, Central Coast Range, and South Coast and Kalmiopsis regions.

DOUGLAS-FIR forest covers more of Oregon than any other, primarily on the west side of the Cascades, though Douglas-fir trees are found in the mixed conifer forest types as well. These forests are dominated by their namesake tree, but in moister and riparian areas there are also western hemlock, western redcedar, Pacific yew, bigleaf maple, and alder; and on drier sites incense cedar, madrone, and chinquapin. Douglas-fir, western hemlock, and red cedar can grow to astounding sizes in these forests if left undisturbed, and hemlocks can take over as the dominant tree after five hundred years or so. These forests often have the best examples of classic ancient forest structure. Featured hikes in this forest type can be found in all regions west of the Cascade Crest.

LODGEPOLE PINE are often found in pure, dense stands originating after a fire or other disturbance. They grow quickly, and once they reach eighty to one hundred years they often experience disturbance from fire and/or insect outbreaks. If this doesn't happen, they often get overtopped by shade-tolerant species like white fir, ponderosa pine, or Engelmann spruce, which can live much longer and develop into a more classic old-growth forest. Lodgepole pine forests grow in diverse climates but often grow on pumice or other dry soils, in cold microclimates, and in areas with dry summers and longer, cold winters. Featured hikes in this forest type can be found in the Central Oregon, Klamath-Lakeview, and Northern Blue Mountains regions.

Mixed conifer forest *(Photo by James Johnston)*

MIXED CONIFER forests are generally found east of the Cascades in areas that get more moisture than the ponderosa pine forest type. Mixed conifer forest covers a range of elevations, depending on the slope, aspect, and moisture levels of the area. Tree species are truly mixed, and include Douglas-fir, white fir, Shasta red fir, noble fir, western larch, Engelmann spruce, lodgepole pine, incense cedar, sugar and western white pine, Pacific yew, and ponderosa pine. Western larch trees dominate some mixed conifer areas at elevations between 3000 and 7000 feet and stand out in autumn when their deciduous needles turn brilliant yellow. In riparian areas, these forests can have a mix of large cottonwood, alder, and other hardwood species. These forests can be very long-lived, with dominant species components changing over time and through disturbances like fire. Featured hikes in this forest type can be found in the South Cascades, Klamath-Lakeview, Northern Blue Mountains, Blue Mountains, and Wallowas regions.

OREGON WHITE OAK forests are found throughout the southern portion of western Oregon, spread across the low- and middle-elevation hillsides of the Willamette, Umpqua, and Rogue River valleys. Open oak woodlands were once more common, but fire suppression and agricultural development have reduced their extent. White oak forests can be found in the featured hikes in the Mount Hood region.

PONDEROSA PINE forest, found mostly on drier sites in central and eastern Oregon, covers a vast area. Ponderosa pine dominates, but lodgepole pine, aspen, Douglas-fir, western larch, incense cedar, western white pine, and some other species can be found mixed in. The understory of these forests is often dominated by grasses, and riparian areas have aspen, cottonwood, willows, and other shrubs. Frequent, low-intensity fires historically played a big role in shaping this forest type, clearing out brush and young trees and keeping the forest in a savannah-like state in many areas. Featured hikes in this forest type can be found in the Central Oregon, Klamath-Lakeview, Blue Mountains, and Wallowas regions.

Ponderosa pine forest *(Photo by James Johnston)*

QUAKING ASPEN forest appears on the map, but aspens also grow mixed in with other forest types. Aspens can be found in featured hikes in the Mount Hood, South Cascades, Central Oregon, Klamath-Lakeview, Blue Mountains, and Wallowas regions.

Quaking aspen forest *(Photo by Brizz Meddings)*

SIKIYOU MIXED CONIFER forests comprising hardwoods mixed with conifers are largely confined to southwest Oregon from the Rogue River valley south and inland to the Cascade Crest. They are characterized by diversity: in addition to Douglas-fir, sugar pine, ponderosa pine, incense cedar, various firs, and western white pine, there are also madrone, chinquapin, tanoak, and canyon live oak. Other rare tree species in this forest type in specific microclimates include Jeffrey pine (found on serpentine soils), Port Orford cedar, Oregon myrtle, and Brewer's spruce. Fire historically played a role in maintaining the diversity, but the varied topography, soil types, and microclimates also contribute. Featured hikes in this forest type can be found in the Siskiyou Crest and South Coast and Kalmiopsis regions.

WESTERN JUNIPER forests, the driest forests in the state, blanket a big portion of central and eastern Oregon's high desert region. Junipers tend to grow in hot, dry areas widely spaced from one another and surrounded by sagebrush and grasses. Junipers are also interspersed within other forest types on rocky outcroppings or in other dry microclimates. Frequent fires in this forest type once limited its distribution, but fire suppression has allowed it to expand over the past century. Featured hikes within the Siskiyou Crest, Mount Hood, Central Oregon, and Blue Mountains regions include this forest type.

COMPLEX EARLY-SERAL occurs as a stage after a disturbance when areas are dominated by diverse nonconifer vegetation (shrubs, hardwoods, grasses, and wildflowers) mixed with legacy structures. These areas support abundant birds, insects, and other wildlife.

YOUNG TREE ESTABLISHMENT occurs when seeds left behind in the soil or available from surviving trees begin to grow into a young forest cohort and slowly begin shading out the nontree vegetation.

CANOPY CLOSURE develops as the initial cohort of trees gets bigger and begins to compete for resources. Localized conditions and types of trees determine which species live and die.

COMPETITIVE EXCLUSION can last from thirty to one hundred years and is very dynamic. Biomass accumulates; weaker trees die and become habitat for a variety of species that depend on dead wood; sun-loving trees lose their lower limbs and grow tall. Little grows in the understory because of the dense canopy.

MATURATION takes place as biomass continues to accumulate, even as tree growth slows down. The forest canopy begins to open up as trees succumb to disease, insects, and other factors. Understory and shade-tolerant trees establish themselves in sunny spots on the forest floor and start to grow. The growth forms of individual trees begin to gain more character. At this stage the classic components of an old-growth forest are starting to develop.

VERTICAL DIVERSIFICATION characterizes old growth. A mid- and understory are well-developed; individual trees get thicker and lower branches expand as more sunlight is available. Trees that die are large enough to provide good snag and down wood structure.

HORIZONTAL DIVERSIFICATION is reached between 250 and 350 years, depending on the forest. This stage has a lot of large snags and down wood structure. Large trees that die create gaps that fill in with other trees and shrubs. These gaps can then experience the full range of stages described here at a small scale, perpetuating the old-growth forest for a very long time.

PIONEER TREE LOSS occurs after five hundred to a thousand years as the initial cohort of trees is reaching the end of its life. Younger trees of all sizes and species vie for their space and live off their structure.

Of course, the process isn't really so simple as having a beginning and an end—not if a forest is healthy and functioning as it should. Forests are constantly experiencing disturbance at different scales, which restarts the cycle of stages. Some of these stages happen at a small scale, a forest might not start at the beginning of these stages or succession might be reset when it's partway through, and climatic factors will influence how things progress.

Different disturbances restart succession in different ways with different effects and are more or less common in different forest types. Windstorm events are more common on the coast, for example, and have more of an effect on trees with shallower root systems. Insect outbreaks are more common in eastern Oregon and might target certain species more than others, resulting in a major shift in forest species while not killing a whole forest stand. Both of these disturbances leave a lot of dead and down wood as legacies that the growing forest will build on.

Human-caused disturbances (primarily logging) lead to successional pathways that are different from natural ones. In the case of a clear-cut, replanted, and reharvested forest, the natural successional stages are artificially accelerated, the complex early-seral stage is purposefully skipped, and forest development is not allowed to proceed even to the maturation stage. Few if any legacy structures are left behind when the process starts anew with another clear-cut.

A healthy forest with a full complement of plant and wildlife species, healthy soils, connectivity to other ancient forests, and legacy structures is incredibly resilient to disturbance. As it recovers, a forest may not look the same, but the ecosystem continues to function. In a forest that has been significantly altered by human activities, however, healthy structure, soils, and biodiversity can take centuries to recover.

FIRE AS AN AGENT OF CHANGE

Fire is by far the most significant disturbance in Oregon's forests in terms of scale, effects, and how humans relate to it. Humans tend to see forest fires as a destructive force, but fire represents another way that nature renews itself and shapes our living landscapes. It is a key process that affects forest succession, structure, and biodiversity.

For as long as there have been trees in Oregon, fire has been part of our forests. Historically, different forest types and climates in Oregon have experienced different fire regimes. In some forests, fire tends to burn infrequently and more severely, while other forests tend to burn more frequently and less severely—and everything in between. The fire regime in a moister forest type and climate like the Coast Range, for example, would likely recur at a long interval of a few hundred years but at a high severity where many of the trees would die. In a dry ponderosa pine forest, we would expect fire frequency to be much higher—every five to fifteen years—but fires would be less severe, mostly killing small trees along the ground.

While different regions and forest types evolved with different fire regimes, individual tree species are also adapted to fire in different ways. Some species, such as ponderosa pine,

evolved to be tolerant of fire. These trees have thick bark to protect their cambium (the living layer of a tree just under the bark) from the frequent, generally low-intensity fires that tend to burn in the dry ponderosa pine forest type. Other species like lodgepole pine have adapted to unlock their cones to release seeds after a fire to quickly begin the process of regrowth. With thick bark and a love of growing in sunny, open areas, Douglas-fir trees, though often found in moister forest types that don't experience fire often, are also well-adapted to fire. In an ancient Douglas-fir forest, the biggest, oldest trees often have blackened bark near their base, showing that they lived through a fire, while tree species typically found in moister environments or at higher elevations might not have such adaptations and tend to perish in a high-severity fire.

While fire does kill trees—sometimes just a few and sometimes vast landscapes depending on the severity and intensity of the fire—it also has a rejuvenating effect on forests. The trees that die in a fire are recycled naturally as snags and down logs, stabilizing and enriching the soil and providing much-needed habitat for species like woodpeckers, bluebirds, and bats that depend on abundant dead trees. Fires reset the understory where it may have grown very dense, allowing different species to thrive in burned patches.

Unfortunately, the natural cycles of fire have been disrupted—significantly in some areas—since Oregon's settlement by Euro-Americans. Over the past century, logging has removed the largest and most fire-resistant trees in many areas, making forests less resilient to fire. Even more damaging are fire management policies that

OPPOSITE: Fire can be used as a tool by forest managers to reintroduce or maintain historic fire regimes, as here in a ponderosa pine forest adapted to frequent, low-severity fires. (*Photo by Brett Cole, www.vikasproject.org*)

sought to prevent and put out fires whenever and wherever they started. This approach has led to an unnatural buildup of fuels and dense undergrowth in areas where frequent fire was the norm. While these changes in fuels and forest structure can affect fire severity, weather conditions determined by climate are more of a deciding factor than fuels in how fires burn. Over the long term, we still need to work to reduce the impacts of climate change, as well as prepare for them.

Removing burned trees in postfire logging operations—salvage logging—has also altered natural forest structures in the aftermath of fires. This management practice destroys valuable structure and kills young seedlings and sprouts just as they are emerging, while replanting displaces diverse native vegetation with conifer monocultures. It can also require damaging roads to remove logs, which threatens soil and water quality.

To have thriving ancient forests, fire needs to be both tolerated in and restored to its natural role. In dry forests in southwest, central, and eastern Oregon, efforts to restore a more natural, more frequent fire regime include removing small fuels that have grown in as a result of fire exclusion, using controlled fires to reduce fuels, and making homes and communities more fire-resilient so they are not threatened by natural processes like fire. These treatments can help forests that have been thrown out of whack by grazing, logging, and fire exclusion to attain a more natural vegetation condition and become more resilient to natural fires. They can also help keep communities safe from uncharacteristic fires. In moister climates, like western Oregon's Douglas-fir and hemlock forests or in the moist mixed conifer forests of the Blue Mountains, it can make sense to reduce fuels only if fire exclusion and suppression have significantly altered the natural fire regime and if large trees and other fire-resilient structures are not removed.

OREGON'S ANCIENT FORESTS HIKE REGIONS

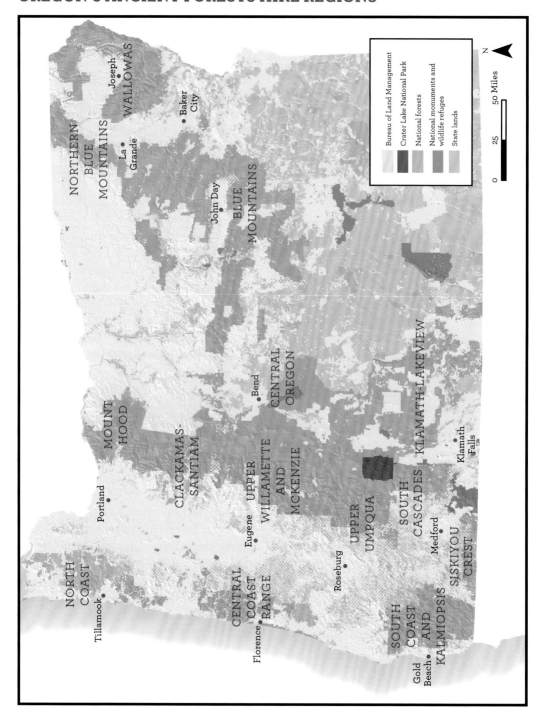

Legend:
- Bureau of Land Management
- Crater Lake National Park
- National forests
- National monuments and wildlife refuges
- State lands

N

0 — 25 — 50 Miles

Regions:
NORTH COAST
NORTHERN BLUE MOUNTAINS
WALLOWAS
BLUE MOUNTAINS
MOUNT HOOD
CLACKAMAS-SANTIAM
CENTRAL OREGON
CENTRAL COAST RANGE
UPPER WILLAMETTE AND MCKENZIE
KLAMATH-LAKEVIEW
UPPER UMPQUA
SOUTH CASCADES
SOUTH COAST AND KALMIOPSIS
SISKIYOU CREST

Cities:
Tillamook
Portland
Joseph
Baker City
La Grande
John Day
Bend
Eugene
Florence
Gold Beach
Roseburg
Medford
Klamath Falls

HOW TO USE THIS GUIDE

The first part of the book has prepared you with background and context including the ecology of ancient forests. In the pages ahead, you'll find some of the best ancient forest hikes in Oregon. They explore diverse geography, forest types, structure, and elevation, at a variety of difficulty levels that are largely accessible without special equipment or skills.

There is no comprehensive list of all the remaining ancient forests, old-growth groves, or trails in the state. The hikes featured in this book are my personal favorites, unique examples of a particular type of forest, or an area with particular significance in the history of forest advocacy. Travel to these hikes will also show you how forests in the vicinity are managed—from wild, native forests to extensively logged areas.

HIKE ORGANIZATION

The ninety-one featured hikes are divided into fourteen geographic regions across the state. Regions, and their featured hikes, are generally presented from west to east and north to south. Each regional chapter offers information about the forests of that area, including protected areas, general ecology, and forest management. Each featured hike includes a detailed description about the trail and how to get there, as well as other key information to help you prepare for your hike.

DISTANCE refers to total distance, round-trip, for the recommended hike. If there are additional opportunities for longer hikes, I include those in the hike description.

TRAILHEAD LOCATION is the trailhead's GPS location in decimal minutes for latitude (north) and longitude (west) using WGS 84 (World Geodetic System of 1984) data.

STARTING ELEVATION AND ELEVATION GAIN or loss on the trail can also help you gauge likely snow levels and temperatures as well as the difficulty or potential ecological changes along the

About the Maps

The maps that appear at the beginning of each region indicate trailhead location only. You can find more detailed maps of featured hikes from a variety of sources: Free trail maps are available online at www.oregonhikers.org. Purchase national forest and BLM maps from any national forest headquarters office or ranger station, from BLM district offices, or online from the Forest Service websites listed in the Resources section of this book. Other good resources are your favorite outdoor store, the National Geologic Map Database (https://ngmdb.usgs.gov), or www.natgeomaps.com.

way. Elevation gain is the total for the trail; if it is under 100 feet, it is listed as minimal.

DIFFICULTY categories for the hikes are generally defined as:

- **EASY** Under 4 miles in distance and up to 500 feet elevation gain
- **MODERATE** 4 to 8 miles and up to 1000 feet elevation gain
- **DIFFICULT** Over 8 miles, or over 4 miles and over 1000 feet elevation gain, or trail for experienced hikers only

SEASON may come into play. Many of the hikes in this guide are accessible for much of the year. Many others are accessible only when roads are free from snow—which can vary from year to year. For some of the hikes, there is a best time of year to really experience and enjoy all the hike has to offer. I've included a general note on what this season is and why.

FOREST TYPE corresponds to the forest types described in the Oregon's Forest Types sidebar earlier in this section.

PROTECTIONS lets you know what level of protection, if any, is afforded the hike area. This includes wilderness protection, wild and scenic river corridors, and roadless area status, as well as whether an area is reserved from logging in the managing agency's management plan. Unprotected roadless areas do not have protections based on their roadless status, but they may be reserved from logging under current management plans.

MANAGEMENT lists the government agency responsible for managing the area described in this hike. Contact information for each managing agency can be found in Resources.

NOTES indicate whether there are restroom or other facilities at the trailhead and any fees or permits that are required. Specific hazards may also be mentioned here.

GETTING THERE provides the directions to each hike and indicates the easiest route from the closest large town. If you plan to come from a different location, be sure to use detailed maps and trusted directions from another source. Mileages should be considered estimates, but pay attention to those given, as not all roads are well signed.

I have noted rough roads and other hazards as well as parking limitations. Conditions can change, so use caution at all times; many roads on public lands are not maintained in the winter. Check www.tripcheck.com for major highway conditions, and contact the local national forest or other agency office listed in Resources for current conditions on local roads.

Driving to trailheads on forest roads can take more time than you might expect and can come with some hazards. To be safe, leave yourself plenty of time to get to and from a trailhead; drive defensively, being prepared to pull over on narrow roads to avoid collisions; and don't take any unnecessary chances on bad roads or in bad weather.

Generally roads in national forests are numbered, with primary routes (those in the best condition) having two digits. Tributary roads to primary routes usually have two or more extra digits and are not as well maintained. For example, Forest Road 42 would be a primary route, while FR 4235 is a secondary route off FR 42. BLM road names do not use the same system.

ABOUT THE HIKE

Each hike description offers context for the hike and describes the area and trail in some detail, including trail junctions and distances. Notes about forest ecology, tree and wildflower species, and individual trees you might see are included, but keep in mind that what you see along the trail could be quite different from what is described, since these forests are constantly changing. Trees die and fall, storms and fires happen, and vegetation grows. Trails can go unmaintained for years, especially in more remote areas, so expect that down trees may create obstacles.

OUTDOOR SAFETY AND ETHICS

No guide is a substitute for using your own common sense and taking your own precautions to stay safe while traveling to and while on the trail. You must take personal responsibility for your safety and well-being as you explore Oregon's ancient forests.

Please remember that these forests are a legacy both for future human generations and for the plants, animals, fungi, and microscopic life that live there, so it's important to respect all life-forms on the forest trails. Leave No Trace principles should be practiced while visiting the forests. Learn more at Leave No Trace and the Center for Outdoor Ethics: www.lnt.org.

PLAN AHEAD AND PREPARE

To get ready for a hike, doing a little research and preparing the right gear can mean the difference between a great forest experience and one turned memorable for all the wrong reasons.

SCHEDULE YOUR TRIP FOR THE BEST TIME. This can mean planning to avoid high-elevation areas during mosquito season, aiming to do a waterfall hike when water levels are high, or avoiding a popular hunting area during elk season. It can also mean avoiding the highest use times for a better experience, like avoiding popular swimming holes on warm summer weekends. In general, stream levels are highest in spring; wildflower displays are best before late summer; mosquitoes are typically worse in early to midsummer; fall is best for leaf color; and hunting seasons, when it is best to wear bright colors, range from late summer through fall. (Learn more at https://myodfw.com /big-game-hunting/seasons.)

KNOW WHAT PERMITS AND REGULATIONS APPLY TO AN AREA. At some trailheads, a fee or permit—usually per vehicle—is required to park and use the area. These are included in the Notes section of each hike description. Generally, if a fee or permit is required, a sign at the trailhead will make that clear. Most places that require a fee also have a fee box and envelope. A Northwest Forest Pass generally covers the fee charged on national forest lands, while national parks are covered by an America the Beautiful Pass. Golden Eagle passes also work for all of these. State parks are a different entity, and permits may be different.

Regulations in designated wilderness areas limit group size to no more than twelve people, and a free self-issued permit is often required. Mountain bikes and any motorized equipment are not allowed in designated wilderness. Mushroom gathering is also prohibited in wilderness areas.

WEAR THE RIGHT CLOTHING. It's best to be prepared with layers of appropriate clothing for sun, shade, rain, snow, and a variety of temperatures. Avoid wearing cotton if it will be wet or cold.

Wear comfortable and sturdy shoes, preferably closed-toed to avoid getting poked or punctured.

KNOW WHAT OTHER USERS YOU MIGHT ENCOUNTER. Regulations for each trail are often posted at the trailhead, but it's a good idea to be aware of the types of activities an area is open to before you go. If you're heading to a popular trail that might have a mix of trail users, consider visiting on a weekday when it is less likely to be busy.

CARRY ESSENTIAL GEAR THAT CAN HELP YOU IN CASE OF EMERGENCY. The point of the Ten Essentials, originated by the Mountaineers, has always been to answer two basic questions: Can you prevent emergencies and respond positively should one occur (items 1–5)? And can you safely spend a night—or more—outside (items 6–10)? Use the list below as a guide and tailor it to the needs of your outing.

BE SURE TO LET SOMEONE KNOW WHERE YOU ARE GOING and when you plan to be back, so that if you get stuck or lost someone knows that you are missing.

DON'T ASSUME YOU WILL HAVE CELL PHONE COVERAGE and keep in mind that batteries drain faster when searching for a signal. Consider bringing an external charger or setting your phone to airplane mode to save battery when there is no cell service.

DON'T LEAVE VALUABLES IN YOUR CAR at the trailhead—break-ins can happen.

CHECK THE WEATHER AND ROAD CONDITIONS in advance, and be prepared for the conditions you might encounter. This includes being prepared for snow, mud, high water in streams, or storms that may come in during your trip. To

The Ten Essentials

1. **NAVIGATION.** The essential basics are a reliable map and a compass (and the knowledge to use it). Be prepared with a physical or pre-downloaded map and directions.

2. **HEADLAMP OR FLASHLIGHT.** Include spare batteries.

3. **SUN PROTECTION.** Wear sunglasses, sun-protective clothes, and broad-spectrum sunscreen rated at least SPF 30.

4. **FIRST-AID BASICS.** Include bandages; skin closures; gauze pads and dressings; roller bandage or wrap; tape; antiseptic; blister prevention and treatment supplies; nitrile gloves; tweezers; needle; nonprescription painkillers; anti-inflammatory, antidiarrheal, and antihistamine tablets; topical antibiotic; and any important personal prescriptions, including an EpiPen if you are allergic to bee or hornet venom.

avoid heat- and cold-related illnesses, consider timing your hike to avoid the hottest or coldest time of day, or foregoing your planned hike in bad weather conditions.

KNOW WHAT TO DO IN EMERGENCIES. Know what's in your first-aid kit, and brush up on your first-aid knowledge or consider taking a first-aid course. A good resource is the National Outdoor Leadership School's (NOLS) Wilderness Medicine Institute: www.nols.edu/en/about/wilderness-medicine/.

DO NO DAMAGE TO LAND, TRAILS, OR WATER

To avoid doing damage to soil and water, don't build any structures or dig holes or trenches unless necessary in an emergency or to bury waste. Stay on designated trails and do not cut switchbacks, as this increases soil erosion and creates unsightly multiple paths.

PACK IT IN, PACK IT OUT

Leave no waste or litter behind, not even compostables like apple cores and toilet paper. Be sure to pack out feminine hygiene products. Bring a sealed plastic bag or other bag to pack out everything. If you can, pick up litter left behind by people who don't care about the forest as much as you do.

When you need a restroom and there isn't one nearby, do your business off the trail and at least two hundred feet from any body of water. Do not leave toilet paper on the forest floor and do not bury it; toilet paper should be packed out in a sealed plastic bag. Deposit solid human waste in a hole dug six to eight inches deep, at least two hundred feet from water, camp, and trails. Cover and disguise the hole when finished.

LEAVE WHAT YOU FIND

Things found in the forest generally belong in the forest and should not be picked up or

5. **KNIFE.** Also consider a multitool, strong tape, some cordage, and gear repair supplies.

6. **FIRE.** Carry at least one butane lighter (or waterproof matches) and firestarter, such as chemical heat tabs, cotton balls soaked in petroleum jelly, or commercially prepared firestarter.

7. **SHELTER.** Carry at all times (can be lightweight emergency bivy sack).

8. **EXTRA FOOD.** For shorter trips a one-day supply is reasonable.

9. **EXTRA WATER.** Carry sufficient water and have the skills and tools required to obtain and purify additional water.

10. **EXTRA CLOTHES.** Pack additional layers needed to survive the night in the worst conditions that your party may realistically encounter. And because this is Oregon, a rain jacket and rain pants are always a good idea.

removed. In particular, do not pick flowers and plants. They may be pretty, but they belong where they are. Picking plants can disturb the soil and other plants around them.

RESPECT WILDLIFE

The most common wildlife you will encounter in the forest are birds and small mammals. Observe wildlife from a distance and do not follow or approach them. You should never feed any wild animal as feeding wildlife damages their health, alters natural behaviors, and exposes them to predators and other dangers. If you are hiking with a dog, keep it on a leash to avoid conflicts with wildlife.

BE CONSIDERATE OF OTHER TRAIL USERS

It's best to follow the golden rule when it comes to other trail users: treat them as you would like to be treated.

KEEP LOUD VOICES AND NOISES TO A MINIMUM and let nature's sounds prevail.

KEEP DOGS UNDER CONTROL. Dogs can be great companions on hikes, but it's important to realize that they can have an impact on plants, wildlife, and other trail users. Keep dogs on-leash and on-trail to prevent conflicts and ecological damage.

SHARE THE TRAIL. Many trails are used by people on horseback, mountain bikes, and sometimes even motorized vehicles—not just hikers. To avoid conflict, be aware of your surroundings and follow right-of-way etiquette.

- Hikers going uphill are working hard and should be given the right of way over hikers coming downhill. Sometimes uphill hikers will prefer to stop and let you pass coming down so they can get a short break. The uphill hiker should get to make the call.
- Hikers should yield to backpackers.
- Get off the trail on the downhill side when horses or other livestock approach. Quietly greet the rider and ask if you are okay where you are. Hold still, but do not hide, until they are past. Speaking softly in a calm voice will help stock animals identify you as human and not a "pack monster."
- Watch and listen for mountain bikers, who can move quite quickly. Bikes should generally yield to hikers, but if it makes sense in the moment, step off the trail to let bikes go by.

PLAYING IT SAFE

Specific hazards associated with certain trails are included in the Notes section of each hike. Generally, though, trail and forest hazards fall into a few major categories. With proper preparation and knowledge, hikers can often avoid injury and accidents.

POISONOUS PLANTS

Some plants can cause a rash or other skin reaction in many people. In Oregon the most common plant in this category is poison oak, but eastern Oregon also has western poison ivy. Both plants grow in diverse environments; their leaflets grow in groups of three and are sometimes shiny. They usually grow as low shrubs but can also climb trees as a vine. Avoid touching or rubbing up against this plant if you can. If you are exposed, wash your skin with soap and cold running water, and wash clothing in hot water when you return home.

Avoid eating any plant, berry, or mushroom that you can't positively identify as edible and safe. If you're not sure, don't eat it.

HEAT- AND COLD-RELATED ILLNESSES

You can generally avoid heat- and cold-related illnesses by following the preparedness tips just described. However, in extreme heat or in wet, cold weather, the life-threatening conditions of heat exhaustion, heatstroke, or hypothermia can occur.

Heat exhaustion and heatstroke can result from extreme external temperatures or physical exertion causing internal body temperature to rise too high. Signs of heat exhaustion can include nausea, dizziness, headache, excessive sweating, and other symptoms of dehydration. It can often be treated by drinking fluids and resting in a cool place. Left untreated, the condition can progress to the more serious heatstroke, indicated by dry, red skin and worsening symptoms of heat exhaustion. In the event of heat exhaustion or heatstroke, get to a cool place, preferably in or near a stream, and bathe your skin with cool water.

Hypothermia occurs when a person's body temperature drops too low, caused by exposure to extreme cold or when body heat is lost too fast. Initial symptoms include shivering and mental confusion that can worsen if shivering stops. In the event of hypothermia, the key is to get warm and dry as soon as possible. This can mean changing into dry clothes, wrapping in blankets, and drinking warm beverages.

ACCIDENTS, INJURY, AND INSECT BITES

Small cuts, scrapes, and blisters are the most common injuries on the trail and can easily be cleaned and bandaged with items in a basic first-aid kit.

More serious injuries that can occur—from a fall, for example—include sprains and broken bones. If you're out on the trail and do not have cell service, the most important thing to do is to immobilize the injured area and get assistance to return to the car and get medical help. In the field, a sprain can often be treated by wrapping the injured joint with an elastic bandage and carefully, with assistance, walking out. Broken bones or more serious injuries will need medical attention. If possible, send someone to call for help. Remain on the trail and do not move more than necessary while you wait for help.

Stinging and biting insects are common in many areas. Bring insect repellent to avoid bites from mosquitoes and ticks. If you are bitten by a tick, remove it with a pair of tweezers as close to the skin as possible. If you're allergic to bee or wasp stings, be prepared with antihistamine or an EpiPen.

Poison oak can cause an itchy rash and is best avoided when hiking on Oregon's trails.

ENCOUNTERS WITH WILDLIFE

The best way to avoid wildlife-related hazards is to be aware of your surroundings and make noise as you are hiking to alert animals to your presence.

The only poisonous snakes in Oregon are western rattlesnakes. They can be found in warm, rocky areas below about 6000 feet in elevation. If you are in such an area in the summer, look and listen for rattlesnakes, and make noise that will alert a snake to move away. If you see or hear one on or near the trail, give it a wide berth or turn around. Rattlesnakes are generally shy and not likely to strike unless threatened at close range.

The only bears in Oregon are black bears, which are omnivores that live primarily on plants and berries and are quite common across the state. Cougars are not common in Oregon, and you're unlikely to see one on the trail as they are quite shy and stealthy. Wolf populations are growing and expanding in territory in Oregon but are still exceptionally rare. None of these animals is usually interested in being near humans. Confrontations with any of these animals can usually be avoided by making noise as you hike to alert them to your presence, and avoiding hiking near dawn or dusk. If you see a cub or pup, move away, as the mother is likely nearby and will be protective. If confronted by a bear, cougar, or wolf, don't run or turn your back. Stand your ground or back away slowly, raising your arms so you look big, talking firmly, or clapping. Give the animal a way to escape, and it will likely retreat. In the unlikely event that an animal attacks, fight back using your pack, rocks, sticks, or other tools.

MAKING THE MOST OF YOUR ANCIENT FOREST HIKE

Going for a hike in an ancient forest is a lot more interesting if you are armed with an inquisitive attitude, a little knowledge and context, and some extra time to enjoy the special place you are in. Here are a few tips that can help you have the best experience.

LOOK UP! It's all well and good to watch the trail at your feet so you don't trip or fall, and wonderful to admire the girth of trees at eye level, but most of the forest is towering above you. First, stop hiking (walking while looking up is a sure way to

A Note About Safety

Safety is an important concern in all outdoor activities. No guidebook can alert you to every hazard or anticipate the limitations of every reader. Therefore, the descriptions of roads, trails, routes, and natural features in this book are not representations that a particular place or excursion will be safe for your party. When you follow any of the routes described in this book, you assume responsibility for your own safety. Under normal conditions, such excursions require the usual attention to traffic, road and trail conditions, weather, terrain, the capabilities of your party, and other factors. Keeping informed on current conditions and exercising common sense are the keys to a safe, enjoyable outing.   —*Mountaineers Books*

lose your balance). Once stopped, look up at the forest canopy, or follow a particular trunk to its top. Perhaps what you thought was a live tree is actually a snag. You might notice interesting characteristics like twisted branching arms or multistemmed tops, or cavities that owls might nest in.

GET TO KNOW THE TREES OF OREGON'S FORESTS. Being a student of the forest is a fun way to enjoy your hike even more. Become familiar with the different leaves and needles, bark, cones, and shapes of different trees. Even if you don't know what every tree is, exploring the differences between them is a great way to learn. And remember, not all trees in an ancient forest are big and old, and there can be a variety of vegetation. Small trees, shrubs, and wildflowers in the understory are fascinating to learn about as well.

BE A FOREST DETECTIVE. Enjoying the forest can mean thinking about the forest's origins and how it has developed and changed. You don't need to be a scientist to look for signs of past logging (like stumps or same-aged trees), signs of past fire (like burn scars, charred stumps, or down logs), and signs of different successional stages. It can be quite fascinating to think about how individual trees, small stands, and whole vast forests have changed over time—and there's no better time to do so than when hiking through an ancient forest.

DON'T BE AFRAID TO EXPLORE OFF-TRAIL. Trail-builders look for the best route, which doesn't necessarily go by the biggest trees or most scenic vistas. If you see a huge tree, snag, or down log you want to take a closer look at that is near but off the trail, go see it. Just be sure you keep track of the direction and location from which you left the trail, and note nearby landmarks so you don't get lost.

EAT AND BE MERRY! Ancient forests, with their diverse vegetation and network of organisms, offer a smorgasbord of tasty treats if you know what to look for and take the time to properly identify them. From oxalis and wild ginger leaves lining the trail, to multiple types of huckleberries on late-summer shrubs, to chanterelles and morels popping out of the ground, wild foods can be nutritious and delicious. Edible plant and mushroom guidebooks can be found in the Resources section of this book. Remember that mushroom gathering is prohibited in designated wilderness and be sure you know what something is before you eat it.

TAKE YOUR TIME. Enjoying ancient forests isn't just about hiking the trails through them—it's also about just hanging out to get the full experience. Sitting or standing still in the forest—over lunch, while resting, or just because—opens you up to seeing more wildlife, noticing more of the forest floor vegetation, listening to the forest sounds, and really getting a feel for the special place you are in.

Above all, *have fun*, use common sense, and enjoy your adventures in Oregon's ancient forests.

Mountain huckleberries are just one edible treat that can be found in Oregon's ancient forests.

PART 2

ANCIENT FOREST HIKES

NORTH COAST HIKES

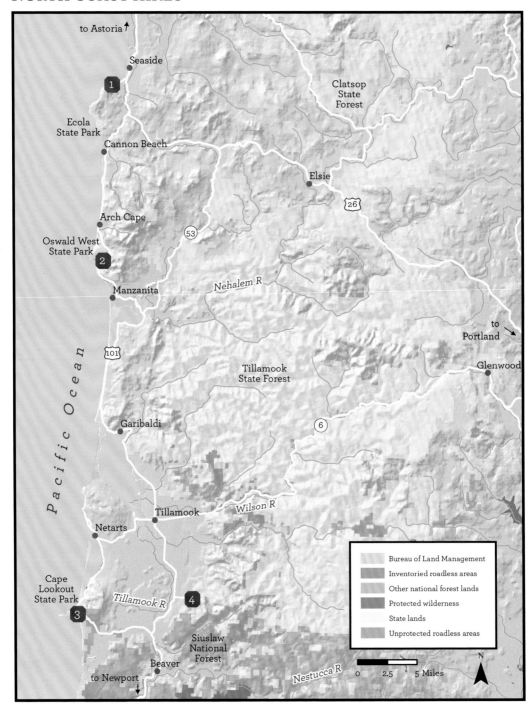

to Astoria↑

Seaside

1

Ecola
State Park

Cannon Beach

Clatsop
State
Forest

Elsie

26

Arch Cape

53

Oswald West
State Park

2

Nehalem R

Manzanita

to
Portland↘

101

Glenwood

Pacific Ocean

Tillamook
State Forest

Garibaldi

6

Tillamook

Wilson R

Netarts

Cape
Lookout
State Park

Tillamook R

4

3

Siuslaw
National
Forest

Beaver

Nestucca R

to Newport↓

	Bureau of Land Management
	Inventoried roadless areas
	Other national forest lands
	Protected wilderness
	State lands
	Unprotected roadless areas

0   2.5   5 Miles

N

NORTH COAST

The northern part of Oregon's Coast Range—from the Columbia River south to Lincoln City and the Siletz River—has a typical moist, temperate climate influenced by the Pacific Ocean. The ancient eroding hills of the northern Coast Range, topping out at just over 3000 feet, have been carved by the Nehalem, Wilson, Tillamook, and Nestucca Rivers, which drain this northern range west to the ocean through tidally influenced estuaries. These estuaries have been manipulated to allow for livestock and other agriculture, an industry the region is known for.

Historically, the low-lying floodplains and surrounding hills would have been covered in Sitka spruce, western hemlock, and hardwood forests, while ancient Douglas-fir and hemlock marched up and over the Coast Range to the Willamette Valley. These forests have been heavily logged over the past century, however, and today this region's forests (primarily managed plantations) are still heavily clear-cut. Only small pockets of ancient forest remain in state parks and on federal public land.

Large rocky headlands and forests reaching right down to the beach are characteristic of the North Coast's shoreline—striking features that state officials deemed worthy of setting aside as part of the state parks and public beach system over the last century. In the northern portion of this region, the only

remaining ancient forests are in these relatively small parks of less than 2500 acres.

The southern half of this region includes the Hebo Ranger District of the Siuslaw National Forest. Unlike every other region in this book, there are no protected wilderness areas, but a few large natural areas can be found in the national forest surrounding Mount Hebo and Cascade Head. Management of the Siuslaw National Forest focuses on the restoration of functioning old-growth forest habitat and streams, which is essential in the context of the rest of the northern Coast Range. There are also scattered parcels of forests managed by the Bureau of Land

Enormous Sitka spruce on the Tillamook Head Trail (Hike 1)

PREVIOUS PAGE: A hiker is dwarfed by towering trees in the Waldo Lake Wilderness along the Black Creek Trail (Hike 48).

Management in the North Coast region, but few of these have been left untouched.

Many coastal communities on the North Coast—including Astoria, Seaside, Cannon Beach, Tillamook, Pacific City, and Lincoln City—rely on state parks and other public forest-lands for their quality of life and drinking water, recreation, and tourism. Without changes to how forests in the North Coast region are managed, all of this will suffer, as water is contaminated, salmon continue to decline, and growing forests that cover the hillsides are turned, again, into clear-cuts.

1. TILLAMOOK HEAD

DISTANCE: 4 miles round-trip
TRAILHEAD LOCATION: 45.9734°, -123.9541°
STARTING ELEVATION/ELEVATION GAIN: 180 feet/1000 feet
DIFFICULTY: Moderate
SEASON: Year-round, but trail can be muddy in all seasons

FOREST TYPE: Coastal fog zone and redwoods
PROTECTIONS: State park, unlikely to be logged
MANAGEMENT: Oregon Parks and Recreation Department
NOTES: No restrooms at trailhead; no parking fee or permit required

GETTING THERE: From the south end of the town of Seaside, turn west off of US Highway 101 onto Avenue U. In a quarter mile turn left on South Edgewood Road, which continues south as Sunset Boulevard. The road dead-ends a little over a mile later near the entrance to a housing development. The trailhead with parking for a few dozen cars is on the left.

Part of Ecola State Park, this strip of ancient coastal forest along Tillamook Head is the Elmer Feldenheimer Forest Preserve, which was dedicated to "the return of Tillamook Head to its pristine state, as it was when so richly endowed by Lewis & Clark with our nation's history," a noble cause and a beautiful forest along the route that the Lewis and Clark Expedition followed in 1806 to Cannon Beach.

The trail to the headlands summit of Tillamook Head, 1100 feet above the ocean, is steep, muddy, and—in areas with roots and rocks—challenging. But it's worth the effort: the whole route, a segment of the Oregon Coast Trail, has a rainforest feel to it with some huge trees to gawk at and ocean views.

The trail ascends through a brushy forest with scattered large Sitka spruce trees for the first quarter mile, and then opens up to a nice western hemlock forest with salmonberry, salal, ferns, and elderberry—classic coastal vegetation. Huge spruces appear after about a half mile—the most impressive is twelve feet across at the base, with a towering and thick trunk heading skyward. Another big spruce greets you at about three-quarters of a mile, and you can keep an eye on it for perspective as the trail switchbacks up above it through a younger forest. Between 1 and 1.3 miles, the forest showcases a diverse structure of down logs, multileveled canopy, and young trees perched on top of old ones, their buttressed roots exposed. This structure changes dramatically when you reach a tree plantation, logged half a century ago. Here the young trees are far more uniform, and stumps and alder (a disturbance-loving tree) are dominant features. At about the 1.7-mile mark, reenter the ancient forest near the top of the headland and check out a big old snag. From here, the trail rolls along the headland through a primarily hemlock forest, with scattered big spruces. Boardwalks grant passage through wet areas with skunk cabbage and tall shrubs, and huge tipped-up root wads of ancient trees dot the understory. You get peeks at the ocean as the trail continues, and you reach a nice overlook and the turnaround point at 2 miles.

If you would like to extend your hike, the trail continues another 1.7 miles to Clark's Viewpoint and, beyond that, descends 2 miles to the southern trailhead at Indian Beach.

The well-signed trailhead for the Tillamook Head Trail

2. CAPE FALCON

DISTANCE: 4.5 miles round-trip
TRAILHEAD LOCATION: 45.7630°, -123.9561°
STARTING ELEVATION/ELEVATION GAIN: 140 feet/480 feet
DIFFICULTY: Moderate
SEASON: Year-round
FOREST TYPE: Coastal fog zone and redwoods

PROTECTIONS: State park, unlikely to be logged
MANAGEMENT: Oregon Parks and Recreation Department
NOTES: No trailhead facilities, but they can be found at the next parking area south of this trailhead; no parking fee or permit required

GETTING THERE: From Cannon Beach, drive US Highway 101 south for about 10 miles to Oswald West State Park. The trailhead is located on the west side of US 101 right at milepost 39: look for beach access parking and Cape Falcon signs. The parking area is a pullout on the side of the highway.

Oswald West State Park is among the most popular destinations on the North Coast, so expect to share this section of the Oregon Coast Trail with other visitors (as well as plenty of squirrels). It has great picnicking, hiking, and beaches to enjoy.

To begin, follow this popular trail along Short Sand Creek at the base of a steep ravine to a trail junction for the beach (left) or to Cape Falcon (right). For this hike, turn right, but visit Short Sand Beach another time. There is great surfing and beachcombing here, but the views inland are a bit gut-wrenching—the hillsides are heavily clear-cut, and local beach users are concerned about herbicide sprays polluting the water.

The forest is dominated by towering Sitka spruce, but it also includes Douglas-fir, western redcedar, and western hemlock. The trail is well maintained: boardwalks cover many of the wet areas, but roots and mud do make it slick and

A small stream crosses the Cape Falcon Trail near a Sitka spruce.

challenging in some places. The trail rolls up and down and in and out of headland forest with tall spruces, a dense salal understory, and some spruces of wide girth also scattered along the way. A few areas along the trail are younger forests replanted after the large old trees were removed following a major windstorm in 1981.

At about 2 miles, the trail narrows and ascends among exposed roots through a tall hedge of salal and other shrubs to an unmarked trail junction. Take a left to head toward the open headland through the shrub tunnel. Rogue trails start to snake through the hedge—but it's hard to get lost if you are seeking the view, which stretches out over a protected marine reserve and south across Smuggler's Cove and Short Sand Beach to Neahkahnie Mountain. Once you've taken it all in, head back the way you came.

3. CAPE LOOKOUT

DISTANCE: Cape Trail, 5 miles round-trip; North Trail, 1 mile round-trip
TRAILHEAD LOCATION: 45.3414°, -123.9746°
STARTING ELEVATION/ELEVATION GAIN: Cape Trail, 875 feet/550 feet; North Trail, 875 feet/200 feet
DIFFICULTY: Moderate

SEASON: Year-round, but trail can be muddy in winter and spring; whale-watching season peaks in January
FOREST TYPE: Coastal fog zone and redwoods
PROTECTIONS: State park, unlikely to be logged

MANAGEMENT: Oregon Parks and Recreation Department

NOTES: Restrooms at trailhead; no parking fee or permit required

GETTING THERE: From US Highway 101 in Tillamook, turn west on 3rd Street, following signs for the Three Capes Scenic Loop. Cross the Tillamook River and keep left to head toward Netarts and Cape Lookout State Park. About 10 miles from US 101, you'll pass the Cape Lookout Campground and day-use area, but continue another 2.8 miles to the large, developed trailhead parking area.

Cape Lookout's 2-mile bluff is the remnant of a huge lava flow from fifteen million years ago. The state park, about two thousand acres, offers camping and a nice beach, but the Cape Trail along the bluff hundreds of feet above the ocean is the real highlight.

From the parking lot, the busy Cape Trail heads to the left and descends gradually (with a few uphills thrown in on the second half of the trail) as it continues to the end of the cape. In the first half of the hike, there are good views to the south through the typical headland forest of spruce, hemlock, and swordferns. Starting at about half a mile, there are a lot of big spruce trees with interesting structure—big arms covered in moss and ferns, multiple tops, and buttressed roots. At 1.3 miles (about halfway to the end of the cape), you'll reach a nice viewpoint and a good place to turn around if you're looking for an easier hike.

If you continue another 1.2 miles beyond this point to the end of the cape, the trail is a bit rougher, with some short climbs as well as a continued overall descent. Be sure to keep an eye out for migrating gray whales from up here.

Back at the trailhead, if you want to check out a less busy (but muddier) trail with spectacular old-growth trees, take the North Trail to the right. This section of the Oregon Coast Trail descends a bit steeply through giant Sitka spruce and hemlocks, with a tall shrubby understory of osoberry and salmonberry in many shades of green. I recommend going at least a half mile to really enjoy the forest.

If you have the energy to climb back up, you can take this trail another 2.3 miles one-way down to a day-use area and beach. Either way, you just retrace your steps to return to your car.

A hiker takes in a large Sitka spruce on the Cape Trail.

State and Private Lands Management

About half of Oregon's forested land is owned by private timber corporations or by the state. In the northern Coast Range, this percentage is closer to 90 percent. These forests are managed primarily for producing timber and are subject to the Oregon Forest Practices Act passed in 1974. This law allows for clear-cut logging (meaning almost zero trees are left standing in an area) of up to 120 acres at a time. They later must be replanted, usually with a single type of tree that grows in a monoculture, much like a corn crop. The dominant practice on these lands is to then add herbicides to kill competing natural vegetation and fertilizer to keep young trees growing as fast as possible. They are then typically cut again in thirty to fifty years.

The ecological consequences of these logging practices at a huge scale are devastating. Legacy structures like snags and down wood are all removed, no diversity in tree or shrub types that might offer food or shelter to wildlife remains, soil easily erodes without robust root and soil networks, chemicals get into water that flows downstream, streams get no shade from large trees, and thirsty young tree farms deplete stream flows in summer months so there is less water for other uses. "Modern forestry" might result in a profitable wood farm, but it leaves thousands of acres of nearly contiguous land—once covered by ancient forest—that today provide little to no wildlife habitat; lack natural forest, soil, and stream structure; are a net source of carbon emissions to the atmosphere; and are poisoned on a regular basis. Oregon Wild, other conservationists, and local citizens are working to modernize the Forest Practices Act to better protect coastal communities' drinking water, human health, water quality, and fish and wildlife habitat. This industrial landscape may never be an ancient forest again, but it illustrates the need to protect the last remaining ancient forests and restore much of what has been destroyed wherever it can be done.

Clear-cut logging dominates the private and state lands in the northern Coast Range.

4. MUNSON CREEK FALLS

DISTANCE: 0.5 mile round-trip
TRAILHEAD LOCATION: 45.3656°, -123.7736°
STARTING ELEVATION/ELEVATION GAIN: 300 feet/300 feet
DIFFICULTY: Easy
SEASON: Year-round
FOREST TYPE: Coastal fog zone and redwoods

PROTECTIONS: State park, unlikely to be logged
MANAGEMENT: Oregon Parks and Recreation Department
NOTES: No restrooms at trailhead; no parking fee or permit required

GETTING THERE: From Tillamook, travel south 7 miles on US Highway 101 to just north of milepost 73 and turn east at a sign for Munson Creek Falls State Natural Site. Follow state park signs for 0.7 mile of paved and then 0.9 mile of gravel road. The road dead-ends in a large parking area for the trail.

The Munson Creek Falls State Natural Site is just sixty-two acres, acquired from and surrounded by private timberland. Found just a few miles off Highway 101, it's a great stop to stretch your legs on a drive along the coast.

This short, pleasant hike heads up a box canyon lined with ancient red alder and bigleaf maple draped in moss and slopes with big Sitka spruce, hemlock, and western redcedar. Salmon swim up the Tillamook River and find Munson Creek, shaded and nourished by the ancient forest, a perfect place to spawn. The waterfall, viewed from a distance at the end of the trail, is the tallest in the Coast Range at just over 300 feet. Enjoy the view before returning the way you came.

Bigleaf maples, western redcedars, and Douglas-firs frame the view of Munson Creek Falls.

CENTRAL COAST RANGE HIKES

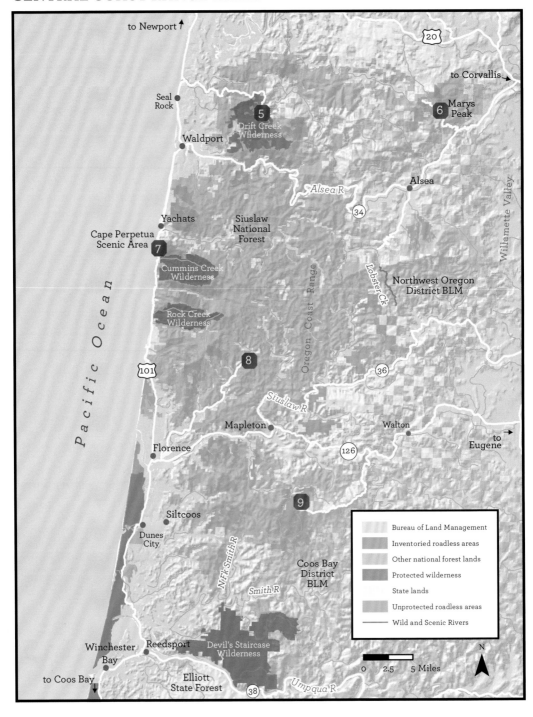

to Newport ↑

〔20〕

to Corvallis →

Seal Rock ●

⬛ 5

⬛ 6 Marys Peak

Drift Creek Wilderness

Waldport ●

Alsea ●

Alsea R.

〔34〕

Yachats ●

Siuslaw National Forest

Cape Perpetua Scenic Area ⬛ 7

Lobster Ck.

Northwest Oregon District BLM

Cummins Creek Wilderness

Oregon Coast Range

Rock Creek Wilderness

〔36〕

〔101〕

⬛ 8

Siuslaw R.

Mapleton ●

Walton ●

to Eugene →

〔126〕

Pacific Ocean

⬛ 9

Siltcoos ●

Dunes City ●

Florence ●

N. Fk. Smith R.

Coos Bay District BLM

Smith R.

Winchester Bay ● Reedsport ●

Devil's Staircase Wilderness

to Coos Bay ↓

Elliott State Forest

〔38〕

Umpqua R.

	Bureau of Land Management
	Inventoried roadless areas
	Other national forest lands
	Protected wilderness
	State lands
	Unprotected roadless areas
—	Wild and Scenic Rivers

0   2.5   5 Miles

N ↑

Willamette Valley

CENTRAL COAST RANGE

The Central Coast Range region spans from Newport to Coos Bay along the coast and stretches inland across the Coast Range toward the Willamette Valley. With its topography shaped by the uplift of ancient sedimentary mountains worn down by flowing water and time, the area is a prime example of Oregon's forest wonders—and horrors. Over a hundred inches of rain fall in this region each year, and with mild temperatures, trees grow here like nowhere else in the state. From massive Sitka spruce in the coastal fog belt to moss-laden bigleaf maple and alders in the lowlands and towering western hemlock and Douglas-fir throughout, the forest ecosystem found here epitomizes a temperate rainforest. The rain feeds major rivers like the Yaquina, Alsea, Siuslaw, and Umpqua, their extensive tributary networks, and countless streams that flow to the ocean out of the Coast Range, supporting chinook and coho salmon, steelhead, and plenty of recreation.

Unfortunately, this productivity means that the federal forests here, managed by the Siuslaw National Forest and the Northwest Oregon and Coos Bay Districts of the BLM, have been at the heart of the clear-cutting epidemic that ravaged the area from the 1960s through 1980s and continues today on private and state lands.

The liquidation of the Coast Range's ancient forests led to drastic declines in populations of native salmon, northern spotted owls, and marbled murrelets, all of which are now listed under the Endangered Species Act. The Northwest Forest Plan came about in response to these population declines and designated nearly all of the Siuslaw National Forest as "reserves," essentially prohibiting any more logging of mature or old-growth forests. Today, the focus of forest management in the Siuslaw has shifted from logging ancient forests to restoring the tree plantations planted in their wake. Whole watershed restoration has been prioritized, and partnerships between conservationists, watershed councils, private landowners, and federal agencies have blossomed around this common ground.

Despite the heavy logging of the past, about 48,500 acres of the Siuslaw's ancient and intact forests have been permanently protected. The Drift Creek, Cummins Creek, and Rock Creek

Some of the largest Sitka spruce trees in Oregon are found in the Cummins Creek Wilderness on the central Oregon coast.

Wilderness areas were designated in 1984 and Devil's Staircase Wilderness in 2019. Some additional large blocks of unlogged forest, including the Elliott State Forest, remain in this region. And scattered throughout the national forest are small pockets of ancient forests to discover that still provide a sample of the primeval rainforest that once dominated the Central Coast Range.

5. DRIFT CREEK WILDERNESS

DISTANCE: 8 miles round-trip
TRAILHEAD LOCATION: 44.4814°, -123.9086°
STARTING ELEVATION/ELEVATION GAIN:
1500 feet/1600 feet
DIFFICULTY: Difficult
SEASON: Year-round

FOREST TYPE: Douglas-fir
PROTECTIONS: Drift Creek Wilderness
MANAGEMENT: Siuslaw National Forest
NOTES: No restrooms at trailhead; no parking fee or permit required

GETTING THERE: From the town of Waldport, drive 7 miles north on US Highway 101 (or, from Newport to the north, drive south 8 miles). Turn east (inland) on North Beaver Creek Road across from Ona Beach State Park and go 1 mile to a fork. Stay left and go 2.9 bumpy miles to a junction. Turn right on paved Forest Road 51 and go another 6 miles. Turn left onto FR 5000 for 1.4 miles, take the right fork onto FR 5087, and follow this for 2.8 miles to where the road ends at the trailhead. Park in the road-end clearing.

The nearly six-thousand-acre Drift Creek Wilderness, just north of the Alsea River, is one of the largest remaining intact blocks of protected ancient forest in the Coast Range and could be even bigger if adjacent roadless areas are added. The steep, densely forested area isn't all super old, but the naturally recovering mature forest, mixed with old growth, is lovely. Horse Creek Trail heads to Drift Creek from the north, while Harris Ranch Trail, which also has nice trees, comes in from the south.

Horse Creek Trail starts out where the road ends and continues up an old road converted to a trail lined with alder and salmonberry, with Douglas-fir and western hemlock forest to the left and right. A signboard along the way has some info and a map. After 0.6 mile, the old road ends and the proper wilderness trail begins—and it's a marked change. The stand you enter in the wilderness is of tall ancient hemlocks, their bases tapered like pedestals. As you walk along, note the tall snags, down wood, pockets of younger hemlocks growing up, and a few scattered giants (like a six-foot-diameter hemlock just before the 1-mile point).

From here, the trail descends a bit into a younger, denser forest with tall snags, some western redcedar, and more shrubs in the understory as it follows the side of a ridge. At around 1.5 miles, Douglas-fir becomes the dominant tree and the forest takes on a different feel: the crowns are higher, it's less dense, and there are more open patches with tangles of shrubs. This transitions at the 2-mile mark when the trail makes a hard right turn, passes a huge cedar, and enters an old-growth Douglas-fir stand where the massive trees have giant arms and furrowed bark. At a flat, moist area with swordferns, cedars, and a salmonberry patch at about 2.3 miles, consider if you want to start the steep descent to the creek or turn around for a much easier hike that gains only 200 feet in elevation on the way back.

The second half of the trail has most of the elevation loss (and gain, on the way back). To continue—which is worth it if you're up for the elevation and distance—the trail switchbacks to the east and starts a more steady descent through a structure-rich younger-mature Douglas-fir forest with patches of vine maple and scattered large Douglas-firs. At around 2.8 miles, stay to the left at an old trail junction sign and follow short, zigzagging switchbacks down the ridge past giant firs and snags, with glimpses to the south over the Drift Creek drainage in the heart of the wilderness.

As you descend over the next mile, you'll switchback down through a younger (roughly hundred-year-old) but towering Douglas-fir stand, a

Towering western hemlock trees line the Horse Creek Trail in the Drift Creek Wilderness.

large open thicket with alder and salmonberry, and moister areas with large western redcedar and mossy vine maples. As you near the bottom of the ridge, you'll pass a few giant Dougs and cedars before the trail flattens out. A particularly interesting feature of this trail is quite noticeable throughout this descent: short snags (ten to thirty feet tall) topped with miniature gardens—salal, hemlock seedlings, red huckleberry, and ferns—that look like crazy hairdos. See if you can find a favorite.

You reach the pretty obvious destination—a campsite just above the creek—at 4 miles. Here, in the flat bench above Drift Creek, scattered giant Douglas-firs tower above tall ferns and moss-covered logs. Steep side trails lead down to the creek, which is lined with alders and bigleaf maples draped in moss. The one to the far left (facing the creek) gets to the most accessible and gentlest way down, but unless you're prepared to wade or swim, there's nowhere to go from there so just retrace your steps to return to your car.

6. MARYS PEAK: EAST RIDGE-TIE TRAIL LOOP

DISTANCE: 5-mile loop
TRAILHEAD LOCATION: 44.4958°, -123.5435°
STARTING ELEVATION/ELEVATION GAIN:
2550 feet/1250 feet
DIFFICULTY: Difficult
SEASON: Spring to late fall, access
dependent on snow

FOREST TYPE: Douglas-fir
PROTECTIONS: Unprotected roadless area;
Corvallis municipal watershed; old forest
reserved from logging in management plan
MANAGEMENT: Siuslaw National Forest
NOTES: Restrooms at trailhead; $5 fee or
permit required to park

GETTING THERE: Take Oregon Route 34 (US Highway 20) west from Corvallis. From the far end of Philomath, turn left to stay on OR 34 toward Alsea/Waldport. Go 8.8 miles and turn right at a sign for Marys Peak Recreation Area just past milepost 48 onto Marys Peak Road (Forest Road 30). In 5.3 miles, FR 30 turns to the left, but continue on FR 3010 a short ways to Conner's Camp on the right, just before a snow gate at 5.5 miles. The East Ridge Trail starts here from a large parking area. For the other hike options, continue past the Marys Peak Campground entrance to where the road ends at the large Observation Point parking lot.

Though Native peoples valued the area for spiritual purposes and for hunting and foraging going back thousands of years, Marys Peak is best known today for the spring wildflower displays in its summit meadows. But the forests that surround the peak and that shelter the Corvallis water supply are definitely worth exploring too. Most of these forests are publicly owned, but the drive up to the trailhead gives you views of how private lands are managed in the area (hint: they're clear-cut).

Located on the eastern edge of the Coast Range, Marys Peak's forests give rise to streams that feed both coastal and Willamette River systems. The peak, the highest in the Coast Range at just over 4000 feet, is also home to an island of old-growth noble fir.

To begin the 5-mile loop from Conner's Camp, take the East Ridge Trail through a younger forest that has been "thinned"—the most common form of logging on public lands these days—and then through a small grove of old trees before crossing a road marked by a sign for the municipal watershed. After a quarter mile of skirting the plantation, enter a tall, cathedral-like stand of Douglas-fir with a vine maple understory. Chinquapin, salal, Oregon grape, and young western hemlocks fill in the understory, and you'll catch views to the northeast through the trees as the trail climbs steadily to a junction with the Tie Trail at 1.2 miles.

Stay left here and go uphill on a series of long switchbacks that take you through the towering forest farther up the east-facing slope. As you gain elevation the forest gets messier, with snags, down wood, and a thicker understory. At 1.9 miles, the trail transitions to a north-facing slope with rocky outcrops and a steeper drop-off to the right. At 2 miles, there is an almost abrupt transition into a stand of noble firs, their blue-hued needles and gray bark markedly different from the Douglas-firs dominating the forest thus far. Openings along this slope include vine maple, elderberry, and thimbleberry.

Douglas-firs and western hemlocks line the East Ridge Trail on Marys Peak, the understory thick with greenery.

Turn right in the noble fir forest at a sign for the Summit Loop Trail, 1.4 miles past the Tie Trail junction. Then pass through a blowdown patch of forest and come out in the Observation Point parking area. To complete the East Ridge–Tie Trail loop, find the trail at the west end of the parking area in the corner opposite the restroom. This segment of trail parallels the road for a quarter mile through a grove of old noble firs. As you descend a ridge to the north, the forest transitions to hemlocks by the time you get to a junction of the North Ridge and Tie Trails in about 0.6 mile. Turn right to get on the Tie Trail back to Conner's Camp.

From here, the trail traverses the northeast-facing bowl that gives rise to Chintimini Creek through a beautiful Douglas-fir and hemlock forest, with some real giants. After about 0.4 mile on this trail, you'll cross the head of the creek, where water seeps out of the rocky hillside and feeds a peaceful western redcedar grove. Continue on, following the contour with a steep drop-off below, round a rocky outcrop, and then meet the East Ridge Trail after 1.2 miles. Turn left for the final 1.2 miles back to Conner's Camp.

The 2-mile Meadowedge Trail loop and the Marys Peak summit can both be reached from the Observation Point parking lot on their own or as additions to the featured loop. From the Observation Point parking lot, walk up the road. In a quarter mile, turn right at a sign for the Summit Loop Trail and Meadowedge Trail. At the first junction go right to get to the Meadowedge Trail. (To reach the summit, turn left at this junction in the forest.)

The Meadowedge Trail loop starts just below this junction at a large signboard. Heading left to do the loop clockwise takes you through a dense forest with little understory, though in places the forest floor is covered with oxalis and decomposing logs. Cross Parker Creek in a lovely woodland with some short snags left over from a previous iteration of this forest. The trail skirts the base of the large summit meadow, ducking in and out of the forest's edge, around Parker Creek's headwaters, and back to the start of the loop.

Head back up to the road and turn left toward the Observation Point parking lot to continue the East Ridge–Tie Trail loop or to return to your car if you parked there.

Ancient Forest Habitat: Can't Live Without It

While many types and forms of wildlife—from millipedes and salamanders to red tree voles and Pacific fishers—depend on the habitat provided by ancient forests, there are two birds that are particularly well known as old-growth forest "obligates," meaning they can't survive without the particular structure of an ancient forest. Both the northern spotted owl and marbled murrelet are listed as threatened under the Endangered Species Act because they are in danger of going extinct. Their critical status is in large part due to the destruction and fragmentation of the ancient forests they depend on to live. The only way to save them is to protect and reconnect their forest habitat.

Northern spotted owls are well adapted to the complex structure of an ancient forest. They use broken treetops or large brushy side limbs as nest sites; eat flying squirrels, tree voles, and woodrats that live in this type of forest; and use the multilayered canopy as cover for hunting and to evade larger predators. They don't do well in or near large openings like clear-cuts and tend to thrive best where they have large patches of ancient forest to live in. Having plenty of old-growth habitat also helps spotted owls coexist with barred owls, which have recently invaded their range. Larger, bolder barred owls tend to outcompete spotted owls for food and space, especially in less ideal habitat.

Marbled murrelets are seabirds, like puffins and auks—they feed on small schooling fish and spend most of their time on the ocean. But instead of nesting on rocky cliffs along the shore like others in their family, they have evolved to nest high in the canopy of old-growth trees—living cliffs, if you will. They aren't graceful perching birds and lack the physical means to build a nest, so they require wide, moss-covered limbs where they lay their single egg and can land without much agility. Their nest trees can be up to 50 miles from the ocean, and the parents trade off making the round-trip to the ocean for food at dawn and dusk every day to feed their chick.

Northern spotted owls depend on ancient forest structure for nesting, hunting, and escaping predators. *(Photo by Kristian Skybak)*

7. CAPE PERPETUA AND GWYNN CREEK

DISTANCE: 6.4-mile loop
TRAILHEAD LOCATION: 44.2804°, -124.1073°
STARTING ELEVATION/ELEVATION GAIN: 150 feet/1100 feet
DIFFICULTY: Difficult
SEASON: Year-round
FOREST TYPE: Coastal fog zone and redwoods, Douglas-fir

PROTECTIONS: Cape Perpetua Scenic Area; unprotected roadless area; old forest reserved from logging in management plan
MANAGEMENT: Siuslaw National Forest
NOTES: Restrooms and Cape Perpetua Visitor Center at trailhead; $5 fee or permit required to park

GETTING THERE: From the town of Florence, head north on US Highway 101 for 23 miles to signs for the Cape Perpetua Visitor Center between mileposts 168 and 169. From the north, head 3 miles south of Yachats on US 101. Park in the large lot to begin this loop.

The Cape Perpetua Scenic Area has a lot to offer: trails, camping, viewpoints, tidepools, and giant trees. The visitor center here offers information about the area's history and is a great place to look for whales. Just to the south, the Cummins Creek Wilderness protects one of the Central Coast's few intact ancient forest watersheds, but the best trails are on Cooks Ridge and in the little Gwynn Creek drainage between Cummins Creek and Cape Creek.

Start the hike from the Cape Perpetua Visitor Center (at the uphill part of the parking area) to do the loop in a clockwise direction. The trail begins on an old roadbed that climbs up past some impressive Sitka spruce with a tall shrub understory. After crossing a little creek on a bridge, enter an older plantation stand, with scattered big spruce and tall swordferns. As you head up the ridge with Cape Creek to the left, you'll come to the Discovery Loop. Continue straight to more quickly reach the main trail, and wind up steadily through the plantation—its dense canopy preventing much from growing on the ground. A bit over the half-mile point you'll find an interpretive sign near some large snags and legacy trees from the original forest stand, and then at 0.7 mile reach the top of the loop.

Go left to continue up the ridge, where the trees start to get more stately and the climb becomes more gradual for a while. The trail ambles along Cooks Ridge—Cape Creek to the north, Gwynn Creek to the south—up and down ridgetop saddles, gently climbing as you head east through a forest of tall spruce, western hemlock, and Douglas-fir with huckleberry, salal, and swordfern. Patches of dense young hemlock—filling in where ancient trees fell—and larger ones with pedestal bases punctuate the forest. Take some time to rest and catch views of the ocean behind you.

At about 1.8 miles, notice a patch of snags and alder trees on the ridgetop, likely growing here because of unstable soils. Beyond this, the spruce drops out of the forest, and the dense canopy tops an open understory before you finally reach the high point of the hike at about 2.3 miles. Descend a bit from here toward a south-facing slope with a really lovely multileveled canopy before intersecting the Gwynn Creek Trail at 2.4 miles. Turn right to continue downhill through

gawking. Look for the huge, seven-foot-diameter spruce in a wet area below the trail as well. The trail finally gets close to creek-level at about 3.5 miles and flattens into a gradual descent. Over the next nearly 2 miles, the trail dips in and out of little side-ravines, crossing numerous (I counted a dozen) side streams with cedars and salmonberry in their moisture-laden nooks. Gwynn Creek, below, is lined with alder, forming a green tunnel in the summer months. As you continue to head west toward the ocean, more and bigger spruce trees reenter the forest.

The Gwynn Creek Trail meets the Oregon Coast Trail 5.4 miles into the loop. Turn right to go back toward the visitor center through a forest that is now dominated by Sitka spruce and enjoy the sight and sound of the ocean—which almost drowns out the noise of US 101 just below. Cross the Cape Perpetua entrance road and turn right on the Captain Cook Trail to head back to the visitor center and parking area (unless you want to take a side trip to the tidepools, in which case, turn left).

Douglas-fir and hemlock, with only some small spruce and redcedars.

At about 2.8 miles, the trail begins to switch-back down the ridge to Gwynn Creek below. Between 3 and 3.5 miles, the trail descends more gradually toward the stream, with spectacular views through the forest of old-growth Douglas-fir trees with massive arms and furrowed, fire-scarred bark—some near the trail for close-up

8. PAWN GROVE

DISTANCE: 0.8 mile round-trip
TRAILHEAD LOCATION: 44.1267°, -123.9124°
STARTING ELEVATION/ELEVATION GAIN: 200 feet/Minimal
DIFFICULTY: Easy
SEASON: Year-round

FOREST TYPE: Douglas-fir
PROTECTIONS: Old forest reserved from logging in management plan
MANAGEMENT: Siuslaw National Forest
NOTES: No restrooms at trailhead; no parking fee or permit required

GETTING THERE: From Oregon Route 126, 1 mile east of Florence and US Highway 101, turn north on North Fork Siuslaw Road, just west of the big bridge over the North Fork Siuslaw River. Follow this paved road 11 miles up the North Fork valley to a junction, and continue straight on the Upper North Fork Road another 5.4 miles. Turn right and cross the bridge over the (now much smaller) North Fork Siuslaw River and find the parking area for this trail immediately on the right.

ABOVE: Hikers walk along Cooks Ridge among sword ferns and tapered Sitka spruce trunks.

OPPOSITE: Giant western redcedar, Douglas-firs, and hemlocks tower over evergreen huckleberry shrubs on the PAWN Trail.

The ten-acre PAWN Grove, named for four families that homesteaded in the area (Poole, Ackerly, Worthington, Norland), is a wonderful little gem. Once upstream of the cattle pastures that have severely altered the North Fork Siuslaw's lower reach, the stream is home to salmon and remnants of ancient forest that escaped the homesteaders' axes and the Siuslaw National Forest's timber boom.

Start the hike by crossing a footbridge over a small creek and passing an exposed rock wall that was once a quarry. Pick up a brochure here from a wooden box (if they aren't all gone) so you can follow along with the interpretive signage. The trail climbs past some big Douglas-firs and western redcedars, with an understory thick with vine maple and salmonberry. The North Fork Siuslaw flows below, lined by bigleaf maple and red alder.

After about 900 feet, cross two little bridges over trickling streams and then find the junction for the short loop. Stay straight here and enter a towering stand with a lot of western redcedar and western hemlock mixed in with the Douglas-fir. Swordfern and evergreen huckleberry dominate the understory. At a post marked number 6,

check out the giant Douglas-fir with a double top starting about 40 feet off the ground.

The trail continues with a steep forested slope to the left and the river's deciduous gallery to the right, with a view down over huge Douglas-firs with shattered tops and giant arms reaching out and up to the sky—perfect roosts for bald eagles. Big redcedars with gnarled arms are also found along the trail, and a few down logs across the trail (cut for passage) give good perspective on the size of the trees here. The trail then turns sharply right and down toward the river to head back on the loop, in close range of some huge trees that you saw from above. At post 9 a large hemlock is growing out of a nurse log—a perfect illustration of ancient forest structure. As you complete the loop, turn left to head back to the car.

Devil's Staircase Wilderness

Ancient Douglas-fir trees can be found deep in the Devil's Staircase Wilderness.

The largest contiguous forested area in the Coast Range that has never been logged is nestled in the rugged landscape between the Umpqua River and Smith River, east of the town of Reedsport. For many years forest advocates worked toward protection of the twenty-six-thousand-acre area, finally succeeding in 2019 when the Devil's Staircase Wilderness was designated by Congress, named after a stairstep waterfall on Wassen Creek that is notoriously hard to reach.

Much of the wild forest here isn't incredibly old—it originated after a large fire in the Coast Range between 150 and 200 years ago.

There are still some pockets of old-growth forest, however, with trees up to ten feet in diameter and likely four hundred years old. There are no official trails into this wild, rugged area, though advocates for the place use a few unofficial routes to reach some remarkably beautiful forests. Its inaccessibility is probably for the best: northern spotted owls and marbled murrelets make their home here, and the more intact and undisturbed it remains, the better for these sensitive creatures.

9. KENTUCKY FALLS

DISTANCE: 4.4 miles round-trip
TRAILHEAD LOCATION: 43.9282°, -123.7939°
STARTING ELEVATION/ELEVATION GAIN: 1550 feet/800 feet
DIFFICULTY: Moderate
SEASON: Early spring to late fall; roads not maintained for winter travel. Waterfalls most impressive in spring, but lower water in summer and fall make it easier to explore the base of the falls

FOREST TYPE: Douglas-fir
PROTECTIONS: Unprotected roadless area; Kentucky Falls Special Interest Area; old forest reserved from logging in management plan
MANAGEMENT: Siuslaw National Forest
NOTES: Restrooms at trailhead; no parking fee or permit required

GETTING THERE: From Eugene, go west on Oregon Route 126 for 33 miles. Turn left at the Whittaker Creek Recreation Area sign between mileposts 26 and 27. Continue for 1.6 miles, and turn right to cross a bridge onto BLM Road 18-8-28 (there will be another sign for Whittaker Creek). Continue for 1.5 miles, and then turn left onto Road 18-8-28.1 (Dunn Ridge Road). Continue on this road for 7 miles until you reach a T intersection where the pavement ends; then turn left onto Knowles Creek Road (Road 18-8-9). Continue for 2.8 miles and then veer right onto Forest Road 919. Continue for 1.6 miles to a second T intersection and turn right onto paved FR 23. Continue for 2.8 miles to Kentucky Falls Trailhead, on the right. Some of the logging roads can be bumpy and potholed, so drive with care.

In many ways the Kentucky Falls area represents a step back in time to an earlier day in Coast Range history, a period before intense timber harvesting reduced thousands of acres to a cutover maze of roads and clear-cut-scarred hillsides. To be sure, the drive to the area is through a patchwork of privately owned and BLM-managed lands that have been heavily logged. But the Kentucky Falls area was largely untouched by the logging that decimated other areas of the Siuslaw National Forest. It is, in fact, part of a four-thousand-acre unprotected roadless area— one of the largest intact forest areas in the Central Coast Range.

The trail begins across the road from the parking lot after you cross Kentucky Creek. Starting out in an ancient Douglas-fir forest along Kentucky Creek where spring wildflowers bloom in April and May, the trail then descends along a seeping rock wall to the base of the hundred-foot Upper Kentucky Falls in about three-quarters of a mile.

About another 1.4 miles in, after a switchbacking descent through the Douglas-fir and western hemlock forest, the trail ends at an observation deck overlooking the impressively tall and powerful Lower Kentucky Falls and the North Fork Smith Falls at the confluence of Kentucky Creek and North Fork Smith River. A smaller trail scrambles down from the deck (be careful on the slick rocks) to the river's edge and a better view of the colossal twin falls.

To return, head back uphill, being sure *not* to take the right-hand (downhill) trail about a quarter mile uphill from the falls. That beautiful trail—the North Fork Smith River Trail—continues through ancient riparian and Douglas-fir forests along the river another 6.5 miles to its trailhead along FR 23. You can get there by turning left onto FR 23 at the T intersection where you would go right to get to the Kentucky Falls Trailhead, and continuing for 6 miles.

Upper Kentucky Falls is the first of three tall waterfalls along the Kentucky Falls Trail.

SOUTH COAST AND KALMIOPSIS HIKES

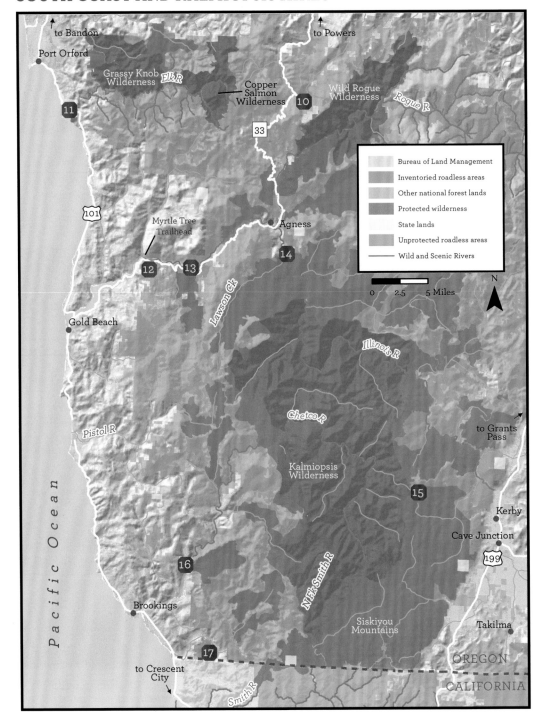

to Bandon

Port Orford

Grassy Knob
Wilderness *Elk R*

Copper
Salmon
Wilderness

to Powers

Wild Rogue
Wilderness

Rogue R

10

33

11

101

Myrtle Tree
Trailhead

Agness

Lawson Ck

14

12 **13**

Gold Beach

Illinois R

Chetco R

Pistol R

Kalmiopsis
Wilderness

to Grants
Pass

15

Kerby

Cave Junction

199

16

N Fk Smith R

Brookings

Siskiyou
Mountains

Takilma

17

to Crescent
City

Smith R

OREGON

CALIFORNIA

Pacific Ocean

	Bureau of Land Management
	Inventoried roadless areas
	Other national forest lands
	Protected wilderness
	State lands
	Unprotected roadless areas
———	Wild and Scenic Rivers

0   2.5   5 Miles

N

SOUTH COAST AND KALMIOPSIS

The South Coast and Kalmiopsis region fills in the southwest corner of the state and is home to the unique forests of the Siskiyou mixed conifer forest type. Though encompassing the Oregon Coast, this region is part of the Siskiyou Mountains (a subset of the Klamath Mountains), not the Coast Range. The climate is warmer and drier, and the ecosystem in this crossroads location has evolved separately from its surrounding mountain ranges and over a longer period of time, making it one of North America's most diverse botanical landscapes. Along the Coquille River, for example—which bridges the gap from north to south between the Umpqua and Rogue Rivers—the transition from the classic Douglas-fir and hemlock rainforest to the north and the mixed conifer and hardwood forest to the south is fairly pronounced. While Douglas-fir is still ubiquitous, even the coastal region loses Sitka spruce as hardwoods like myrtle and tanoak become more dominant. Areas of serpentine soil (with a high concentration of heavy metals) support unique plants and trees like Jeffrey pine not found elsewhere in Oregon.

The tallest trees on Earth, coast redwoods are the ultimate ancient trees, sometimes living more than two thousand years. Most people think of the towering coastal redwood forests of California, but these mighty trees also sneak into Oregon at the northern limit of their range, within the coastal fog zone in the lower Chetco River and Winchuck River watersheds. Adapted to withstand fire with thick bark and the ability to resprout from their base and trunk, redwoods often take on amazing shapes where they've been scarred by fire or deformed at their base by

massive burls caused by localized stress or infection. Oregon's redwoods faced near extinction from logging in the 1970s and 1980s, but thanks to Wendell Wood and other forest advocates who drew attention to the plight of Oregon's redwoods at that time, additional logging plans were dropped. Today, public awareness and pressure on federal managers means these remaining redwood stands are off the chopping block, but they are still in need of lasting and official protection.

The 180,000-acre Kalmiopsis Wilderness is the crown jewel of this region, spawning several world-class wild and scenic rivers (the region has been called the Wild Rivers Coast for good reason). The Elk and Chetco Rivers flow west from these mountains, while the Rogue and Illinois cut right through.

Several other large forested wilderness areas are also found here, including the Grassy Knob and Copper Salmon Wilderness areas, which protect the headwaters of the Elk River. But additional wild forestlands both east and west of the Kalmiopsis Wilderness are in need of lasting protections to preserve these ancient and diverse forests. The Wild Rogue Wilderness surrounds a spectacular river canyon, but its boundary should be doubled to truly protect this forested landscape. Efforts to do so have been under way for years.

Some unique challenges face the forests of this region. Not only have they been heavily logged outside of protected areas but two invading diseases threaten the continued existence of forest diversity. A type of root rot, spread through water and mud and initially introduced by logging equipment, has been killing Port Orford cedars (a species found only in a narrow band from Coos

Bay to the California border) for years. Another similar microbe causes the disease sudden oak death in tanoak and live oak and could dramatically change the vegetation of the region if unchecked.

Fire naturally plays a bigger, more frequent role here than farther north—and certainly has in recent years with the giant Biscuit Fire in 2002 and Chetco Bar Fire in 2017. The trees are well-adapted to fire, but in this era of a changing climate with longer summer droughts and less snowfall, forests of this region are likely to see worsening outbreaks of stress-caused diseases and perhaps hotter, more intense fires.

ABOVE: Fog hangs on the trees and hills surrounding the Kalmiopsis Wilderness.

OPPOSITE: The path to Coquille River Falls features layers of vine and bigleaf maples under tall Douglas-firs.

10. COQUILLE RIVER FALLS

DISTANCE: 1 mile round-trip
TRAILHEAD LOCATION: 42.7171°, -124.0216°
STARTING ELEVATION/ELEVATION GAIN:
1300 feet/440 feet
DIFFICULTY: Easy
SEASON: Year-round
FOREST TYPE: Douglas-fir, Siskiyou mixed
conifer

PROTECTIONS: Research natural area;
unprotected roadless area
MANAGEMENT: Rogue River–Siskiyou
National Forest
NOTES: No restrooms at trailhead; no
parking fee or permit required

GETTING THERE: From Interstate 5 south of Roseburg, take exit 119 for Oregon Route 42 toward Winston and Coos Bay. Follow OR 42 for 68 miles until it merges with OR 542 and turns south toward Powers. Go through the town of Powers and continue south, following the South Fork Coquille River, first on County Road 219, which turns into Forest Road 33 at the national forest boundary. At 16 miles past Powers, cross a bridge over the South Fork Coquille just past an informational sign and restroom, continue a half mile more, then turn left on FR 3348 at a sign for Glendale and Eden Valley. Find the trailhead at a small pullout on the left 1.5 miles up this paved road. FR 3348 can be accessed from the south by driving north of Agness on FR 33. Turn right to reach the trailhead.

The drive to this trailhead along the Rogue-Coquille Scenic Byway from Powers is delightful, following the South Fork Coquille River into the Rogue River–Siskiyou National Forest and leaving the Oregon Coast Range behind as you head into the Siskiyou Mountains. This transition means the forest has Port Orford cedar, Oregon myrtle, and tanoak mixed in to the classic Douglas-fir forest type. If you continue south from here into the Rogue River basin, the change becomes even more obvious. Though Port Orford cedars are in decline from the spread of a root rot disease, those in the Coquille River Falls Research Natural Area are still healthy—and beautiful.

This short but pleasant hike is a great stop on the drive between OR 42 and the Rogue River—illustrating the vegetative and climatic transition between the Coast Range and Siskiyou Mountains. The trail descends, gradually at first, through tall Port Orford cedars, Douglas-firs, and western hemlocks, with young cedars and hemlocks, swordfern, moss, and oxalis covering the ground. It passes through an opening with tall shrubs and a noticeable tanoak, which has lost its top and grown bushy, at the beginning of a series of switchbacks. Large cedars and Douglas-firs with fire scars indicate a past fire that the biggest trees in this forest survived (though some have since succumbed). As you descend toward the roaring river, some large bigleaf maple and tanoak lean toward the light. The falls plummet over huge rocks, and smaller rivulets join the main river near the trail—dripping over rocks that the adventurous and sure-footed could climb down for a closer look before heading back up the trail.

11. HUMBUG MOUNTAIN STATE PARK

DISTANCE: 5.3 miles round-trip
TRAILHEAD LOCATION: 42.6875°, -124.4393°
STARTING ELEVATION/ELEVATION GAIN: 80 feet/1600 feet
DIFFICULTY: Difficult
SEASON: Year-round
FOREST TYPE: Siskiyou mixed conifer

PROTECTIONS: State park, unlikely to be logged
MANAGEMENT: Oregon Parks and Recreation Department
NOTES: No restrooms at trailhead; no parking fee or permit required

GETTING THERE: Drive US Highway 101 north from Gold Beach 21 miles, or south from Port Orford 6 miles. Look for the large gravel parking area at the base of Humbug Mountain about a quarter mile north of the entrance to the Humbug Mountain State Park Campground and milepost 307 at a sign for the Humbug Mountain Trailhead.

Humbug Mountain State Park stands out as the last ancient forest left along a huge stretch of the Pacific Coast—from Cummins Creek Wilderness north of Florence to Redwood National Park south of Crescent City, California. Humbug Mountain stands out in a more literal way as well: the tall, hump-shaped, forest-covered mountain can be seen for miles along the coast from both the north and south. The hike to the top of the 1756-foot mountain features some huge trees in a diverse forest and trickling, fern-lined streams.

The trail up Humbug Mountain is steep from the beginning, climbing past large bigleaf maple and myrtle trees on a moist, north-facing slope. As you climb, you'll pass five-foot-diameter Douglas-fir trees and tall tanoaks. Turn up a drainage past a spectacular, spreading bigleaf maple, cross the creek at 0.7 mile, and climb again through a forest dominated by western hemlock.

Just shy of the 1-mile mark, there is a grove of big Douglas-firs and then a trail junction for the main loop. Take the west trail, to the right, and pass still more giant trees, with a mix of hemlock and myrtle with the Douglas-firs. Views of the ocean to the north appear here and there for the first half mile from the junction, and then the trail turns to the southwest where the forested slope is covered in smaller Douglas-fir—stunted a bit by conditions on this slope. At 1.9 miles, reach a ridge and continue to follow it gradually upward.

To check out the true summit of Humbug Mountain, go straight at the junction at the 2.3-mile point for just under a tenth of a mile, but don't expect much of a view. Continue on the big loop on the East Trail, descending a bit through a pure tanoak forest before traversing the top of the long north-facing slope covered in mixed-species forest and large, fire-scarred Douglas-firs. Switchback down this slope a ways, passing through patches of tanoak, madrone, rhododendrons, and tall hemlocks as the trail follows the mountain's east side. At about 3.8 miles, enter a wide ravine, with a lot of down wood and ferns and a view north to the ocean. After crossing the creek, the trail turns back across the bottom of the north slope it crossed much higher up. It returns to the junction with the West Trail at 4.3 miles, and then it's all downhill for the mile back to the parking area.

Humbug Mountain dominates the view south of the town of Port Orford.

12. SHRADER OLD-GROWTH GROVE

DISTANCE: 1-mile loop
TRAILHEAD LOCATION: 42.4907°, -124.2843°
STARTING ELEVATION/ELEVATION GAIN:
1100 feet/100 feet
DIFFICULTY: Easy
SEASON: Accessible year-round
FOREST TYPE: Siskiyou mixed conifer

PROTECTIONS: Old forest reserved from logging in management plan
MANAGEMENT: Rogue River–Siskiyou National Forest
NOTES: No restrooms at trailhead; no parking fee or permit required

GETTING THERE: From US Highway 101 in Gold Beach, just south of the Rogue River, turn inland on Jerry's Flat Road (which becomes Forest Road 33). Follow this road for about 10 miles. Just past the entrance to the Lobster Creek Campground, turn right on FR 090. Don't let the steep-grade sign scare you—the road is steep but well maintained. It's even paved for the first half mile, then good gravel for another 1.5 miles before you come to the trailhead parking area on the left.

This small ancient forest grove on the western edge of the Rogue River–Siskiyou National Forest, just south of the Rogue River, is simply spectacular. Classic ancient forest structure is on display at every turn—with evidence of multiple disturbances that continue to reshape the area. If one is available, pick up an informative interpretive brochure.

Tall Douglas-firs, Port Orford cedars, and riparian shrubs in the Shrader old-growth grove

From the parking area, cross the road to begin the packed-gravel trail in a grove of alder trees. Large Douglas-firs, tanoak, rhododendron, and evergreen huckleberry line the trail. Look also for the shredded-looking bark of the Port Orford cedars in the forest. A short way down the trail through the forest to the right, you'll get a glimpse of a massive Douglas-fir with huge branching arms, but stay to the left at the junction (you'll have a chance to get closer to it at the end of the loop). The layered forest includes a lot of large Port Orford cedar snags, which have succumbed to a root rot disease that is harming their population all over southern Oregon.

On a bridge cross a small creek that pours down through the forest and ferns. The opening here is piled with down logs, blown over in a windstorm in the winter of 2001–2, and tanoaks are responding by filling in the canopy. Pass by some large Douglas-firs, their tops broken in places and large upper branches reaching for the sky, and descend to another creek-crossing at about a half mile. Along the creek there are large bigleaf maples, overtopped by cedar snags, with myrtle and salmonberry in the understory. Cross the creek again at 0.6 mile, with views up and down this little drainage.

From the other side, the trail heads uphill, crossing another bridge and a big burnt-out Port Orford cedar snag with a tall fire scar from 100 years ago. At a split in the trail, you've reached Laddie Gale—the giant Douglas-fir noted at the beginning of the loop. This tree, named for a player on the 1939 University of Oregon basketball team known as Tall Firs, is over ten feet in diameter and 220 feet tall. A tall fir indeed! Go either way at the split to walk around and explore the base of the tree before meeting the loop, turning left, and returning to the trailhead.

13. LOWER ROGUE RIVER

DISTANCE: 3.4 miles round-trip
TRAILHEAD LOCATION: 42.4958°, -124.2096°
STARTING ELEVATION/ELEVATION GAIN: 580 feet/500 feet
DIFFICULTY: Easy
SEASON: Year-round
FOREST TYPE: Siskiyou mixed conifer

PROTECTIONS: Wild and scenic river corridor; unprotected roadless area; old forest reserved from logging in management plan
MANAGEMENT: Rogue River–Siskiyou National Forest
NOTES: No restrooms at trailhead; no parking fee or permit required

GETTING THERE: From US Highway 101 in Gold Beach, just south of the Rogue River, turn inland on Jerry's Flat Road (which becomes Forest Road 33). Follow this road for about 10 miles to the Lobster Creek Bridge on the left, just past Lobster Creek Campground. Cross the bridge and take the first right onto gravel Silver Creek Road (FR 3533). Pass the Myrtle Tree Trail after a quarter mile (but consider taking it later) and keep going another 6 miles on FR 3533, following signs for the Lower Rogue River Trail. Park on the side of the road at the trailhead sign.

The Lobster Creek bridge crosses the lower Rogue River on the way to the Lower Rogue River Trail.

The Rogue River is one of Oregon's gems. While the upper river is amazing (see Hike 60, Upper Rogue River Trail), the lower river—after gaining size and volume and cutting through the Siskiyou Mountains—is truly impressive at another scale. The river, designated as a wild and scenic corridor for 84 miles of its length below Grants Pass, passes through the Wild Rogue Wilderness and many surrounding roadless, wild forestlands on its way to the ocean in Gold Beach.

This stretch of the Lower Rogue River Trail runs from the town of Agness near the confluence with the Illinois River downstream for 12 miles. The best ancient forest on this trail is most accessible from the lower end described here.

The first section of the trail is actually on an old road, but it soon becomes more trail-like and passes through a beautiful forest of four-foot-diameter Douglas-fir trees, myrtle, and tanoaks. Hazelnut, evergreen huckleberry, ferns, and a mixture of young trees fill in the multilayered understory. In about a half mile, enter a stellar grove of giant Douglas-firs before passing through a disturbed area thick with blackberries and shrubs. At the 0.8-mile mark, follow a sign to go toward Agness and reenter the native forest.

At a little over a mile, the trail dips into a ravine with two small streams lined with maidenhair ferns and salmonberry. Enjoy a patch of pure hardwood forest of tanoak, madrone, and bigleaf maple before passing through a blowdown area on a wet hillside with a view over the river canyon.

At 1.5 miles the trail turns up a large ravine with gorgeous ancient trees—Douglas-fir, alder, and bigleaf maple—and comes to a busted up (in the summer of 2017) bridge over Slide Creek at 1.7 miles. The trail leading up Slide Creek's canyon is made of crumbling rocks, and large boulders in the creek below the bridge indicate that this area is prone to rockslides. This is a good place to turn around, even if the bridge is repaired, for a short hike. The ancient forest does continue, with some of the nicest examples another 3.5 miles up the trail above Tom East Creek, if you are out for a longer hike.

Lobster Creek Myrtle Grove: The Myrtle Tree Trail

TRAILHEAD LOCATION: 42.5043°, -124.2890°

Some of the oldest and most unusual trees in southern Oregon aren't what you might expect. Oregon myrtle, or California laurel, is found mixed in with Douglas-fir, tanoak, hemlock, and cedar forests in the South Coast and Kalmiopsis region, but it isn't a generally dominant tree in size or prevalence. Excellent ancient examples of these really interesting (and wonderful-smelling) trees can be found on the way to the Lower Rogue River Trail (Hike 13).

The whimsical trunks and base of a myrtle tree on the Myrtle Tree Trail

The Myrtle Tree Trail, located in the 445-acre Lobster Creek Botanical Area, is well marked on the side of the road. (Grab a brochure, if one is available, to learn more about this grove.) It switchbacks up through a nearly pure myrtle grove. It's hard not to think about J. R. R. Tolkien's inspiration for his ents as you walk among these gnarled, hollowed-out monsters, with burls and conch fungi adding to the feeling that each one is its own unique character.

The largest specimen in Oregon is found at the end of the trail, in just 0.2 mile. This giant had multiple trunks growing out of a huge, thirteen-foot-diameter base, hollowed out by past fires but now crushed by one of its neighboring tanoaks. Myrtle trees are adapted to resprout from their bases, so a new canopy will develop. Head back down the trail when you're done gawking and return the brochure for the next visitor to use.

14. ILLINOIS RIVER TRAIL: BUZZARDS ROOST

DISTANCE: 6 miles round-trip
TRAILHEAD LOCATION: 42.5190°, -124.0420°
ELEVATION GAIN: 230 feet/850 feet
DIFFICULTY: Moderate
SEASON: Year-round
FOREST TYPE: Siskiyou mixed conifer

PROTECTIONS: Inventoried roadless area
MANAGEMENT: Rogue River–Siskiyou National Forest
NOTES: Restrooms at nearby Oak Flat campground; no parking fee or permit required. Beware of ticks.

GETTING THERE: From US Highway 101 in Gold Beach, just south of the Rogue River, turn inland on Jerry's Flat Road (which becomes Forest Road 33). Drive 27 miles up this paved road to the confluence of the Rogue and Illinois Rivers. Just after crossing a tall bridge over the Illinois, turn right on Oak Flat Road. Follow this narrow, winding paved road for 3 miles to the trailhead and small parking area on the left, just before the road turns to gravel and heads downhill to Oak Flat Campground and a large gravel bar.

The 27-mile-long Illinois River Trail follows the rugged and magnificent wild and scenic river through the north end of the Kalmiopsis Wilderness and surrounding designated roadless areas. Much of the trail's length has burned in fires—first in the Silver Fire of 1987 and then in the Biscuit Fire of 2002—but the naturally recovering forest can be interesting, the views expansive, and wildflowers wonderful.

The Wild and Scenic Illinois River is visible through snags burned in the 2002 Biscuit Fire.

The trail starts out in a dense Douglas-fir and myrtle forest with an open understory and climbs gently to a bench covered in three-foot-diameter Douglas-firs with a smattering of canyon live oak, tanoak, and ponderosa pine. Along the ridge-top overlooking the river are some impressive red-barked madrones and small black oaks, with wildflowers lining the trail.

At about 0.4 mile, look across the river to see where Lawson Creek enters the Illinois, and note the blackened bases of the tree trunks in the forest along the trail—a low-intensity fire burned here, killing small trees and shrubs but leaving most trees unharmed.

Coming up on 0.7 mile, enter a riparian area with incense cedar and an opening with oaks up to the left. This area is just outside of the protected roadless area, and plans (in 2018) to do some logging could change the forest here. Hike up along lovely Nancy Creek, which pours down boulders past myrtles, madrones, tanoaks, and alders, and then cross the creek on a bridge near where a logging road comes down the hill.

Heading back out toward the Illinois, on a rocky section the trail passes more hardwoods and then follows the river past canyon live oak, incense cedar, and madrone below a grassy slope. At 1.3 miles, pass a big ponderosa pine snag and turn up another side drainage (Rattlesnake Creek) where Douglas-fir, western redcedar, and bigleaf maple are thriving. Cross the creek and head back toward the river, where you'll get a nice view downstream. The trail continues upstream, with a steep drop-off to the river below, and at 1.6 miles finally enters the high-severity burn area. Tall blackened snags dominate the slopes in every direction (with some green Douglas-firs scattered here and there), with a dense, rapidly growing understory of madrone, tanoak, ceanothus, and Douglas-fir seedlings.

Entering a small riparian area at 1.8 miles, you'll get some shade and find tall shrubs, myrtle, and cedars where the wetland protected the area from the fire. This forest continues a little way toward Ethels Creek, which you'll cross on a small bridge at about 2 miles. From there, enter an area dominated by tanoak overhanging the trail, pass a stand of live Douglas-firs, and then climb gently through an exposed rocky slope high above the river. Ahead, you'll spot Buzzards Roost—a tall rocky outcrop—and look across the river to the unburned forest. Use caution on this narrow stretch of trail leading to Buzzards Roost, and beware of ticks that like to jump off of the grasses that line the trail here. Reach Buzzards Roost at 3 miles—a good place to turn around for a day hike. Retrace your steps to your car.

15. BABYFOOT LAKE

DISTANCE: 2.5 miles round-trip
TRAILHEAD LOCATION: 42.2247°, -123.7928°
STARTING ELEVATION/ELEVATION GAIN:
4300 feet/300 feet
DIFFICULTY: Easy
SEASON: Late spring to fall, access dependent on snow

FOREST TYPE: Siskiyou mixed conifer
PROTECTIONS: Inventoried roadless area; Kalmiopsis Wilderness
MANAGEMENT: Rogue River–Siskiyou National Forest
NOTES: Restrooms at trailhead; no parking fee or permit required

A diversity of trees, living and dead, are reflected in the waters of Babyfoot Lake.

GETTING THERE: From Grants Pass, drive US Highway 199 south 24 miles, or from Cave Junction, drive US 199 north 5 miles. Turn west on Eight Dollar Road, which is paved at first, becomes Forest Road 4201 and narrows after a mile, crosses the Illinois River at just under 3 miles, then turns to gravel. From here, the road climbs for 11.9 gravel miles above the Illinois River valley from US 199. As you approach the 12-mile mark, turn left on marked FR 140 at a fork in a pass. Then keep right at another fork and continue for 0.7 mile to the well-marked trailhead and parking area on the right.

The drive to the Babyfoot Lake Trailhead is scenic and quite educational for the observant person. The views over the Illinois River valley are impressive, and as the road winds its way up toward the east side of the Kalmiopsis Wilderness it passes sparse serpentine slopes (where scattered Jeffrey pines grow on the mineral-rich soil) and continues across Fiddler Mountain into areas that burned in the 2002 Biscuit Fire. There is a mix of unburned forest, areas that burned and were logged in the aftermath, and places where standing snags indicate that the forest is recovering naturally.

When you arrive at the trailhead, note the lack of snags. After the Biscuit Fire in 2002, the edge of the Kalmiopsis was ground zero in the fight over salvage logging, because even protections for designated roadless areas are subject to loopholes big enough to drive logging trucks through when it comes to postfire logging.

Despite the high-severity burn in this area, the short hike to Babyfoot Lake, on the east side of the vast Kalmiopsis Wilderness through the recovering forest, is lovely and the lake itself stunning. Please keep in mind that this area is both very sensitive and very popular and avoid camping close to the lake or blazing new trails.

Starting out through an area logged after the fire, you get sweeping views of the burned landscape and some of the damage done in the aftermath—with logging roads and the removal of legacy trees. Note the vegetation here. After entering the unlogged, naturally recovering stand covered in tall snags, you'll see young conifers and a whole host of shrubs, hardwoods, and wildflowers taking over the understory. Compare this diversity and lush growth with the first stretch of logged trail.

In a little over a quarter mile, stay to the right at a trail junction to go downhill, and pass a rocky outcrop. Cross a small stream at 0.7 mile. Round a corner to face the rock wall that forms Babyfoot Lake's backdrop; still-green trees perch on the ridgetop and steep walls. Catch your first glimpse of the lake below just over a mile into the hike, and descend the last 1000 feet to its shore.

Here in the cool lake basin, many trees survived the fire, and the lakeshore is a great place to put some tree identification skills (or just curiosity) to work. Douglas-fir, Port Orford cedar, sugar pine, and Brewer's spruce are the largest living trees, while young true firs, tanoak, chinquapin, azaleas, and willows line the shore in the understory. (Brewer's, or weeping, spruce, found only in the Klamath Mountains, has gray, flaky, puzzle-piece bark and sharp-tipped needles.) Explore the shore carefully to enjoy the wildflowers, reflections, and shade before heading back the way you came.

16. REDWOOD NATURE TRAIL

DISTANCE: 1-mile loop
TRAILHEAD LOCATION: 42.1184°, -124.1959°
STARTING ELEVATION/ELEVATION GAIN:
Sea level/290 feet
DIFFICULTY: Easy
SEASON: Year-round
FOREST TYPE: Siskiyou mixed conifer, coastal fog zone and redwoods

PROTECTIONS: Old forest reserved from logging in management plan
MANAGEMENT: Rogue River–Siskiyou National Forest
NOTES: Restrooms at trailhead; no parking fee or permit required

GETTING THERE: In Brookings on US Highway 101, turn east (inland) at the stoplight just north of the Chetco River Bridge onto North Bank Road. Travel up the Chetco River for 8 miles to find the trailhead on the left, about a half mile past the entrance to Alfred A. Loeb State Park. Parking is limited on the roadside and in the trailhead pullout.

This is the most easily accessible redwood trail in Oregon, just a fifteen-minute drive from US 101, up the Chetco River. It's in the Rogue River–Siskiyou National Forest but is adjacent to Alfred A. Loeb State Park and a mixture of BLM and private lands that lie between the bulk of the national forest and the coast.

The route starts by following a small, boulder-strewn creek, with a salmonberry thicket covering its riparian area. Just below a bridge and waterfall, the trail splits for the loop—head left to hike

Fighting for Natural Fire Recovery

The Biscuit Fire, which burned much of the Kalmiopsis Wilderness and adjacent road-less (but unprotected) forests in the summer of 2002, was huge and hot. Afterward, the Forest Service proposed logging thousands of acres of burned trees in the sensitive area. This resulted in citizen protest, direct action blocking access to the area, and litigation. Activists were somewhat successful, but some areas, as illustrated at the Babyfoot Lake Trailhead, were logged.

Why were forest advocates, including a huge number of scientists, so keen on pre-venting postfire logging here and in other areas like the forest burned in the Warner Creek Fire in the Willamette National Forest in the early 1990s? Forests naturally grow back on their own after a fire, setting in motion the classic stages of succession. Because humans have been actively suppressing fires and insisting on salvage logging across the forested landscape for the past century, naturally recovering postfire forests are now rare. Yet they are an essential element of the ancient forest ecosystem, providing snags and down wood legacies for the next iteration of the forest.

After fire, federal agencies have traditionally shown a tendency to rush to remove burned trees that would otherwise "go to waste" from a wood-products perspective. But in nature, there is no waste. Dead trees are recycled naturally—stabilizing and enrich-ing the soil and providing much-needed habitat for species such as woodpeckers that depend on abundant dead trees. Experts agree that "salvage" logging and associated road building and replanting sets back ecological recovery after a fire and leaves the future forest with a lack of biodiversity building blocks.

Many of these transgressions and their impacts can be seen near the Babyfoot Lake Trailhead, where the unlogged forest—with snags still standing—is thriving, while the logged forest has been set back and has no legacies to rebuild from. The area is a great illustration of what activists and scientists have been standing up for: the best thing to do after fire is to let nature heal itself.

Shrubs and small trees regrow at the base of fire-killed trees on the trail to Babyfoot Lake.

Giant coast redwood trees stand out among smaller trunks on the Redwood Nature Trail.

clockwise, following the numbered posts that correspond to an interpretive brochure (if there are any in the box at the trailhead).

The trail follows a contour above the road a short way, with views through the trees of the clear green water of the Chetco River, before climbing up and away from the river corridor through a tanoak and Douglas-fir forest. The first big redwood is on the side of the trail just 600 feet or so into the forest—a taste of what's to come. Just beyond that, you'll climb through an opening dominated by shrubs and seedlings, then enter a denser forest of Douglas-fir, myrtle, tanoak, and redwoods. Cross a creek on a bridge in a bit over a quarter mile, then follow the drainage to a lovely redwood grove with ten- to twelve-foot-diameter trunks. These ancient specimens are likely five to eight hundred years old.

Continuing to climb, you'll reach another bridge at the halfway point and then begin to descend on the other side of the creek, with nice views through the forest from this vantage point. Descend past big double- and triple-stemmed redwoods, five to eight feet in diameter, then cross the creek again at about 0.7 mile.

From here, the trail switchbacks down through towering (if not super thick) trees, past moss-covered rocks, and through a lush green understory.

This trail saves some of the best for last: in the final quarter mile, pass a huge double-trunked redwood with a twelve-foot-diameter base and finally a giant burned-out redwood with a cavity going up twenty feet. Finish the loop by crossing the creek one more time where it tumbles over boulders as a small waterfall.

17. OREGON REDWOODS TRAIL

DISTANCE: 2-mile loop
TRAILHEAD LOCATION: 42.0086°, -124.1470°
STARTING ELEVATION/ELEVATION GAIN:
1130 feet/260 feet
DIFFICULTY: Easy
SEASON: Year-round, but roads may be muddy in winter and spring
FOREST TYPE: Siskiyou mixed conifer, coastal fog zone and redwoods

PROTECTIONS: Unprotected roadless area; old forest reserved from logging in management plan
MANAGEMENT: Rogue River–Siskiyou National Forest
NOTES: Restrooms at trailhead; no parking fee or permit required

GETTING THERE: One mile north of the Oregon–California border on US Highway 101 (6 miles south of Brookings) turn east (inland) on Winchuck Road (County Road 896) and travel 1.4 miles. Turn right on unmarked Peavine Ridge Road (Forest Road 1101) to cross the Winchuck River on a concrete bridge. Drive up this gravel road, which is a bit rough and muddy in areas (in the wet months, consider four-wheel drive), for 4.1 miles to the end of the road and a large parking area.

When forest advocate Wendell Wood explored the region inland of the southern Oregon coast in the 1980s looking for redwoods that had survived logging, he found a mere 1300 acres of small groves scattered on the western edge of the Siskiyou National Forest, on some BLM lands, and in the Alfred A. Loeb State Park, some of them still threatened by logging plans.

The redwoods in the Peavine Ridge area, between the California border and the Winchuck River, were among the stands slated for logging. In response to the public outpouring of care for these forests, the logging plans were dropped and the Forest Service built this trail on Peavine Ridge.

Despite being a bit off the beaten path, the trailhead on Peavine Ridge is well-developed. The trail starts out from the parking area past a signboard with information (and possibly interpretive brochures) about redwoods. This first part of the trail begins the half-mile accessible loop—a great way for people of all abilities to enjoy this spectacular forest. Tall snags are mixed with tall living trees—redwoods, Douglas-firs, tanoak, and myrtle—along with rhododendrons and evergreen huckleberry for a nice layered effect. Ignore the trail that heads downhill a short way into the hike—that's the return part of the larger loop. As the trail follows the ridgetop, pass a few small openings with bigleaf maple, salmonberry, and western hemlock all seeking the sun.

Just 0.4 mile into the trail, the short loop begins in a grove of truly enormous redwoods with blackened bark going up thirty feet. Stay to the right and continue to the highlight of this loop: a burnt-out snag, at least twelve feet in diameter, that you can walk right into (along with a handful of friends) to explore the fire-sculptured interior. Arrive at a picnic table shortly after the big tree—a good place to sit and enjoy the forest—and then the trail junction for the longer loop.

This longer trail descends through a dense forest of younger trees, and switchbacks down,

Blooming rhododendrons mix with giant redwoods on Peavine Ridge. *(Photo by Wendell Wood)*

following a headwater tributary to Moser Creek. Fat redwoods, some with large burls at their base, are scattered along the trail among Douglas-firs and tall rhododendrons. The trail turns to the south and descends toward another small drainage, with a flatter bench downhill between the two. The forest here is a lovely mix of sizes, the smaller trees making the giant ones really stand out.

After about three-quarters of a mile on this longer loop, the trail begins to climb up another arm of Moser Creek past some gorgeous trees. Look for the twelve-footer just off the trail to the left, and not long after hopping over a small stream look for a five-foot-wide trunk with a huge burl encircling the tree about thirty feet off the ground, with huckleberries growing from the platform. To finish the loop, the last quarter mile climbs up more steeply through a mostly younger Douglas-fir forest with a sparse understory and a few scattered giants, before you reach the main trail, turn right, and head back to the trailhead.

SISKIYOU CREST HIKES

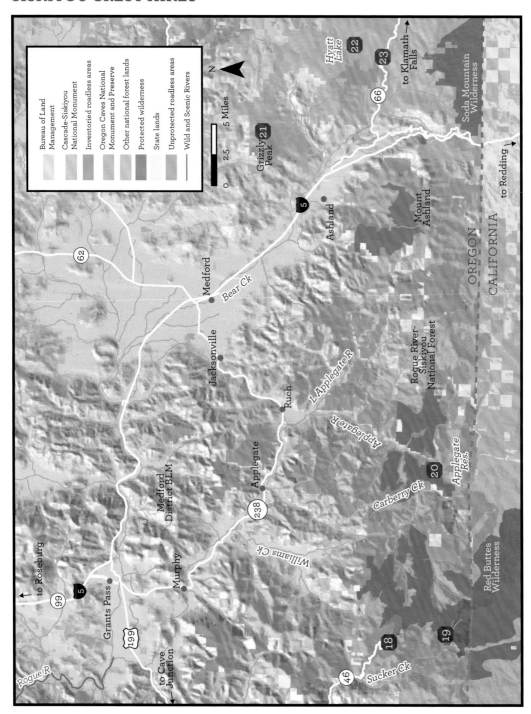

SISKIYOU CREST

The Siskiyou Crest region, as defined here, bridges the divide between the Siskiyou Mountains (a subset of the Klamath Mountains) to the west and the southern Cascade Range to the east of Ashland. The mountains in this area run mostly east–west, spanning the border between Oregon and California and dividing the huge Rogue and Klamath River watersheds. The rivers that dissect the area head in every direction—Sucker and Deer Creeks flow west to the Illinois River; the Applegate River and its tributaries flow north off of this crest to the Rogue River; Ashland and Emigrant Creeks drain the mountains above the wide Bear Creek valley, which also feeds the Rogue; and Jenny and Keene Creeks flow east into the Klamath River drainage.

Its unique position, and a range from low to higher elevations, means that the region supports a wide diversity of tree species, the forest types falling within both the Siskiyou mixed conifer and the Douglas-fir zones. The ecological importance of the area has been recognized through protections of the Soda Mountain Wilderness and Cascade-Siskiyou National Monument (CSNM), the first national monument ever designated for its unique biological diversity.

Important as this ecosystem is, protected forests are not the rule here. Much of this region is managed by the BLM, where logging of ancient forests is still an

emphasis and the Roadless Rule does not apply. Several large undeveloped, wild forest areas are found on BLM lands here, forming the backdrop for many rural homes and communities and offering great trails through diverse landscapes, including those in the Cascade-Siskiyou National Monument. Outside the CSNM (where forests

Ponderosa pines and oak trees line the ridge on Green Springs Mountain on the Siskiyou Crest.

are generally protected from logging other than for restoration purposes), some of these forests are zoned for protection under the BLM's management plan, but many are not.

Protected forests are primarily limited to national forestlands in this region. The Red Buttes Wilderness, which bridges into both Oregon and California, and Oregon Caves National Monument protect forests on the west side of this region. The forests surrounding Mount Ashland and the streams that supply Ashland with drinking water also have some special protections.

18. OREGON CAVES NATIONAL MONUMENT

DISTANCE: 4-mile loop
TRAILHEAD LOCATION: 42.0982°, -123.4066°
STARTING ELEVATION/ELEVATION GAIN:
4000 feet/1100 feet
DIFFICULTY: Difficult
SEASON: Late spring to fall, access dependent on snow

FOREST TYPE: Siskiyou mixed conifer
PROTECTIONS: Oregon Caves National Monument and Preserve
MANAGEMENT: National Park Service
NOTES: Restrooms at trailhead; no parking fee or permit required

GETTING THERE: From Cave Junction on US Highway 199, 29 miles south of Grants Pass, turn east onto Oregon Route 46 at signs for Oregon Caves National Monument. Drive 20 miles on this lovely paved road, which gets narrow and windy after passing Greenback Campground at about 12 miles. Park in the large parking area before the narrow bridge and roadway that goes to the visitor center, where the trail begins.

Originally designated a national monument in 1909, the Oregon Caves protected barely over five hundred acres right around the cave system's access point. In 2014 the underground river that flows through the cave system was designated a wild and scenic river, and the renamed Oregon Caves National Monument and Preserve was expanded to over four thousand acres. The monument now protects more of the diverse ancient forest and watershed that feeds the cave system. When you plan a visit here, it's well worth allowing enough time to both tour the caves and hike in the ancient forest.

The Big Tree Trail begins behind the visitor center —past the restrooms at a large signboard— but the recommended hike actually begins on the Cliff Nature Trail. This paved path, lined with a wooden railing, starts in front of the visitor center. It goes uphill a bit steeply to start, passes the cave's official exit, takes a sharp right at the base of a marble cliff, and switchbacks up through a middle-aged forest of Douglas-fir, madrone, and bigleaf maple, with canyon live oak in rockier areas. The trail climbs to a spectacular overlook of the surrounding peaks, forests, and drainages, showing especially the many snags present in the surrounding forest. From there, the trail descends through a pleasant mixed fir and cedar forest—both Port Orford and incense cedar are found here—with down wood littering the forest floor. Rocky steps lead down to the junction with

A diverse forest, including both Port Orford and incense cedars, is found on the Big Tree Trail in the Oregon Caves National Monument and Preserve.

the Big Tree loop at 0.8 mile. Turn right to join the Big Tree loop.

From here the trail ascends through a dense Douglas-fir, white fir, and cedar forest, with some large specimens. On some of the more exposed slopes, shrubby alders form dense thickets. As you head up, you'll pass some really large Douglas-firs and cedars, as well as some snags, with burn scars. A spur trail to the left goes to the edge of the creek, but the main trail goes up and to the right, and switchbacks up to cross this gully farther up. About a mile along the trail, look for a seven- to eight-foot-diameter Douglas-fir, its top broken 60 feet up, with a new one taking over. Open slopes and meadows filled with wildflowers and patches of shrubby alder are interspersed with forest after about 1.5 miles, with large snags lining the edges of these openings.

In an opening with rocky mountain maples, at 1.7 miles, you'll pass the Mount Elijah Trail junction. From here the trail descends a bit into the denser forest, emerges again onto a slope full of alders, crosses a stream and wet area on a boardwalk, and then—don't forget to look up—you're struck with The Big Tree. This seriously impressive Douglas-fir has lost its top but has massive limbs and a fourteen-foot girth near the base—it is likely over a thousand years old.

After marveling at this tree's base, follow the trail downhill, past some large white fir and moist areas with rhododendron and Pacific yew. More of the classic ancient forest—with snags, patches of young fir saplings, and a grove of large cedars—awaits as you work your way down. When you come to a road junction, switchback down to the left on a drier southwest-facing slope with more ponderosa pine, madrone, canyon live oak, and manzanita. Stunted Douglas-firs also grow on this rocky, drier slope. You'll get views across the Cave Creek canyon to the Cliff Nature Trail overlook as you switchback down, then encounter a junction with the Old Growth Trail that goes to the right. Despite its enticing name, this trail doesn't offer much old growth. Turn left instead to head 0.2 mile back to the visitor center.

19. SUCKER CREEK

DISTANCE: 6 miles round-trip
TRAILHEAD LOCATION: 42.0304°, -123.3898°
STARTING ELEVATION/ELEVATION GAIN: 3900 feet/1300 feet
DIFFICULTY: Difficult
SEASON: June through late fall; mosquitoes in early summer

FOREST TYPE: Siskiyou mixed conifer
PROTECTIONS: Red Buttes Wilderness
MANAGEMENT: Rogue River–Siskiyou National Forest
NOTES: No restrooms at trailhead; no parking fee or permit required

GETTING THERE: From Cave Junction on US Highway 199, 29 miles south of Grants Pass, turn east onto Oregon Route 46 at signs for Oregon Caves National Monument. At a hairpin turn 1.7 miles past Greyback Campground (13.3 miles from Cave Junction), turn right onto unmarked Forest Road 4612. Drive through a gate (which should be open) and continue a total of 9.6 miles on this road—staying right at junctions at 2 and 3.4 miles and left at 6.7 miles. Stay left on FR 098, heading south along Sucker Creek. Stay straight on this road at a junction at 3.4 miles and then look for a small pullout on the right a quarter mile later to find the nearly hidden, unmaintained trailhead, a total of 13.2 miles from the turnoff of OR 46. Most of the route is on good gravel, but the last few miles are a bit bumpy.

The Sucker Creek Trail follows Sucker Creek, a tributary of the Illinois River, through an exceptional ancient forest and then climbs to wildflower meadows in the Red Buttes Wilderness. Most of the Red Buttes Wilderness is in California, but about four thousand acres slop over the border to protect this unique area. The trail to the Sucker Creek shelter, on the edge of a high-elevation meadow, offers a lot of diversity and all the classic components of an ancient forest—down wood, snags, disturbance patches, and trees of varied ages.

Look for the battered signpost in the bushes to find the trail at the trailhead pullout. This section hasn't been maintained in quite some time, so be prepared for down logs and brush, though the trail is still evident and features an impressive ancient forest. The trail descends gradually toward Sucker Creek, though never reaches it, into a diverse mixed forest of chinquapin, sugar pine, Douglas-fir, white fir, dogwood, and Pacific yew. Patches of bigleaf maple punctuate openings along the trail as you pass several small springs and streams, easily crossed on some of the many down logs littering the forest floor.

A mile into the hike, cross a wet meadow area filled with wildflowers and sedge before coming to the Fehley Gulch Trail junction.

Continue straight on the main trail and head up Thirteenmile Creek's gulch, passing some impressive examples of Douglas-fir infected with dwarf mistletoe—of which there are a lot in this forest. Look for the elongated, drooping branches that give the lower limbs of the tree a weeping look, and for witches' brooms—dense clumps of branches—higher up. (Dwarf mistletoe is a parasitic plant that stimulates excessive growth that leads to these strange formations.)

The trail then travels side-slope past some big snags and sugar pines. You might start to notice incense cedar, with its stringy and furrowed bark, as it starts to make an appearance in the forest. Some of the biggest you pass, after about 1.3 miles, have visible burn scars. A little farther, pass some

really large pine snags and one giant living pine amid smaller incense cedars.

At about 1.6 miles, the hillside flattens to a gentle slope with large cedars and Douglas-fir and an open forest floor. The big trees continue, with white fir mixed in. After crossing a spring, you'll find the nicest cedars yet (four feet in diameter) in a grove mixed with dogwood and bigleaf maple at just under 2 miles. From here, it's another quarter mile to the junction with the connector tie trail that leads down from a second trailhead at the end of FR 098, passing an old mining area.

From the tie trail junction, cross a fork of Sucker Creek in under a quarter mile and start to climb. This last three-quarters to a mile of

A worn-out sign indicates the way along Sucker Creek in the Red Buttes Wilderness.

the hike to the Sucker Creek shelter gains 1200 feet of elevation, so you may need to stop and catch your breath. It's worth it though—huge incense cedars line the trail as you reach the high elevation meadows and find the Sucker Creek

shelter off the trail to the left near a spring. This trail connects to much longer backpacking options a bit farther on at Sucker Creek Gap, but turn back here for a day hike and return the way you came.

20. COLLINGS MOUNTAIN

DISTANCE: 4.2 miles round-trip
TRAILHEAD LOCATION: 42.0512°, -123.1315°
STARTING ELEVATION/ELEVATION GAIN:
2130 feet/1330 feet
DIFFICULTY: Difficult
SEASON: Early spring through late fall

FOREST TYPE: Siskiyou mixed conifer
PROTECTIONS: Inventoried roadless area
MANAGEMENT: Rogue River–Siskiyou
National Forest
NOTES: No restrooms at trailhead; no parking fee or permit required

GETTING THERE: From Medford and Interstate 5, follow signs west to Jacksonville and continue on Oregon Route 238 to Ruch. Or from Grants Pass, from the intersection of OR 99 and US Highway 199, follow signs south to Murphy and then follow OR 238 to Ruch, between mileposts 25 and 26. Turn south on Upper Applegate Road and drive 15.9 miles. A mile past the Applegate Dam, just past the entrance (on the left) to Hart-Tish Park and just before milepost 16 and a guardrail, park on the right shoulder of the road.

The Collings Mountain Trail follows Grouse Creek, climbs above the canyon's headwalls, and follows a ridge to Collings Mountain. The wild forest west of the Applegate River isn't what I'd call a classic ancient forest, though there are pockets of big, old trees. It is, however, a forest unique in its naturalness and a great representative of this region's fascinating Siskiyou mixed conifer forest type.

Start out by descending into a forest of tall madrone, chinquapin, Douglas-fir, and big-leaf maple. Canyon live oak, with its tiny, holly-shaped leaves, and ponderosa pine are also mixed in. The trail crosses Grouse Creek—dry in the late summer and fall—several times as it gradually ascends, passing three-foot-wide Douglas-firs with deeply furrowed bark. Close to the creek, firs and alders soak up the moisture, while ash, ninebark, and wild roses line the banks.

After a quarter mile, cross a wooden bridge over a side channel; then continue up the main channel. In a half mile, you'll come to a side trail that goes uphill a short 0.1 mile to the legendary Bigfoot trap (an actual trap designed to catch, you guessed it, Bigfoot) among fat ponderosa pines. Take it—why not? Better to do so now than on the way back when a little bit of uphill won't be as appealing.

Back on the main trail, more pines enter the forest mix before the route crosses a side channel and starts to climb more steeply. As you ascend, you'll catch glimpses across the ravine of the oak woodland that dominates many of

The canopy of a canyon live oak and ponderosa pine filters the sun along the Collings Mountain Trail.

the slopes here. Just before three-quarters of a mile, cross the creek again and enter a dense oak-madrone woodland with canyon live oak and Douglas-fir mixed in, the black oaks and madrones often growing in clumps. At about 0.9 mile, pass the opening to an old gold mine and a bedrock outcrop.

From here, the trail starts to switchback up, with views across the Grouse Creek ravine to the ridge where the trail eventually leads. Atop this rocky slope, big canyon live oak, pines, sage, and bunchgrasses indicate the dry climate. By 1.3 miles, the forest has more of a thick shrubby quality with red-stemmed manzanita, short oak trees, and bushy madrones. After reentering a dense fir forest, the trail curves to the left to begin traversing the headwalls of the Grouse Creek canyon. Continuing to climb, enjoy (while you catch your breath) the madrone forest and the views back across the canyon, before switchbacking steeply to the top of the ridge, lined with big canyon live oaks at just under 2 miles. Openings at and beyond the 2-mile mark on this ridge offer lovely views to the west over the Carberry Creek drainage and Siskiyou hills.

The trail continues, descending slightly and then following the ridge toward Collings Mountain, but since the view from the top of the ridge is lovely, it's a good place to turn around. The descent back to the trailhead is nearly as tough as the uphill if your knees are anything like mine—not as young as they once were.

As the forest atop Grizzly Peak recovers from a 2002 fire, the openings provide views over the Bear Creek valley east of Ashland.

21. GRIZZLY PEAK

DISTANCE: 5.3 miles round-trip
TRAILHEAD LOCATION: 42.2719°, -122.6060°
STARTING ELEVATION/ELEVATION GAIN:
5300 feet/900 feet
DIFFICULTY: Moderate
SEASON: Late spring through fall, access dependent on snow; best wildflowers in June and July

FOREST TYPE: Siskiyou mixed conifer
PROTECTIONS: Cascade-Siskiyou National Monument
MANAGEMENT: Medford District BLM
NOTES: Restrooms at trailhead; no parking fee or permit required

GETTING THERE: Take Interstate 5 to exit 14 on the south side of Ashland, and head east on Oregon Route 66 toward Klamath Falls for just 0.7 mile. Turn left on Dead Indian Memorial Highway (yes, it's a terrible name) and go 6.7 miles. Turn left on Shale City Road and travel 3 miles; then turn left on BLM Road 38-2E-9.2 at a less-than-obvious sign on the right-hand side of the road. Follow this gravel road for 1.7 miles, staying straight at a junction at 0.8 mile, to a large parking area and the trailhead.

Located on land managed by the Bureau of Land Management, Grizzly Peak overlooks Bear Creek Valley and the city of Ashland. Rising to 5900 feet, its slopes give rise to Antelope Creek and Walker Creek flowing in different directions from this prominent peak. In addition to old trees and wildflower meadows, this hike offers a glimpse at a rare, unlogged postfire landscape. BLM lands here form the edges of the big river valleys of southern Oregon, intermixed with private lands.

Grizzly Peak was designated as part of the expanded Cascade-Siskiyou National Monument in 2017. Despite broad local public support, this expansion has been controversial, with its fate still up in the air as of 2019. Without the protections of the national monument designation, parts of this hike area could be subject to logging under the BLM's management plan of 2016.

The well-traveled trail sets out, for the first quarter mile, through an impressive stand of Douglas-fir, three to four feet in diameter, with an understory of young grand fir. Multitudes of wildflowers—from tall purple delphiniums to more subtle wild onion—line the trail and populate several small meadows as the trail climbs through lichen-draped ancient forest of grand and Shasta red fir. At this elevation, trees grow more slowly, so it's important to appreciate the size and structure that has developed over a few hundred years here. Some of the largest trees are beginning to literally fall apart as the younger trees begin to take over.

Just over a mile into the hike, stay left at the trail junction to begin a 3-mile loop. In another half mile, you reach a rocky outcrop with manzanita, oak, and stunted Douglas-fir. The view from this area to the west is over Ashland, Emigrant Lake, and south to Mount Shasta.

From here, the trail passes through a forest that burned in 2002. Early successional shrubs like ceanothus and elderberry form the understory, while young ponderosa pine and cedar saplings jockey for space. The trail leads past another rocky outcrop—a good place to venture off-trail a bit to find the best view—before it heads downhill through the burned forest again to complete the loop. Lupine, elderberry, and thimbleberry dominate this stretch. Wildlife—including songbirds and squirrels, deer and elk—seem to be thriving in the recovering burn area. After about a mile of the fire area, the trail heads back into the cool, mixed fir forest with scattered meadows to complete the loop. Turn left at the junction to head back down to the trailhead.

22. PACIFIC CREST TRAIL: HYATT LAKE

DISTANCE: 8.5 miles round-trip (Hyatt Lake, 1.5 miles; Little Hyatt Lake, 7 miles)
TRAILHEAD LOCATION: 42.1644°, -122.4653°
STARTING ELEVATION/ELEVATION GAIN: Hyatt Lake, 5100 feet/Minimal; Little Hyatt Lake, 5100 feet/500 feet
DIFFICULTY: Moderate
SEASON: Spring to late fall

FOREST TYPE: Ponderosa pine, Siskiyou mixed conifer
PROTECTIONS: Cascade-Siskiyou National Monument
MANAGEMENT: Medford District BLM
NOTES: Restrooms at nearby entrance to Hyatt Lake Campground; no parking fee or permit required

GETTING THERE: Take Interstate 5 to exit 14 on the south side of Ashland, and head east on Oregon Route 66 toward Klamath Falls. Travel up this narrow, winding highway just under 15 miles to the summit of Green Springs Mountain. A mile and a quarter past this summit, turn left on East Hyatt Lake Road and go just under 3 miles. At the intersection with Hyatt Dam Road and before passing an entry station for the Hyatt Lake Campground, you'll find parking for the Pacific Crest Trail where it crosses this road, on the left.

East of Ashland the Pacific Crest Trail (PCT) passes through the heart of the BLM-managed Cascade-Siskiyou National Monument, and several sections between the California border and the national forest feature ancient forest groves. In between, past logging has fragmented the forest and scenery near the trail. Following the PCT in either direction from the trailhead on the south end of Hyatt Lake (also called Hyatt Reservoir) will get you to some terrific mixed conifer old-growth groves, big ponderosa pines, and stunning views.

For the shorter stretch (1.5 miles round-trip), head east, across the road from the parking area. You'll hike along the edge of a pine plantation to the right for a quarter mile, with huge stumps showing what the forest was like before it was logged. Soon, though, the trail enters a beautiful ancient forest stand of large-diameter Douglas-firs, a mix of younger trees in the understory, and a lot of down logs. Continue through this lovely forest, taking it all in, for about a half mile before heading back to the trailhead.

Going west on the PCT from the trailhead offers a longer and more diverse hike toward and beyond Little Hyatt Lake. The first mile passes under a powerline right-of-way and goes through some younger Douglas-fir, incense cedar, ponderosa pine, and lodgepole pine forests that have seen some logging, though there are some scattered larger trees and more down logs and diversity as you approach the mile mark. At about 1.2 miles, begin to descend toward a large meadow, with a lot of wildflowers in the

spring and early summer and a huge ponderosa pine snag.

When you come to a road, cross it, turn right, and then turn left on the trail to cross a wooden bridge over the outlet of Little Hyatt's dam. Past this point, the forest becomes much nicer, though some of the nicest groves are not right along the trail. The trees are of mixed sizes and spacing, with down logs and an open understory. At about the 2.2-mile point, you'll come to a series of scattered meadows, wildflowers and butterflies adding color to the grasses, and stringers of old-growth ponderosa pine and Douglas-fir forests. One really large meadow, which crosses a sometimes-wet gully, is crowded with zipping dragonflies.

As the trail turns south over the next mile or so, you'll pass through a gate (at the 3-mile mark) and traverse a moist slope of undisturbed forest with oak, incense cedar, and Douglas-fir. You'll catch some nice views to the west, then shift to a south-facing slope where the forest opens up to lovely oak savannah with tall grasses. At this point, unless you're through-hiking to the Green Springs Summit a few more miles away, it's best to turn back after taking in the views of Mount Ashland and the Siskiyou Mountains.

OPPOSITE: A tall snag contributes to the forest canopy on the Pacific Crest Trail near Hyatt Lake.

23. PACIFIC CREST TRAIL: GREEN SPRINGS SUMMIT TO HOBART BLUFF

DISTANCE: 7.3 miles round-trip

TRAILHEAD LOCATION: 42.1300°, -122.4827°

STARTING ELEVATION/ELEVATION GAIN: 4500 feet/1300 feet

DIFFICULTY: Difficult

SEASON: Spring to late fall; best wildflowers in May and June

FOREST TYPE: Siskiyou mixed conifer

PROTECTIONS: Cascade-Siskiyou National Monument

MANAGEMENT: Medford District BLM

NOTES: No restrooms at trailhead; no parking fee or permit required

GETTING THERE: Take Interstate 5 to exit 14 on the south side of Ashland, and head east on Oregon Route 66 toward Klamath Falls. Travel up this narrow, winding highway just under 15 miles to the summit of Green Springs Mountain. Park on the right at the Pacific Crest Trail parking area and trailhead.

Though only stretches of this hike are in ancient forest, it is some of the best remaining old growth along southern Oregon's PCT, and the killer views from atop Hobart Bluff make the rest of the hike worthwhile.

For this stretch of trail, head south on the PCT (on the same side of the road as the parking area). The trail climbs slowly and steadily above Keene Creek through private land, protected by a conservation easement, and through meadows and logged areas. In 0.6 mile, emerge into the first of several rocky scablands with shrubby and woodland oaks and a grassy ground covering. The trail then follows this ridge on its west side, through a young stand of fir and pine, enters another opening with oaks and pines, and enters a fir plantation at the 1-mile point.

At 1.2 miles, leave the private land through a gate and continue, on BLM land now, through alternating oak woodlands and dense, logged forest stands. Eventually, after 1.5 miles, the forest surrounding the meadows gains some bigger ponderosa pine trees, though they are lacking some of the characteristics that would indicate that they are very old. Going on, however, the trail passes some much older pines, three feet in diameter with more old-growth character, mixed with spreading oaks in a flat meadow. Then the forest closes in again, now with tall Douglas-firs and large incense cedars, as you begin to climb toward a ridgetop through this old forest—which is most impressive at around the 2-mile point. Grand fir fills in parts of the understory, with scattered Douglas-firs four feet in diameter.

From here, the trail climbs up through a younger Douglas-fir stand and then a plantation before cresting the ridge at 2.4 miles. The next half mile travels in and out of denser forest with evidence of past logging and rocky open areas with stunted cedars and Douglas-firs, oak, juniper, and manzanita.

Beginning at about 3 miles, you'll round the northeast slope of Hobart Bluff and start to get views over the Soda Mountain Wilderness. Hike under a dense oak canopy to reach the junction for the Hobart Bluff viewpoint at 3.3 miles. Take this up to the right, climbing steadily for 0.4 mile until you come out on the top where twisted juniper, manzanita, mountain mahogany, and wildflowers cover the rocky bluff. Views in every direction take in the southern Cascades and nearby Pilot Rock. Return the way you came.

OPPOSITE: A grassy understory and ponderosa pines line the Pacific Crest Trail on the way to Hobart Bluff.

MOUNT HOOD HIKES

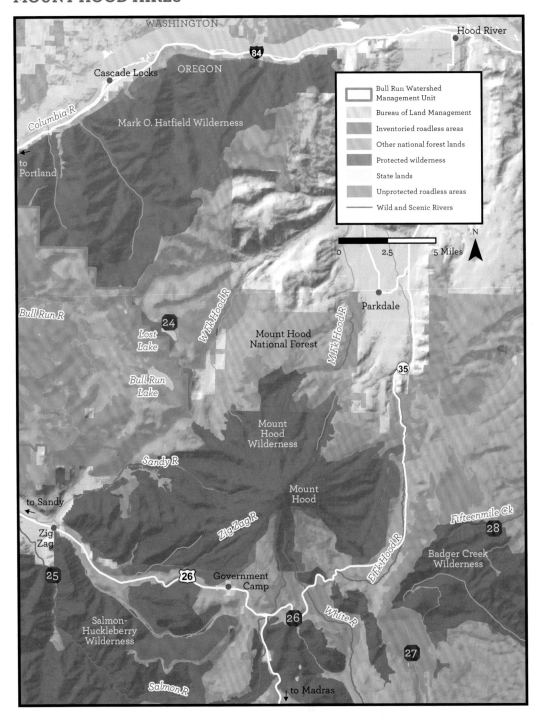

WASHINGTON

Hood River

84

Cascade Locks   OREGON

Columbia R.

Mark O. Hatfield Wilderness

to
Portland

	Bull Run Watershed Management Unit
	Bureau of Land Management
	Inventoried roadless areas
	Other national forest lands
	Protected wilderness
	State lands
	Unprotected roadless areas
	Wild and Scenic Rivers

N

0   2.5   5 Miles

Bull Run R.

24

Lost Lake

W. Fk. Hood R.

Mount Hood National Forest

M. Fk. Hood R.

Parkdale

Bull Run Lake

35

Mount Hood Wilderness

Sandy R.

Mount Hood

to Sandy

Zig Zag R.

Zig Zag

Fifteenmile Ck.

28

25

B. Fk. Hood R.

Badger Creek Wilderness

26   Government Camp

Salmon-Huckleberry Wilderness

26

White R.

27

Salmon R.

to Madras

MOUNT HOOD

Mount Hood is Oregon's iconic peak and its highest, the source of the short but mighty Sandy, Salmon, White, Roaring, and Hood Rivers, as well as Eagle Creek. The mountain also stands guard over diverse forests that include lush Douglas-fir and cedar rainforests barely above sea level, alpine forests just below timberline, and drier forests of ponderosa pine east of the mountain. Some forests on the west side of Mount Hood are part of the Bull Run watershed, which serves a special purpose: protecting and providing drinking water for the city of Portland.

This region also includes another major icon of the state: the Columbia River Gorge. Known for its forest-covered and waterfall-cut cliffs along its namesake river, the gorge's forests, largely protected as part of the national scenic area or wilderness, are generally eighty to one hundred years old. Fires in the early 1900s reset large areas of forest but left a few pockets of old-growth and scattered legacy trees. The Eagle Creek Fire of 2017 burned some of these forests again and left many popular trails in the gorge inaccessible at the time of this writing.

Located so close to Oregon's biggest population center, the trails here are heavily used but also appreciated. Portland's love of the Mount Hood National Forest, and the mountain's iconic nature, means that much of it has been protected—though the focus has been largely on scenery, not on forest ecosystems. The Mark O. Hatfield, Salmon-Huckleberry, and Badger Creek Wilderness areas protect the forests near the base of the mountain, while the Mount Hood Wilderness captures a mixture of the peak and its forested shoulders. Unfortunately, significant parts of the national forest have also been cut, and nearby privately owned timberlands, especially in the Hood River valley, have been heavily logged, fragmenting the forests surrounding the mountain.

A towering western redcedar along the Salmon River delights forest lovers on the slopes of Mount Hood. *[Photo by Katie Kepsel]*

24. LOST LAKE

DISTANCE: 3.2-mile loop
TRAILHEAD LOCATION: 45.4955°, -121.8223°
STARTING ELEVATION/ELEVATION GAIN:
3185 feet/Minimal
DIFFICULTY: Easy
SEASON: Late spring through fall, access
dependent on snow
FOREST TYPE: Douglas-fir

PROTECTIONS: Inventoried roadless
area; old forest reserved from logging in
management plan
MANAGEMENT: Mount Hood National Forest
NOTES: Restrooms in nearby parking area;
$9 day-use fee required to park (Northwest
Forest Pass does not apply)

GETTING THERE: From Interstate 84, take exit 62 in Hood River for US Highway 30 east
(Westcliff Drive). Turn right on US 30, and then turn right on Mount Adams Avenue. Mount
Adams turns to the right and becomes Wine Country Avenue and then Country Club Road.
Follow this road for about 3 miles and turn left onto Barrett Drive. In 1.2 miles, turn right onto
Tucker Road (Oregon Route 281). Two miles later, stay right toward Odell, Dee, and Parkdale
to stay on OR 281. Drive along the Hood River for 6 miles and then turn right at a sign for Dee
and Lost Lake. Cross the East Fork Hood River, stay left on Lost Lake Road, and follow curves
and signs to stay on Lost Lake Road.

Eight miles after turning onto Lost Lake Road, turn right at a sign for Lost Lake Resort 6
miles, and continue. You'll reach the entrance station a total of 13.8 miles after turning off
OR 281. After paying the entrance fee, proceed ahead and stay to the right toward the general
store and boat rental area. Continue left to cross the small bridge at Lake Branch Creek and
park in the large parking loop at the end of the road.

The drive to Lost Lake is quite educational. The road passes through miles of clear-cut private
land, managed exclusively for timber production on the fertile north slopes of Mount Hood. The
contrast as you enter the national forest is stark—huge old trees draped in lichen line the last
five miles of the drive.

While Lost Lake's resort and campgrounds are a favorite destination for families and others
seeking tranquil waters for nonmotorized boating, classic views, and pure mountain air, the ancient
forests here steal the show. The forested ridge to the west of Lost Lake divides the Hood River
drainage from the Bull Run watershed just to the west—the source of Portland's drinking water.

From the parking area, take in the view of Mount
Hood through the trees, then proceed down
the trail that begins at the end of the parking
loop. For the first half mile, follow the level path
through a western hemlock and noble fir forest
with fat Douglas-firs and western redcedars
scattered along the trail. The canopy towers
overhead, while the green shades of vine maple,

huckleberry, and bunchberry form the lower
layers. In this stretch, the trail crosses several
boardwalks and offers good places to step down
to the lakeshore to catch mountain views before
Mount Hood disappears behind the butte on the

OPPOSITE: Breathtaking views of Mount Hood are framed
by beautiful ancient forests along Lost Lake's shore.

lake's southwestern shore. In about a third of a mile, look for some especially big cedars and old gnarled hemlock trees.

Starting at about three-quarters of a mile, the trail crosses a series of wet, boggy areas with large, tapered cedars and snags and patches of dense water-loving vegetation, including skunk cabbage, salmonberry, red-twig dogwood, mountain ash, and alder for a quarter mile. Continue on through the Douglas-fir, noble and silver fir, and hemlock forest, some hemlocks featuring huge, low-hanging branches. After a mile, the trail passes closer to the lake and alternately through dense patches of salmonberry, devil's club, alder, thimbleberry, goatsbeard, and elderberry—their

flowers laden with pollen for bees—and through towering Douglas-firs and hemlocks.

In 1.5 miles, the trail climbs onto the north side of a lakeside butte, a steep slope of dense hemlocks with scattered bigger Douglas-firs rising to the right. Cross a rocky gully—with flowing water during spring's snowmelt—and descend right to the lake's shore, skirting a rocky slope edged with vine maple and continuing past clumps of alders.

Pass a wet area where a spring enters the lake, and at 1.7 miles, climb again into the edge of the forest and pass a few huge tree specimens: noble and silver firs and a redcedar over four feet in diameter. As you round the south end of

the lake a short way later, young and old trees tower over the trail, snag-filled openings appear, and you'll reach another boardwalk in another wet, flat area.

After the junction with the Huckleberry Mountain Trail at about the 2-mile point, the area along the trail becomes more developed and the forest a little younger. Stay on the shoreline trail at a sign for the old-growth trail and day-use area, and over the next mile you'll get views of Devils Pulpit butte and the rocky slope you hiked below on the southwest side of the lake, and pass campsites as the trail alternates between boardwalk and natural surface. Stay on the unpaved path along the shore as you pass picnic sites to reach the boat rental area and a sasquatch statue, continue to the left to cross the lake's outlet stream on a bridge, then pass another picnic area to finish the loop back to the parking area.

25. SALMON RIVER

DISTANCE: 6.2 miles round-trip
TRAILHEAD LOCATION: 45.3084°, -121.9429°
STARTING ELEVATION/ELEVATION GAIN:
1590 feet/Minimal
DIFFICULTY: Moderate
SEASON: Year-round
FOREST TYPE: Douglas-fir

PROTECTIONS: Wild and scenic river corridor, surrounded by Salmon-Huckleberry Wilderness
MANAGEMENT: Mount Hood National Forest
NOTES: Restrooms at trailhead; $5 fee or permit required to park

GETTING THERE: Travel east out of Portland on US Highway 26 through Sandy and toward Mount Hood. As you approach the town of Zigzag, turn right onto Salmon River Road just before the Zigzag Ranger Station. Drive 2.7 miles to the first trailhead and roadside parking area on the right.

The Salmon River is designated as wild and scenic; just outside of the road corridor, the forest here is also part of the Salmon-Huckleberry Wilderness, protected in 1984. Somehow, despite the easy access and frequent views of the road, the trail still feels wild and enchanting. In the spring and early summer, wildflowers cover the forest floor, but any time of year is perfect to explore this low-elevation forest wilderness.

This is easily one of the most accessible and gorgeous of all the trails featured in this book. The forest is simply spectacular along the entire length of the trail. Begin by descending toward the Salmon River and then following it through massive Douglas-firs, western redcedars, and some hemlock. All the classic and essential elements of an ancient forest are present, including large down wood, snags, a mixture of tree species and ages, and multiple canopy layers. After 0.6 mile, the trail crosses a small creek on a bridge and then passes several side trails for accessing the river. When it climbs some steps leading away from the river, be prepared to get up close and personal with an incredible cedar tree—ten to twelve feet in diameter and impossible to miss.

With the trail so close to the river, many tall bigleaf maples draped in moss contribute to the feeling of being in a rainforest.

Past the 1-mile point, side trails from the road join the main trail, and you'll cross a small bouldery creek (dry in the summer) after 1.3 miles. At about 1.7 miles, the trail joins the road, where you need to walk for a short way before ducking back into the forest—here not as old, but at about 2 miles you are back among ancient trees and have a view across the river. Pass by the Green Canyon Campground at 2.5 miles and through more of a riparian forest before climbing back up to the road and following that for another short stretch. Just over 3 miles, the "Old" Salmon River Trail ends at a large parking area right before a bridge over the river.

This is the logical turnaround point, but if you want to go farther, the "New" Salmon River Trail continues on the other side of the road, following the base of a rock cliff along the river, past an island covered with ancient trees at a half mile, and then into the Salmon-Huckleberry Wilderness.

Trees along the Old Salmon River Trail are draped in greenery, an ancient-forest-lover's paradise. *(Photo by Katie Kepsel)*

26. BARLOW PASS

DISTANCE: 4.6 miles round-trip (Barlow Creek, 2.4-mile loop; Pacific Crest Trail, 2.6 miles round-trip)
TRAILHEAD LOCATION: 45.2825°, -121.6849°
STARTING ELEVATION/ELEVATION GAIN: Barlow Creek, 4150 feet/450 feet; Pacific Crest Trail, 4150 feet/200 feet
DIFFICULTY: Moderate

SEASON: Early summer through fall, access dependent on snow
FOREST TYPE: Alpine and subalpine
PROTECTIONS: Mount Hood Wilderness; unprotected roadless area where old forest reserved from logging in management plan
MANAGEMENT: Mount Hood National Forest
NOTES: Restrooms at trailhead; $5 fee or permit required to park

GETTING THERE: Travel east out of Portland on US Highway 26 through Sandy and toward Mount Hood. Drive 3 miles east of Government Camp, take the exit for Oregon Route 35 north toward Hood River, and go 2 miles. Turn right (south) onto Forest Road 3531 at Barlow Pass at milepost 60 and a sign for the Pacific Crest Trail. Go a quarter mile to a large parking area on the right.

Barlow Pass, where the Pacific Crest Trail crosses OR 35 on the southeast flank of Mount Hood, is a great example of a subalpine ancient forest. Though they may not look it, many trees in this area are hundreds of years old. The cold, higher-elevation growing conditions mean they grow more slowly than those at lower elevations and take longer to get really large.

While much of Mount Hood and its surrounding slopes have been protected as wilderness for years, the forests here surrounding Barlow Butte and at nearby White River were newly designated only in 2009. Most of this hike is through roadless forests popular for hiking and skiing; though not officially protected, they are at least unlikely to be logged.

This area has two interesting hikes to do: first through Barlow Creek and then on the Pacific Crest Trail. Combine them for a 4.6-mile trek, or split them into two segments.

Start the Barlow Creek hike at the Old Barlow Road gate near the trailhead and walk down this old road. Pass a trail that heads downhill to the left (that's the return loop) and continue down

Subalpine forests of noble fir, silver fir, and hemlock are found near Barlow Pass along the Pacific Crest Trail.

Drinking from the Forest Faucet

When properly protected, ancient forests play the underappreciated role of natural reservoirs—absorbing, storing, filtering, and gradually releasing pure water to forest streams. In the face of a warming climate and the changes that come with it, this role of water regulator will become increasingly essential.

The water that two-thirds of Oregonians draw from their taps comes from our state's rivers, streams, and lakes. In particular, the residents of Ashland, Baker City, Bend, Corvallis, Cottage Grove, Eugene, La Grande, Medford, Mill City, Portland, Sweet Home, The Dalles, West Linn, and a host of other communities across the state depend on our national forests for their drinking water.

Logging, road-building, and other development damages the forest's ability to produce clean water. Water runs off more quickly from compacted soils affected by roads and logging, carrying with it soil and debris that can foul water filtration systems farther downstream. The volume of runoff also increases, reducing the amount of water available during the dry summer months when water demand is higher and supplies are lower.

Trees also add to water supplies by capturing water out of the air. The high surface areas of conifers, especially, capture fog and create localized rain that adds to water heading downstream. This source is significant, accounting for as much as one-third of all precipitation in Portland's Bull Run watershed. Cutting too many trees reduces the amount of water that a forested landscape can gather in this way.

The Bull Run watershed, on the western slope of Mount Hood, has been the primary source of Portland's drinking water since the late 1800s. Bull Run was set aside to protect the water until the post–World War II logging frenzy led to a lifting of regulations. Public outcry over the treatment of the growing city's water supply finally led to a halt of logging in 1996. Today the watershed is recovering and provides nearly 1 million people with some of the purest water of any major US city.

In contrast, coastal Oregon communities that rely on surface water get a particularly bad deal. Many drinking watersheds are wholly owned by timber companies and have been heavily clear-cut and sprayed with herbicides to limit vegetation that might compete with the farmed trees. The water system in Rockaway Beach, for example, has been so polluted with chemicals and sediment washing off of private land clear-cuts that it's been shut down several times. Local citizens are encouraging their watershed's owners to change their practices to better protect the community's water.

The ancient forest along Alice Creek filters and cools its water as it flows downstream. *(Photo by Pamela Winders)*

the road through a noble fir, western hemlock, Douglas-fir, and silver fir forest. At about a mile, the road bends to the left at a large meadow that has some dispersed camping sites (it's drivable with high clearance to this point). Follow the road as it continues across Barlow Creek through a lovely riparian area and then turn left at a sign for Devil's Half Acre Campground (a defunct Forest Service facility).

Before you reach the abandoned campsites near the creek, find Barlow Trail to the right by looking for an old signpost in the meadow uphill at about 1.2 miles. This trail passes through a nice meadow and then enters a dense forest without much ground cover. As the trail ascends gradually, the forest gets more remarkable, with some really big Doug-firs scattered throughout and then a concentration of gorgeous noble firs with their mosaic bark. Particularly noteworthy is a stand at about 1.9 miles—giant Engelmann spruce, noble fir, Douglas-fir, and hemlock.

Along the way, pass signposts for the original Barlow wagon road, cross some small creeks, and then intersect Barlow Butte Trail to the right at about 2 miles. Continue up to the intersection with Barlow Road through a silver fir forest with many down logs and some huge Douglas-firs. Turn right at the road to get back to the trailhead or continue to the Pacific Crest portion of this hike.

To continue, follow the Pacific Crest Trail north from the gate at Old Barlow Road. At another old road, turn right and head toward OR 35, which you reach after about a quarter mile from the trailhead. Scurry across the highway at an angle to the right to pick up the trail just to the left of the guardrail. The trail climbs up through silver fir, noble fir, Douglas-fir, and western hemlock.

After another quarter mile, you reach a rocky meadow with views down the East Fork Salmon River to the west and through a sparse, dry forest with beargrass and huckleberries before reaching a logged plantation. Past the plantation, enter a natural forest again. Between 0.8 and 1.3 miles, ancient noble firs and other diverse species stand out. Enjoy this beautiful stand before turning back.

27. BOULDER CREEK AND BOULDER LAKE

DISTANCE: 5 miles round-trip (Boulder Creek, 3 miles; Boulder Lake, 2 miles)
TRAILHEAD LOCATION: 45.2588°, -121.5595°
STARTING ELEVATION/ELEVATION GAIN: Boulder Creek, 4330 feet/450 feet; Boulder Lake, 4330 feet/450 feet
DIFFICULTY: Moderate
SEASON: Early summer through fall, access dependent on snow; best wildflowers in early July; late summer better to avoid mosquitoes

FOREST TYPE: Douglas-fir
PROTECTIONS: Mount Hood National Recreation Area; unprotected roadless area where old forest reserved from logging in management plan
MANAGEMENT: Mount Hood National Forest
NOTES: No restrooms at trailhead; no parking fee or permit required

GETTING THERE: Travel east out of Portland on US Highway 26 through Sandy and toward Mount Hood. Drive 3 miles east of Government Camp, take the exit for Oregon Route 35 north toward Hood River. Go 4.5 miles on OR 35 and cross the big bridge over the White River.

Tall trees cast shadows on the water of Boulder Lake.

Immediately after crossing the bridge, turn right onto Forest Road 48, which starts at the far (east) side of the large White River East Sno-Park at milepost 68.

Continue approximately 14 miles on FR 48 and then turn left onto FR 4880. (There's a sign for this road. If you see a sign for Boulder Ditch you've gone too far.) Stay on narrow FR 4880 for 2.5 paved miles; then stay to the right where the road splits and turns to gravel. Go another 4 miles on the now bumpy and potholed gravel road to the trailhead where the road widens, providing room for parking cars on the left. This road dead-ends shortly after, an easy place to turn around.

This relatively pristine area off Mount Hood's southeast flank lies between two units of the Badger Creek Wilderness, but the wonderful ancient forests along upper Boulder Creek are unprotected. The most popular destination in this area is Boulder Lake, a short walk through a beautiful forest, with Bonney Meadows a close second. But if you're here for the ancient forest, the biggest trees in the area are down along Boulder Creek, so the featured hike is really two out-and-backs. Do the creek section first so that your return trip is all downhill.

For the Boulder Creek Trail, head downhill from the road, opposite the Boulder Lake trailhead, and descend half a mile to the stream. After crossing a footbridge, you'll intersect Forest Service Trail 478, which parallels the east side of Boulder Creek. Turn left to go upstream (and uphill) past some huge, fire-charred Douglas-firs near a rocky slope with shimmering quaking aspens. Large white pines, larch, and Douglas-firs continue, but over the next mile, the ancient forest transitions to more silver and noble fir and Engelmann spruce as you gain elevation. Eventually this trail reaches Crane Prairie, a series of wet meadows, where the trail becomes boggy and hard to follow. Turn back at about the 1.5-mile point before it gets too bad.

For Boulder Lake, follow the well-traveled trail from the main trailhead through a delightful forest of Douglas-fir and noble fir past tiny Spinning Lake, for just 0.4 mile. At the trail junction when you reach the lake, you can follow the lakeshore a half mile around, or just turn right to stay on the east side. The lake can be busy on summer weekends, but if you don't have much company, listen for pikas (mammals related to rabbits) giving their high-pitched one-note calls from the rocky talus slopes above the lake. Continue for 0.6 mile from the lakeside trail junction over a rise to Kane Springs, where the wet area supports big noble fir, Engelmann spruce, Pacific silver fir, and mountain hemlock. This is a great turnaround for an easy forest hike.

To trade ancient forest for views and wildflowers, you can continue another mile (gaining significant elevation) past Kane Springs, uphill past rocky slopes, to Bonney Meadows, which is chock-full of wildflowers in late June and July. To explore a quieter lake on the way back to the trailhead, head down the half-mile trail to Little Boulder Lake from the southeast corner of Boulder Lake.

28. FIFTEENMILE CREEK

DISTANCE: 11.3-mile loop
TRAILHEAD LOCATION: 45.3502°, -121.4744°
STARTING ELEVATION/ELEVATION GAIN: 4590 feet/1940 feet
DIFFICULTY: Difficult
SEASON: Late spring through fall, access dependent on snow
FOREST TYPE: Mixed conifer, ponderosa pine, Oregon white oak

PROTECTIONS: Wild and scenic river corridor; unprotected roadless area where old forest reserved from logging in management plan
MANAGEMENT: Mount Hood National Forest
NOTES: Restroom at trailhead; no parking fee or permit required

GETTING THERE: From Interstate 84, take exit 64 in Hood River and drive south along the East Fork Hood River on Oregon Route 35. About 25 miles south of Hood River, turn left on Forest Road 44, a quarter mile south of milepost 71 and just past a Junction 44 sign. Follow this paved road 8.5 miles; then turn right onto unmarked but paved FR 4420. In just over 2 miles, stay straight to stay on pavement onto FR 2730. The trailhead is 2 miles farther at Fifteenmile Campground, just before you cross Fifteenmile Creek, a total of 12.7 miles from the OR 35 turnoff. Parking is limited to pull-offs in the campground and along the roadside.

The ancient forest of the Fifteenmile Creek drainage lacks protection as a roadless area, but eleven miles of its pristine channel and bordering forest, beginning at its headwaters in Badger Creek Wilderness just west of the trailhead, gained wild and scenic river status in 2009. The creek flows east and north into the Columbia near The Dalles, cutting through the eastern slope of the Cascades from west to east. This makes the drainage unique geographically, but also ecologically: the forests here represent the vegetative transition from moister and higher-elevation to drier lower-elevation forests, offering diverse wildlife habitats.

The loop trail loses roughly 1900 feet of elevation on the first half and gains it all back on the second, making it challenging but enjoyable in its variety. It also gets a fair amount of mountain bike use, so stay alert.

The trail begins within the small campground near the restroom and immediately passes a few ancient, twisted ponderosa pines in small openings beside the trail—a taste of what's to come farther down the trail. As you gradually descend, the forest is mostly a mix of mountain hemlock, subalpine fir, and grand fir, with spruce and larch mixed in near the stream.

In a half mile, go right at a trail junction for the Cedar Creek Trail to begin the long loop that makes up most of this hike, and descend farther to cross Fifteenmile Creek on a bridge—a truly wild and scenic spot. Climb to the slope on the other side and leave the sound of the creek behind as you pass in and out of denser and more sparse, younger and older, living and dead patches of trees: a few white, lodgepole, and ponderosa pines mixed in and wild strawberries and lupine lining the trail.

Begin a gradual descent through this mixed forest at about 1.6 miles. Around the 2-mile point, the forest opens up on the ridge with only low-growing plants and a few scattered and stunted pines, allowing views of volcanic peaks to the north over the Fifteenmile Creek canyon. Over the next 2.3 miles, the trail continues its gradual descent on this ridge that separates Fifteenmile from Cedar Creek. It winds past boulder outcrops, huge orange-barked ponderosa pines,

stunted juniper, and grassy wildflower meadows with fluttering butterflies, these openings alternating with denser, moister areas with more firs and vine maple. Occasional views over the Cedar Creek canyon to the right reveal the extent of this wild, ancient forest.

After 4.7 miles, the descent steepens even further as you drop down the spine of the ridge—the south side to the right drier and sporting white oaks, manzanita, and pine, while the north slope is a moister mixed conifer forest marching down toward Fifteenmile Creek. The trail's rocks and loose dirt make this steep stretch—lasting a half mile or so—challenging. You reach the valley's bottom, near where Cedar and Fifteenmile Creeks converge, at 5.3 miles in a moist stand with redcedar, more firs, and vine maple. Cross Fifteenmile Creek on a little bridge. A campsite on the other side is a good place to rest or have a snack to prepare for the second half of the hike.

Continue the hike by following Fifteenmile Creek upstream, following the sign for the campground through a younger forest of redcedars and firs. The trail climbs very gradually near the creek, with vine maples forming a green tunnel, a few scattered cottonwoods, and a grove of big redcedars at about the 6-mile point. Larch and ponderosa pines are scattered among the

other mixed conifers as you continue, with large specimens of every tree species and patches of thimbleberry and huckleberry lining the trail.

At 6.5 miles the trail gets farther away from the creek, still gradually climbing, and crosses the rocky channel of a seasonal stream at about 7 miles. A little farther, cross a flowing creek on rocks and logs in a cedar grove and then begin to climb more steeply through a younger, denser forest as Fifteenmile Creek's sounds fade into the distance and the forest begins to take on a drier condition with more pines and oceanspray lining the trail.

At around the 8-mile point, pass through a denser forest patch, then begin a switchbacking slog up the ridge for nearly half a mile, beginning to parallel an old logging road partway up. You'll reach a wide, sparse area, a natural rock garden on the ridge, with big ponderosa pines and an understory of red-stemmed manzanita shrubs, lupine, sunflowers, yarrow, and grasses. To the left, a rock wall drops off steeply into the Fifteenmile Creek canyon; to the right, a pine plantation (previously logged) drops off to the north. A ridgetop spring pops out of the ground and flows downhill

to the left, surrounded by cedar, spruce, and big Douglas-firs at 8.8 miles.

Beyond this, the trail follows an old logging road a half mile in and out of a young plantation, some scattered large trees remaining. Climb gradually again to the ridgetop rock garden ringed with big pines, then more steeply through a narrow meadow with giant rocks and the ancient twisted skeletons of long-dead pines at 9.3 miles. Pass through a mixture of denser fir forests and open ridgetops with rock walls forming little fortresses along the edges and scattered, twisted juniper trees adding to the sparse vegetation. Views across the Fifteenmile Creek canyon and east to the dry plateau beyond the forest make the arduous climb to this 10-mile point worthwhile.

You get a reprieve from all the climbing over the next half mile, descending into the moister mixed-fir forest, with cedars mixed in as you near the main stream and some side channels you cross along the way. Just before reaching the trail junction at 10.8 miles, you begin to follow Fifteenmile Creek. Stay to the right at the junction (the loop now complete) and continue, brutally uphill again, for the final half mile back to the trailhead.

OPPOSITE: Ponderosa pines thrive along the Fifteenmile Creek Trail, which bridges from wet to dry forest types on the east side of Mount Hood.

CLACKAMAS-SANTIAM HIKES

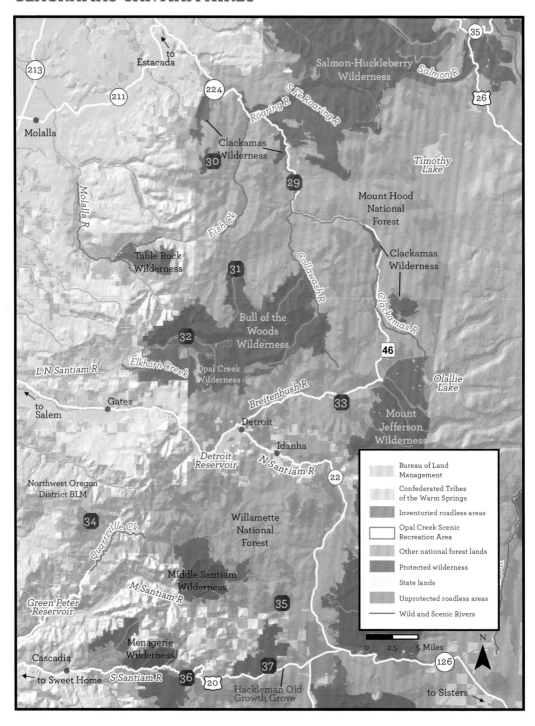

to
Estacada

213

211

224

Molalla

30

Clackamas
Wilderness

Roaring R

S.Fk.Roaring R

Salmon-Huckleberry
Wilderness

Salmon R

35

26

29

Timothy
Lake

Mount Hood
National
Forest

Clackamas
Wilderness

Molalla R

Fish Ck

Table Rock
Wilderness

31

Collawash R

Clackamas R

32

Bull of the
Woods
Wilderness

46

L N Santiam R

Elkhorn Creek

Opal Creek
Wilderness

Olallie
Lake

to
Salem

Gates

Breitenbush R

33

Mount
Jefferson
Wilderness

Detroit

Idanha

Detroit
Reservoir

N Santiam R

22

Northwest Oregon
District BLM

34

Quartzville Ck

Willamette
National
Forest

Green Peter
Reservoir

Middle Santiam
Wilderness

M Santiam R

35

	Bureau of Land Management
	Confederated Tribes of the Warm Springs
	Inventoried roadless areas
	Opal Creek Scenic Recreation Area
	Other national forest lands
	Protected wilderness
	State lands
	Unprotected roadless areas
	Wild and Scenic Rivers

0   2.5   5 Miles

N

Cascadia

Menagerie
Wilderness

to Sweet Home

S Santiam R

36

20

37

Hackleman Old
Growth Grove

126

to Sisters

CLACKAMAS-SANTIAM

The Clackamas-Santiam region, named for the two major river basins it drains, is part of the vast Douglas-fir-dominated forest ecosystem on the west side of the Cascades. This region, especially on the southern half, showcases the western (or Old) Cascades. Much older geologically than the tall peaks of the High Cascades, the western Cascades act as a bridge between lower and higher elevations. They provide a range of diverse habitats across this elevation gradient, with pockets of unique forest types and a lot of diversity in conifer species (not to mention amazing wildflower meadows and rocky outcrops with stunning views).

The Clackamas River begins in the Olallie Lake basin just north of the Mount Jefferson Wilderness and flows mostly north to the Willamette River, picking up major tributaries—the South Fork, Collawash, and Roaring Rivers—on the way. With most of the drainage lying within Mount Hood National Forest, the Clackamas is heavily used by hikers, anglers, campers, and

Ancient western redcedars, with an understory of sword ferns, is one of the classic forests that can be found in the Clackamas-Santiam region.

boaters. It also provides drinking water for more than three hundred thousand people in the Portland metro area.

The Santiam River and its major tributaries—the Little North Santiam, North Santiam, Middle Santiam, South Santiam, and Breitenbush Rivers—get their start on the western slopes of Mount Jefferson. Primarily in the Willamette National Forest, these streams eventually flow through more of a mix of private and BLM-managed land before joining the Willamette River. The river system provides drinking water for communities in the heart of the Willamette Valley.

Both watersheds have been heavily logged and roaded, and restoration efforts for damaged forests and streams are essential for threatened fish and wildlife populations in the region. But despite the severe fragmentation of the forests here, the region also has quite a few ancient forests protected as wilderness. Opal Creek, Menagerie, the Middle Santiam, Table Rock, and Bull of the Woods Wilderness areas are in this region, along with more recently protected wilderness in the headwaters of the Clackamas watershed that includes groves of ancient trees in Big Bottom. Protecting these low-elevation wilderness areas took quite the fight—early tree-sit protests occurred in these forests in the 1980s and 1990s when it seemed like the appetite for old-growth forest logging would destroy these special places forever. These and other public awareness efforts set the stage for the decade-long effort to designate many of these remaining forests as wilderness, though some are still not officially protected.

29. CLACKAMAS RIVERSIDE TRAIL

DISTANCE: 5.2 miles round-trip
TRAILHEAD LOCATION: 45.0578°, -122.0526°
STARTING ELEVATION/ELEVATION GAIN: 1500 feet/300 feet
DIFFICULTY: Moderate
SEASON: Year-round
FOREST TYPE: Douglas-fir

PROTECTIONS: Wild and scenic river corridor
MANAGEMENT: Mount Hood National Forest
NOTES: No restrooms at trailhead but toilets at trail ends in campgrounds; no parking fee or permit required

GETTING THERE: From southeast of Portland, follow Oregon Route 224 to the town of Estacada. Continue on OR 224 a beautiful 25 miles up the Clackamas River to the Ripplebrook Guard Station, and turn right to cross a bridge over the Oak Grove Fork of the Clackamas River. Just over the bridge by Rainbow Campground, Forest Roads 46 and 57 split—stay to the right on FR 46. Travel 1.7 miles to the turnoff with a rustic sign on the right for the trailhead.

This trail, part of the National Recreation Trails system, and nearby campgrounds are a great way to experience the Wild and Scenic Clackamas River corridor. If you stay at either the Riverside or Rainbow Campgrounds, you can head out along the trail right from your tent. The trail is 4 miles long between the two, but there isn't parking for day hikes. If you're just out for a day hike, consider the route described here.

From the trailhead parking area, it's just about 100 yards down the trail to a junction with the Riverside Trail. The nicer stretch from this point is downstream toward Rainbow Campground, a 5.2-mile round-trip. At the junction, turn right. This lovely trail rolls up and down along the Clackamas River from cliffs to rocky beaches, ducking in and out of lush green ravines and drainages with towering Douglas-fir and, in places, western redcedar and hemlock. Vine maple, rhododendrons, hazelnut, chinquapin, and Pacific yew form the understory in varying patches.

For the last quarter of the first mile, the ridge-top forest is dominated by Douglas-firs between 200 and 250 years old, with scattered giant hemlocks likely spared in the last fire cycle, after which the trail enters a truly spectacular ancient forest, several hundred years old. The trail then approaches the river again, in an area along a small creek with evidence of ancient, short snags and Douglas-firs with fire scars. Hemlocks are beginning to take over as dominant understory trees, regrowing after a past fire. At 1.5 miles in, there is another magnificent Douglas-fir grove, and then a boardwalk leads through an area of monster cedar trees and towering bigleaf maple.

Just shy of 2 miles, the trail climbs again to a bluff where a small fire created a snag patch, and you get a good view across the river to the west. Descend from here to the Oak Grove Fork of the

Ancient forest structure is on full display on the Riverside Trail along the Clackamas River.

Clackamas—a narrower, steeper river with big log-jams and a streamside forest of alders, big Pacific yew trees, and a messier feel. The trail crosses a side channel in a ferny grotto and then follows a wet slough on the right as it heads toward its terminus. It reaches Rainbow Campground at 2.6 miles, just past an incredible giant of a Douglas-fir.

Back at the junction for the trailhead parking area, you can elect to continue upstream toward Riverside Campground. This 1.6-mile addition (one way) leads through a similar forest of Douglas-fir, western redcedar, western hemlock, and rhododendrons, with both river views and access points.

30. MEMALOOSE LAKE

DISTANCE: 3 miles round-trip
TRAILHEAD LOCATION: 45.1000°, -122.2187°
STARTING ELEVATION/ELEVATION GAIN: 3440 feet/640 feet
DIFFICULTY: Moderate
SEASON: Late spring to fall, access dependent on snow; best wildflowers in June; October for fall color

FOREST TYPE: Douglas-fir
PROTECTIONS: Clackamas Wilderness
MANAGEMENT: Mount Hood National Forest
NOTES: No restrooms at trailhead; no parking fee required but self-issued, free wilderness permit required at trailhead

GETTING THERE: The easiest route to Memaloose Lake is closed as of 2018 because of damage from a 2014 fire. The detour takes you to the lake from the west. Both the detour and more direct routes lead past gravel-pit shooting ranges that can be a bit scary.

From southeast of Portland, follow Oregon Route 224 to the town of Estacada. Continue on OR 224 another 4 miles, and turn right onto OR 211 toward Molalla. Go 4.7 miles and turn left on Hillockburn Road. In a mile and a quarter, stay to the left at a junction with South Horner Road just before the little settlement of Dodge. In 5 miles, Hillockburn Road becomes Forest Road 45 at the Mount Hood National Forest boundary. From here, continue for 15 miles on the mostly paved, but slow and winding, road. The trailhead is on the right just after you cross Memaloose Creek.

If the easier route opens, from Estacada, continue 9.2 miles on OR 224. Between mileposts 33 and 34, turn right across a big green bridge on Memaloose Road (FR 45). Travel just over 11 miles on the paved road; then keep right at a 90-degree turn to stay on FR 45 as it changes to gravel. The trailhead is about a mile farther, just before the road crosses Memaloose Creek.

Lovely Memaloose Lake was formed when South Fork Mountain was carved by glaciers long ago. The mossy forests here, on the western edge of Mount Hood National Forest, are the source of Memaloose Creek, a major tributary to the South Fork Clackamas River. Though much of the surrounding forest has been logged, after decades of work by forest advocates the ancient forests around the lake were finally protected, as part of the Clackamas Wilderness, in 2009.

Rhododendrons bloom along Memaloose Lake amid tall silver firs. *(Photo by John Sparks)*

Though a small protected area, the classic example of a Douglas-fir forest was worth the efforts to save it—as is the short but sweet hike that is great for kids. Start out on the trail by climbing gradually past big old-growth Douglas-firs, western redcedars, and noble firs, with wildflowers lining the trail. Cross a few tiny streams and then after about three-quarters of a mile, the trail steepens up a series of switchbacks another 0.4 mile to the edge of Memaloose Lake. Here, wildflower meadows, wet areas of skunk cabbage, and huckleberries abound. At the right time of year—usually around June—you'll find rough-skinned newts floating in the shallow waters of the lake. (Look, but please don't touch these critters—they can secrete a highly toxic substance through their skin.)

To explore a bit, take a left at the lake and cross the outlet creek, and if you're up for more of a climb—and a view—continue another mile on the unmarked trail through more ancient forest to the top of South Fork Mountain. From there, you'll get views of the Cascade peaks, the lake below, and the stark contrast between the protected ancient forest and the sea of plantation forests surrounding it.

31. BAGBY HOT SPRINGS

DISTANCE: 3 miles round-trip
TRAILHEAD LOCATION: 44.9537°, -122.1704°
STARTING ELEVATION/ELEVATION GAIN:
2000 feet/200 feet
DIFFICULTY: Easy
SEASON: Spring through late fall, access
dependent on snow
FOREST TYPE: Douglas-fir

PROTECTIONS: Surrounded by Bull of the
Woods Wilderness; old forest reserved from
logging in management plan
MANAGEMENT: Mount Hood National Forest
NOTES: Restrooms at trailhead; no parking
fee or permit required, but $5 fee per person
to soak in the hot springs

GETTING THERE: From southeast of Portland, follow Oregon Route 224 to the town of
Estacada. Continue on OR 224 for 25 miles up the Clackamas River to the Ripplebrook Guard
Station, and turn right to cross a bridge over the Oak Grove Fork of the Clackamas River. Just
over the bridge by Rainbow Campground, Forest Roads 46 and 57 split—stay to the right on
FR 46. After 3.5 miles, turn right onto FR 63 at a fork and sign for Bagby. Go 3.5 miles on FR
63, a beautiful drive up the Collawash River, then turn right on (possibly unmarked) FR 70.
Follow FR 70 for 6 miles to a sign pointing left to the Bagby Hot Springs Trailhead and large
parking area. The route is paved the whole way, and the trailhead is 39 miles from Estacada.

**The Hot Springs Fork of the Collawash River is aptly named. The springs in this area feed the
beautiful river where they rise from the western slopes of the Cascade foothills. The area around
Bagby Hot Springs has been popular for over a century—the Forest Service built its first guard
station near the springs in the early 1900s, and the first bathhouse was built in the 1920s.**

**Somehow the accessibility of this spot didn't translate to logging it, and in 1984, the Bull of the
Woods Wilderness was designated to protect the last large area of low-elevation ancient forest
on the south end of Mount Hood National Forest. The Bagby Hot Springs Trail and development
is surrounded by this wilderness area, which stretches south and connects to the Opal Creek
Wilderness.**

You will have to share this gorgeous trail with the
hot-springs users who frequent the area, but it's
well worth the walk regardless of whether you
plan to soak (carry a towel, just in case). The nearly
flat 1.5 miles to the hot springs is entirely through
an ancient forest of giant Douglas-firs and western redcedars, with smaller western hemlock
and vine maple filling in the understory. At 0.7
mile, the trail begins following the Hot Springs
Fork of the Clackamas River, a stream with huge

boulders and some obvious swimming holes near a
bridge-crossing at 1.2 miles. Continue for another
0.3 mile to Bagby Hot Springs, where you can fill
a hollowed-out cedar log with piping hot water
from the nearby spring or join fellow trekkers in
round, communal tubs before heading back to the
trailhead. If you're out for a longer hike, the trail
continues for many miles beyond the hot springs
into the ancient forest that dominates the Bull
of the Woods and Opal Creek Wilderness areas.

A bridge crosses the Hot Springs Fork of the Collawash River along the trail to Bagby Hot Springs.

32. OPAL CREEK

DISTANCE: Opal Pool, 7-mile loop; Cedar Flat, 10 miles round-trip
TRAILHEAD LOCATION: 44.8598°, -122.2643°
STARTING ELEVATION/ELEVATION GAIN: Opal Pool, 1950 feet/300 feet; Cedar Flat, 1950 feet/600 feet
DIFFICULTY: Opal Pool, moderate; Cedar Flat, difficult

SEASON: Spring through fall, access dependent on snow
FOREST TYPE: Douglas-fir
PROTECTIONS: Inventoried roadless area; Opal Creek Scenic Recreation Area
MANAGEMENT: Willamette National Forest
NOTES: Restrooms at trailhead; $5 fee or permit required to park. Avoid summer weekends, as parking can fill up.

GETTING THERE: From Interstate 5 in Salem, take exit 253 for Oregon Route 22 (Stayton/Detroit) and go east for 22 miles. At milepost 23, turn left (north) onto Little North Fork Road at a flashing yellow light. The road is paved for just over 15 miles and then becomes gravel Forest Road 2209 as you enter the national forest. Continue another 5.5 miles on this sometimes rough road, staying left at signs for Three Pools at about 1.5 miles, to a parking area and trailhead for Opal Creek and Jawbone Flats. Parking here is limited, so try to avoid summer weekends.

In the late 1980s and early 1990s the ancient forest surrounding Opal Creek became a major battleground and symbol of the conflict between conservationists and the timber industry over the fate of Oregon's remaining ancient forests. One side vowed to see Opal Creek cut, going so far as to plan a road up Opal Creek and clear-cuts throughout the forest. Conservationists were even more committed to protecting it, however. The forests here include trees 250 feet tall and up to a thousand years old, and the Opal Creek drainage was among the few remaining intact forest watersheds in the western Cascades. A lot was at stake.

The 1996 designation of the Opal Creek Wilderness and Opal Creek Scenic Recreation Area, totaling thirty-four thousand acres, was the result of conservation groups raising the issue of protecting ancient forests into a national campaign and a mainstream Oregon value.

From the trailhead, walk through the gate and follow the road along the Little North Santiam River. In just under a half mile, cross Gold Creek on a big bridge. The trail follows the road and climbs gradually but steadily through a gorgeous Douglas-fir forest, which, to the left, is protected in the Opal Creek Wilderness area. To the right, and including the rest of this hike, is the Opal Creek Scenic Recreation Area.

At the 2-mile point, you'll reach the site of a historic sawmill and a quarter mile later come to a trail junction on the right. Take it, and cross the river on a log bridge

Opal Creek's pristine waters are filtered by ancient forests, protected after a long struggle.

to follow this trail upriver to the left. Over the next mile, a diverse forest in younger and older patches lines the trail, with views through the trees across the river and the forested hills beyond. As you approach Opal Pool to the left, magnificent trees shade the narrow canyon where Opal Creek flows into the Little North Santiam. Take a moment to enjoy this lovely spot before deciding if you want to complete the 7-mile loop or add on a few more miles to Cedar Flat.

If you decide to go on, turn right at the Battle Ax and Kopetski Trails just past the pool. Follow signs for the Kopetski Trail to continue a rugged mile and a half up the stunningly gorgeous Opal Creek valley. In half a mile you'll need to carefully cross Flume Creek on rocks at the base of Flume Falls. Continue, taking in the views of several falls along Opal Creek before reaching Cedar Flat, a rocky, flat area where nearly millennia-old Douglas-firs and redcedars—some recently dead—stand guard. The trail peters out just past the flat at Beachie Creek and the Opal Creek Wilderness boundary.

If you're not up for the extra mileage or you're on your way back from Cedar Flat, turn left from Opal Pool on the Battle Ax Trail to get to Jawbone Flats, an old mining town at the confluence of Opal Creek and the Little North Santiam. Today it is also home to the Opal Creek Ancient Forest Center, an education outfit that focuses on the ancient forest ecosystem (more info at www.opalcreek.org). Spend some time checking it out, and then hike the 3 miles out the road back to the trailhead along the river and through the ancient forest.

33. SOUTH FORK BREITENBUSH

DISTANCE: 2.8 miles round-trip
TRAILHEAD LOCATION: 44.7754°, -121.9542°
STARTING ELEVATION/ELEVATION GAIN: 2500 feet/200 feet
DIFFICULTY: Easy
SEASON: Spring through fall, access dependent on snow

FOREST TYPE: Douglas-fir
PROTECTIONS: Unprotected roadless area where old forest reserved from logging in management plan
MANAGEMENT: Willamette National Forest
NOTES: No restrooms at trailhead; no parking fee or permit required

GETTING THERE: From Salem, take Oregon Route 22 southeast to the town of Detroit. From the south, travel to Santiam Pass on US 20 and turn north on OR 22 to get to Detroit. Just east of the bridge in town, and at the only gas station, turn onto Forest Road 46 to head east. After 11.5 miles, turn right onto FR 4685 and drive just over a half mile to reach the trailhead and parking pullout on the right side of the road.

The Breitenbush Hot Springs Retreat and Conference Center, a privately owned and managed facility, and nearby summer home community on adjacent Forest Service land have been working to defend the ancient forests in the area for decades. They needed to. The forests here on the edge of the Mount Jefferson Wilderness were heavily logged in the 1970s and 1980s. Protecting the remaining ancient forests in the upper reaches of the Santiam watershed is of utmost

importance for water users downstream, for connecting spotted owl habitat, and for ensuring the amazing recreational opportunities here are not lost.

After following a short spur trail from the road to the main trail, turn left to head toward Roaring Creek. The first half mile is through a gorgeous cathedral-like ancient forest. Sunny openings created from windstorm blowdown are scattered along the way, littered with large down logs, young seedlings, fireweed (look for tall purple flowers in the summer), snags, and tall shrubs and small chinquapin trees growing up. One opening offers a great view of Devils Ridge and giant Douglas-fir on the slope below.

At about 0.9 mile, look down toward the river, which has narrowed into more of a gorge, to see some large logjams and trees blown down on the opposite slope. Pass through another blowdown area at about 1.2 miles, and just beyond that is a good place to take in the view of the river below, or scramble down to its rocky shore when water levels are low enough. The last stretch before reaching Roaring Creek, my suggested turnaround point at 1.4 miles, is through a younger, drier forest. When you reach this destination, the bridge across Roaring Creek may very well be out. The streams and rivers flowing from the slopes of Mount Jefferson are volatile—surging with spring runoff and moving rocks, logs, and bridges with their force.

To extend your visit, the south side of the river provides access to additional trails that were built by the Breitenbush community starting in the 1980s. The Spotted Owl Trail and Emerald Forest Trail, in particular, are really beautiful—though less so after fire

breaks were cut through the forest when the Devils Creek Fire of 2017 threatened to burn the retreat center and summer-home community. A great way to explore all the trails here is to stay at the retreat center, but even if you just pass through the hot-springs area, it's not a bad idea to stop at the information kiosk for trails information, or pay the day-use fee and enjoy a soak in a world-class hot-springs facility (more info at https ://breitenbush.com).

Beautiful forests of Douglas-fir and hemlock along the trail system near the South Fork Breitenbush River

34. CRABTREE VALLEY

DISTANCE: 4.5 miles round-trip
TRAILHEAD LOCATION: 44.6035°, -122.4448°
STARTING ELEVATION/ELEVATION GAIN:
3960 feet/950 feet
DIFFICULTY: Moderate
SEASON: Late spring through fall, access
dependent on snow
FOREST TYPE: Douglas-fir

PROTECTIONS: Area of critical
environmental concern; research natural
area
MANAGEMENT: Northwest Oregon District
BLM
NOTES: No restrooms at trailhead; no
parking fee or permit required

GETTING THERE: From the town of Sweet Home, head 4 miles east on US Highway 20 and turn north onto the Middle Santiam River Road at a sign for Green Peter Dam and Quartzville. Drive 20 miles on what becomes Quartzville Access Road along Green Peter Reservoir. At milepost 20, turn left on Yellowstone Access Road (BLM Road 11-3E-35.3). Follow this paved, but slightly rough, road for a total of 6 miles—staying left at the first Y and right at the second one at 2.8 miles onto Road 11-3E-35.1 (if in doubt at a road junction, stay on the pavement). When you come to a T intersection after 6 miles, turn left onto Road 11-3E-16 and continue on this rough road (go slowly and be careful) for 0.9 mile to its end. Parking is in the road-end clearing.

It's easy to feel a bit lost when you're in Crabtree Valley—in part because the drive through a maze of logging roads and clear-cuts (old and new) can be somewhat disorienting and in part because it truly feels like a valley that time forgot. Carved by glaciers, for nearly a millennium the steep walls of Crabtree Valley and the moist environment around Crabtree Lake and surrounding wetlands have protected pockets of ancient trees from fire.

The heart of the valley was once owned by a timber company and could have suffered the fate of the surrounding forests, but forest advocates worked for years for the BLM acquire it. Today it is designated as an area of critical environmental concern, and part of it is also a research natural area, recognizing the importance and uniqueness of the ancient forest here.

Begin the trail by crossing a rocky barricade and following the old road along a basalt cliff. In a quarter mile, take in the spectacular view of Mount Jefferson to the east before turning sharply to the north and descending gradually into Crabtree Valley along the west face of the wall that protects the valley. The road gets more and more trail-like as it descends—alders, mountain ash, vine maple, and wildflowers are filling in from the edges, and dips in the road where old culverts have been removed are becoming more

like natural streams. (These can be challenging to cross, as some are a bit steep.) Views into the valley, across the tops of old-growth trees, include the interesting peaks of Carolyn's Butte on the north end of the valley, Carolyn's Crown near the lake, and Crabtree Mountain to the south.

When you reach the bottom after about 1.6 miles, scramble down to the gravel road to the left, turn left, and follow this road 0.6 mile south, with Crabtree Creek on the left. The forest of Douglas-firs, western redcedars, and Pacific silver

to a wide open rocky plateau covered in lichen and flowers. Walk north toward its edge to find a patch of Alaska yellow-cedar and a view over the wet meadow, the valley, and Carolyn's Butte. You can also see previously logged plantations lining the slopes.

Head back to the lakeside trail and continue to follow it around to the east side, a quarter mile total. On the way, pass a huge western redcedar on the right side of the trail before entering a towering forest of Douglas-fir and western hemlock. Devil's club, salmonberry, huckleberry, and down logs crowd the trail, making it a little hard to follow. But persevere: near the far southeast corner of the lake, follow a natural left turn to go off-trail into a beautiful open stand of stunning and huge Douglas-firs. In this area the ancient trees are six to nine hundred years old, having lived through past fires—look for burn marks on their bark. Explore the clumps and massive individual trees in this grove (making sure to keep some landmarks in sight so you don't get lost) Other areas of giant, old trees can be found by exploring farther around the lake or down the overgrown old road west of the lake, but extreme caution and excellent routefinding skills are necessary in this off-trail environment. Retrace your steps to return to the parking area.

firs that line the route grew back after a fire three centuries ago. You'll pass an open area where other old roads once connected, and continue to a concrete barricade. Walk around it and follow this old road through a tunnel of alders, gradually uphill another quarter mile to the edge of Crabtree Lake, where rough-skinned newts can be seen floating in the placid water.

At the lake, turn left to cross the outlet creek on rocks. Go a few hundred feet, look for a side trail to the left, and take it through a patch of trees

King Tut, a thousand-year-old Douglas-fir tree found off the beaten path in Crabtree Valley, has many admirers.

35. THREE PYRAMIDS

DISTANCE: 5.6 miles round-trip
TRAILHEAD LOCATION: 44.4989°, -122.0622°
STARTING ELEVATION/ELEVATION GAIN: 4040 feet/1700 feet
DIFFICULTY: Difficult
SEASON: Early summer to fall; early July for best wildflowers

FOREST TYPE: Douglas-fir, alpine and subalpine
PROTECTIONS: Unprotected roadless area reserved from logging in management plan
MANAGEMENT: Willamette National Forest
NOTES: No restrooms at trailhead; no parking fee or permit required

GETTING THERE: From Salem and Interstate 5, take Oregon Route 22 southeast for about 72 miles. Between mileposts 76 and 77 on OR 22, turn right onto Lava Lake Meadow Road (Forest Road 2067). From the south or east, travel to Santiam Pass on US 20 and turn north on OR 22 for 7.6 miles. Between mileposts 76 and 77 on OR 22, turn left onto Lava Lake Meadow Road (FR 2067). Follow this good gravel road for 1.9 miles and, after crossing the Parks Creek bridge, turn right on FR 560. Continue straight for another 3.5 gravel miles, passing through some logged private land and ignoring FR 840 on the left in 3 miles. The trailhead is at the end of the road, with plenty of parking in the big turnaround.

The Three Pyramids, eroding ancient volcanic plugs, lie at the heart of the spectacular and diverse Old Cascades in the Middle Santiam watershed. The four-thousand-acre, unprotected roadless area surrounding the North, Middle, and South Pyramids lies just east of the Middle

Meadows and diverse forests line the base of the Three Pyramids' eroding peaks. *(Photo by Greg Vaughn)*

Santiam Wilderness and west of the higher-elevation wilderness surrounding Mount Jefferson. This lack of official protection means that some of the natural, mature forests along South Pyramid Creek and other nearby areas have been targeted by logging plans.

On this hike you can take in an amazing ancient forest of noble and silver fir interspersed with alpine meadows and—as a final reward—a mountaintop view of one of the Cascades' largest unprotected roadless areas.

Start the hike by crossing the small North Fork Parks Creek and turning right at a junction with the South Pyramid Trail. Climb gradually but steadily along the stream's gorge through a forest of old-growth noble fir, hemlock, silver fir, and Douglas-fir full of snags, down logs, woodland wildflowers, and patches of devil's club. After 0.9 mile, cross the stream on rocks and logs and begin the climb up through a brushy meadow full of bracken ferns, salmonberries, and tall wildflowers.

From here, the trail switchbacks up a steep ridge with views of the large meadow at the base of the eroding cliff that forms the southeast slope of South Pyramid. The lush shrubs and wildflowers overhanging the trail here are teeming with pollinators and hide some sections of rough trail, so watch your footing.

Continue climbing in and out of forest and wildflower-filled openings, with huge noble firs standing out among the diverse species. Around the 1.6-mile point, the openings become rockier and the forest gains more Alaska yellow-cedar and mountain hemlock. Finally, at 2.4 miles, emerge onto a rocky ridge with views of mountains to both the left and right. The trail traverses this ridgetop to the west side of Middle Pyramid, passing the base of a tall cliff and then following a cool, north-facing slope, before climbing to a trail junction at 2.7 miles. Turn left to make the final quarter-mile push up the steepest part of the trail to reach the rocky saddle atop the Middle Pyramid. Here dwarf juniper and a whole host of alpine plants grow in the rocky crags.

To reach the old lookout site on the summit, continue to the right and pick your way up through the rocks on the faint trail. From the top you can see most of the route you just followed, as well as Three Sisters, Three Fingered Jack, Mount Jefferson—and farther on a clear day.

On the way back to the trailhead, consider turning down the South Pyramid Creek Trail to enjoy more of the lower-elevation old-growth forest that lines this trail for another mile or so. This trail continues on for many miles (enough for a multiday backpack trip), eventually connecting with trails into the Middle Santiam Wilderness, with stunning ancient forests as well.

36. HOUSE ROCK

DISTANCE: 1-mile loop
TRAILHEAD LOCATION: 44.3930°, -122.2457°
STARTING ELEVATION/ELEVATION GAIN:
1640 feet/120 feet
DIFFICULTY: Easy
SEASON: Early spring through fall

FOREST TYPE: Douglas-fir
PROTECTIONS: Unprotected roadless area where old forest reserved from logging in management plan
MANAGEMENT: Willamette National Forest

NOTES: No restrooms at trailhead but available in adjacent campground; no parking fee or permit required

GETTING THERE: From the town of Sweet Home, follow US Highway 20 east for 26 miles. Between mileposts 54 and 55, turn right on Latiwi Creek Road (Forest Road 2044). Continue on Latiwi Creek Road for a half mile and turn right toward House Rock Campground; then descend a quarter mile. Park in the wide spot in the road just before the bridge into the campground.

This area near the South Santiam River has remnants of the old Santiam Wagon Road, the primary route from Albany to Sisters from the 1860s to the 1920s. It once held extensive ancient forests, with some of the oldest forests known in Oregon stretching south from current US 20 and surrounding Gordon Lakes. Unfortunately the area has been heavily logged—some of those oldest groves (part of the Millennium Grove) were logged in the 1980s despite a rising tide of forest activism.

Vine maples frame the beginning of the House Rock Loop near a section of the Santiam Wagon Road.

To hike this lovely loop trail, start out heading downstream, away from the bridge to the campground, and cross a large pedestrian bridge over the South Santiam River. From the bridge, you get a good view of some nice swimming holes accessed from the campground and of the stand of ancient forest on the other side of the creek. After crossing the bridge, turn left to reach House Rock—a massive, moss-covered boulder that once sheltered snowbound pioneers. Look for the huge, moss-covered Pacific yew at its base.

The trail, crossing a few wet and muddy spots, follows the river past large Douglas-firs as it makes a big bend.

At about 0.4 mile, follow a side trail to the left at a sign for House Rock Falls. You'll descend into a forest of big western hemlocks scattered with even bigger Douglas-firs, and then into a moist and mossy cedar grove with vine maples in the understory. The falls tumble over large boulders you can scramble around on if you wish to explore.

Head back up to the main trail to continue the loop. When you reach the Santiam Wagon Road (there's a sign), turn right and head down this wide avenue through a towering cathedral forest with a layered canopy. When you come to another Wagon Road sign, turn right, descend past another huge, moss-covered rock, and then turn left at the next junction to complete the loop.

37. ECHO BASIN

DISTANCE: 2.3 miles round-trip
TRAILHEAD LOCATION: 44.4131°, -122.0853°
STARTING ELEVATION/ELEVATION GAIN:
4150 feet/650 feet
DIFFICULTY: Moderate
SEASON: Early summer through fall; best wildflowers in July

FOREST TYPE: Douglas-fir
PROTECTIONS: Inventoried roadless area; area reserved from logging in management plan
MANAGEMENT: Willamette National Forest
NOTES: No restrooms at trailhead; no parking fee or permit required

GETTING THERE: From the town of Sweet Home, follow US Highway 20 east for 38 miles. Just west of milepost 67 on US 20, turn left (north) on Echo Basin Road (Forest Road 055). Follow this rough gravel road for 2 miles—very carefully if you don't have a high-clearance vehicle—to find the trailhead on the right and parking in a wide spot in the road.

This hike, in the heart of the Old Cascades, is short overall, but its diverse scenery and stunning Alaska yellow-cedars make it worthwhile. The Old Cascades, an area west of the newer, taller volcanic peaks that dot the spine of the Cascades today, are probably best known for their wonderful and accessible wildflower meadows like those on Iron and Crescent Mountains and here in Echo Basin.

The trail starts by going pretty steeply uphill for about a half mile through a Pacific silver fir plantation on an old logging road with Echo Creek to the right. After this most arduous part of the hike, the trail begins to climb through alternating wet meadows and natural mixed conifer stands with some big Douglas-fir and western hemlock before getting to a small bridge over the creek. This is where the loop begins.

Turn right to cross the bridge toward a giant Douglas-fir, but don't stand in amazement too long because the trail soon enters a stand of truly spectacular Alaska yellow-cedar. Alaska yellow-cedars are not common south of Mount Jefferson, and here at the southern end of their range they tend to be fairly small and found in rocky, higher-elevation sites. Not in Echo Basin, however: here, they are the true stars of the trail—some as large as six feet wide and likely six hundred years old.

Large silver firs are also scattered at the edge of the cedar grove. Beyond this impressive stand, the trail winds through a wet meadow of tall wildflowers and bracken fern. At about 0.9 mile, pass a nice big Douglas-fir and an alder thicket before finding a true giant—a double-trunked Alaska yellow-cedar, each trunk at least six feet in diameter.

Some of Oregon's largest Alaska yellow-cedars are found in a grove in Echo Basin.

When you are done marveling, follow the trail steeply uphill through a stand of more yellow-cedar and come out into a large wet meadow complex. Even late in the summer, this meadow runs with water, so plan to get a bit wet and muddy as you take in the views of Echo Mountain, a bowl-shaped ridge that rises to the north, and examine the lovely wildflower display including the unique spikes of purple elephant's head and white bog orchids. Boardwalk bridges cross some of the spring-fed streams bubbling out of the meadow, and scattered ancient firs and snags rim the meadows and walls above.

Complete the loop by following the now more overgrown trail through thorny shrubs, big firs, and more huge Alaska yellow-cedars before heading back down through the plantation.

If you are up for an additional short, flat walk near Echo Basin, stop at the Hackleman Old Growth Grove, with a short (0.8-mile) loop from a well-marked parking area just a half mile west of the turnoff for the Echo Basin Trail on US 20.

UPPER WILLAMETTE AND MCKENZIE HIKES

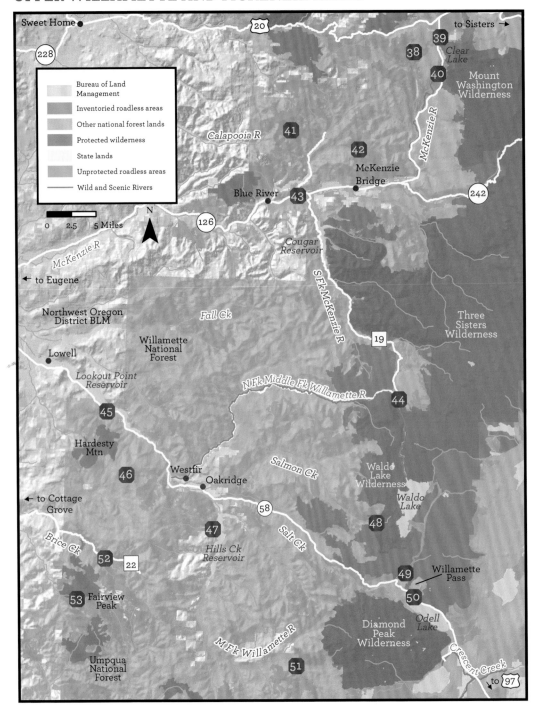

Sweet Home

228

20

to Sisters →

39

38

Clear Lake

40

Mount Washington Wilderness

Bureau of Land Management
Inventoried roadless areas
Other national forest lands
Protected wilderness
State lands
Unprotected roadless areas
Wild and Scenic Rivers

Calapooia R

41

42

McKenzie R

McKenzie Bridge

0   2.5   5 Miles

N

242

Blue River

43

126

Cougar Reservoir

S Fk McKenzie R

McKenzie R

← to Eugene

19

Three Sisters Wilderness

Northwest Oregon District BLM

Fall Ck

Willamette National Forest

Lowell

Lookout Point Reservoir

N Fk Middle Fk Willamette R

44

45

Hardesty Mtn

Westfir

Salmon Ck

Waldo Lake Wilderness

46

Oakridge

Waldo Lake

← to Cottage Grove

58

48

Brice Ck

47

Salt Ck

52   22

Hills Ck Reservoir

49

Willamette Pass

53   Fairview Peak

50

Diamond Peak Wilderness

Odell Lake

Umpqua National Forest

M Fk Willamette R

51

Crescent Creek

to 97

UPPER WILLAMETTE
AND MCKENZIE

The extensive upper Willamette River basin includes several large watersheds that feature the most ancient forest hikes in this book. Dominated by the Douglas-fir forest type at lower elevations, the forests here include a mix of species and types as they transition to higher elevations and to the south. The southern end of this region includes the Calapooya Divide separating the Willamette drainage from the Umpqua with incense cedar and ponderosa pine in the drier forest areas.

To the east the McKenzie River, with its major tributaries the Blue River and South Fork McKenzie, flows through miles of the Willamette National Forest. Designated as wild and scenic for 13 miles from its headwaters at Clear Lake on the edge of the Mount Washington Wilderness to Scott Creek (excluding some small dams and reservoirs), the McKenzie's watershed filters fantastic drinking water for the city of Eugene. Ice cold whitewater, stunning ancient forests, wild fish, and many miles of trails also make it a recreation paradise between Eugene and Bend. Though much of the lower watershed has seen past logging, the upper end of the 26-mile McKenzie River Trail includes several great ancient forest sections for hiking.

Farther south, the Middle Fork Willamette watershed includes the major drainages of the North Fork of the Middle Fork and Fall Creek.

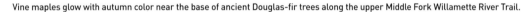

Vine maples glow with autumn color near the base of ancient Douglas-fir trees along the upper Middle Fork Willamette River Trail.

The Middle Fork Willamette's headwaters lie near the base of Diamond Peak; it then flows through the Willamette National Forest and two major reservoirs before it reaches private land and the Willamette Valley. The North Fork of the Middle Fork is one of the wildest rivers in this region (and designated wild and scenic) beginning on the north end of Waldo Lake. Other tributaries like Fall Creek and Winberry Creek begin in the foothills west of the High Cascades and join the Middle Fork downstream of Lookout Point Dam.

This region also includes the Coast Fork Willamette watershed and the Row River. Much of this watershed is managed by the Umpqua National Forest, with low-elevation forests on BLM and private lands. In fact, there are BLM-managed lands downstream of the national forest in all these drainages, but you will find no featured hikes in them. BLM lands in this region have been prioritized for logging, and while some ancient forests remain in small patches on these lands, there are no trails.

Despite a history of extensive logging on public lands throughout this area and continued emphasis on timber production (including some unlogged ancient forests), the Upper Willamette has some of the state's largest protected areas. In the headwaters of the McKenzie and Middle Fork watersheds, the Three Sisters, Waldo Lake, and Diamond Peak Wilderness areas top the High Cascades and include the mountains' western slopes. Bitterly fought battles for forest protections in areas like French Pete Creek, an extension of the Three Sisters Wilderness, set the stage for public awareness of the need to protect ancient forests. For the most part, however, ancient forests in the region remain protected only by changeable policies like the Northwest Forest Plan and Roadless Rule, even when they are adjacent to these wilderness areas.

38. BROWDER RIDGE

DISTANCE: 3 miles round-trip
TRAILHEAD LOCATION: 44.3713°, -122.0551°
STARTING ELEVATION/ELEVATION GAIN:
3700 feet/930 feet
DIFFICULTY: Moderate
SEASON: Early summer through fall, access dependent on snow; best wildflowers in midsummer

FOREST TYPE: Douglas-fir
PROTECTIONS: Unprotected roadless area; most of the old forest reserved from logging in management plan
MANAGEMENT: Willamette National Forest
NOTES: No restrooms at trailhead; no parking fee or permit required

GETTING THERE: From US Highway 20, 3 miles west of the junction with Oregon Route 126 and just east of milepost 69, turn south on Hackleman Creek Road (Forest Road 2672) at a sign for the Santiam Wagon Road and Gate Creek Trail. Follow this good gravel road for 1.7 miles (staying left in a half mile) and turn right on FR 1598 with a sign for Gate Creek. The trailhead is on the right 2.8 miles down this road, with a parking pullout on the left.

From Eugene or Springfield, follow OR 126 east up the McKenzie River. Just past Clear Lake Resort, look for a sign for Ickinick Sno-Park and turn left on Hackleman Creek Road (FR 2672). Drive about 3 miles up this good gravel road, then turn left on FR 1598. The trailhead is on the right 2.8 miles down this road, with a parking pullout on the left.

A clump of Alaska yellow-cedar grows among other diverse tree species on the Browder Ridge Trail.

Part of a 4600-acre unofficial roadless area in the heart of the Old Cascades, Browder Ridge includes headwater tributaries to the McKenzie River drainage. Though the surroundings have been logged, Gate Creek Trail and Browder Ridge include excellent examples of the diverse mid-elevation forest of the western Cascades, with trees several hundred years old.

The trail can be described in thirds: the first section heads steeply uphill through a younger mature forest; the second part is a bit flatter and in the most diverse forest with the biggest trees; and the last section is more of a subalpine forest with meadows and views.

The trail starts out in a lovely forest following the Gate Creek ravine, though you never really see the stream itself. The trail then switchbacks up for a half mile through a mature forest of western hemlock, Douglas-fir, and noble fir, with a fairly open understory that includes wildflowers, vine maple, Pacific yew, rhododendron, and beargrass. This north-facing slope is cooler and moister than the rest of the trail. Once the trail levels out a bit, notice some large snags and look for different trees like Engelmann spruce and Alaska yellow-cedar scattered in the forest (look for their very different bark texture—the spruce gray with small flaky scales, the cedar gray and stringy).

A moist forest stand with pockets of snags and down wood begins after about 0.6 mile, with devil's club (a large, spiny wildflower) and old-growth Engelmann spruce trees. As you continue to ascend, more true firs enter the mix. Around 0.9 mile, enter a large meadow with bracken fern, coneflowers, and flitting butterflies. Pass back into the forest with huge (four-foot-diameter) firs, into another meadow with adjacent tall snags, and then back into a large northeast-facing meadow.

The trail heads back into the forest at 1.2 miles, past a big incense cedar, some Alaska yellow-cedar, and mountain hemlock—an indicator that you've gained elevation. As you turn across a north-facing slope with bigger yellow-cedars, enjoy a view of Echo Basin to the north. Climb a bit higher and crest the ridge on top of the large northeast-sloping meadow where hummingbirds dip in and out of the meadow's edge. This large opening, 1.5 miles into the hike, faces east and gives you views of Mount Washington, the Three Sisters, and Three Fingered Jack. The meadow is a great place to enjoy the antics of grasshoppers, explore the many types of wildflowers in bloom throughout the summer, and gaze down upon the diverse forest and its many hues of green before heading back down.

39. MCKENZIE RIVER TRAIL: FISH LAKE CREEK TO GREAT SPRING

DISTANCE: 3 miles round-trip
TRAILHEAD LOCATION: 44.3936°, -122.0014°
STARTING ELEVATION/ELEVATION GAIN:
3100 feet/280 feet
DIFFICULTY: Easy
SEASON: Spring to late fall, access dependent on snow; fall for color
FOREST TYPE: Douglas-fir

PROTECTIONS: Inventoried roadless area; area reserved from logging in management plan
MANAGEMENT: Willamette National Forest
NOTES: Portable toilet at trailhead; no parking fee or permit required. Watch for mountain bikers on this popular trail.

GETTING THERE: From Eugene or Springfield, follow Oregon Route 126 east up the McKenzie River past Clear Lake Resort. Just south of the 2-mile marker on OR 126, at a trail marker, turn right and go a short way up this potholed road to the trailhead parking area.

The McKenzie River Trail's upper terminus sits in the middle of the (roughly) three-thousand-year-old lava flow that created Clear Lake and nearby Sahalie and Koosah Falls. Amazingly, a forest has been able to establish itself in this harsh environment, replacing the one that lived before the flow. Vine maples in the more exposed parts of the flow turn brilliant yellow and red in the autumn, and stand out against the black rock background. This hike ends at the edge of the spring that feeds Clear Lake—the headwaters of the McKenzie River.

The trail begins a short way from the parking area at a junction with the Santiam Wagon Road. Turn right to cross the footbridge over Fish Lake Creek, which flows only in winter and early spring, as water rapidly drains from the riverbed through the porous lava. The forest along the trail is a mix of Douglas-fir, western hemlock, grand fir, vine maple, Pacific yew, and chinquapin. Follow the dry stream channel, cross a little road, and enter a denser forest with larger trees, tall snags, and a low understory of forest wildflowers.

In a half mile, the forest begins to feel decidedly older, with bigger trunks and more layers. Over the second half mile, the trail gets closer to the streambed and its wall of riparian vegetation, passes some cedar snags and massive Douglas-firs, and enters a denser stand again with a lot of down logs.

In a mile you'll reach the junction with the Clear Lake Trail. Turn left to cross the bridge and continue through the forest and more visible lava rocks another 0.2 mile to the first view of Clear Lake. Follow the stunningly blue lake's shore, passing some massive Douglas-firs growing straight out of the lava as well as elderberry and vine maple. At 1.5 miles from the trailhead, you'll reach Great Spring, where ice-cold water bubbles up from below the lava flow to feed the lake and form the McKenzie River. This is your turnaround point.

If you have the time, you can continue on the Clear Lake Trail to complete the 5-mile loop around the lake for a total of 7 miles. You'll pass through more large trees for a bit, but most of the loop is through younger forest and open lava flows. If you continue, look for the ghostly remnants of the still-standing forest that was drowned when the lake was formed by the lava flow.

The clear, blue waters of Clear Lake are surrounded by ancient forests at the headwaters of the McKenzie River.

40. MCKENZIE RIVER TRAIL: CARMEN RESERVOIR TO TAMOLITCH FALLS

DISTANCE: 5.5 miles with car shuttle; 7 miles round-trip
TRAILHEAD LOCATION: 44.3417°, -122.0041°
STARTING ELEVATION/ELEVATION GAIN: 2650 feet/200 feet
DIFFICULTY: Moderate
SEASON: Spring through fall, access dependent on snow. Flooding can occur along the trail during spring, which is also when water may be flowing over the normally dry Tamolitch Falls into Blue Pool.

FOREST TYPE: Douglas-fir
PROTECTIONS: Wild and scenic river corridor, unprotected roadless area with no specific protection from logging
MANAGEMENT: Willamette National Forest
NOTES: Restrooms at trailhead; no parking fee or permit required but this may change; confirm with Willamette National Forest. Watch for mountain bikers on this popular trail.

GETTING THERE: From Eugene or Springfield, follow Oregon Route 126 east up the McKenzie River. Watch the mileposts on the side of the road, and turn left at the sign for Carmen Diversion Reservoir near milepost 6. Go three-quarters of a mile, cross a bridge over the river where it enters Carmen Reservoir, and park either just past the bridge or a little farther near the toilet.

To leave a shuttle car downstream at the Tamolitch Falls/Blue Pool Trailhead, follow the directions toward Carmen Reservoir, but travel only 10 miles beyond the town of McKenzie Bridge before looking for the Trail Bridge Reservoir sign. Turn left at this sign onto Forest Road 730, cross the bridge, and turn right to get to the trailhead in a half mile. Parking here is limited and gets crowded on weekends.

The stretch of the McKenzie River Trail between Carmen Reservoir and Tamolitch Falls (also known as Blue Pool) has some of the nicest ancient forest, but it is little used by day hikers, possibly because although this stretch follows the wild and scenic river corridor, the river doesn't actually flow in it much of the year. No matter, the forest really shines along this 3-mile stretch of nearly dry river (it does flow in the winter and early spring). While you won't have the river for company, you also won't have the hordes of people that are often found on the 2-mile stretch below Blue Pool.

The ideal way to enjoy this trail is to arrange a car shuttle and walk downhill the 5.5 miles from Carmen Reservoir to the Tamolitch Falls (Blue Pool) Trailhead by Trail Bridge Reservoir. Second best, hike the 3.5 miles from Carmen to the pool and back through spectacular forest, while avoiding the crowds and still seeing the main attraction.

To go downstream on the McKenzie River Trail from this trailhead, enter the forest to the right of the restroom, and then turn left at the junction. The trail climbs to follow the slope above the reservoir, and big Douglas-firs, girthy incense cedars, and a mixture of younger trees and old-growth forest structure line the trail—take note, especially, of a giant Douglas-fir with deeply furrowed bark, woodpecker holes, and fire-scarred bark right about even with the dam. Once you are past Carmen Dam, the forest becomes surprisingly silent after the river disappears—much of the volume is diverted through a tunnel as part of a power-generation development, while the rest soaks through the porous lava rock and travels downstream underground.

The trail descends to river level past the dam through a dense stand, and then alder, bigleaf maple, and dogwoods thrive in the river's riparian zone. At 0.6 mile, in a stand of hemlock with a lot of down wood, pass a tree of much distinction: a giant Douglas-fir with plated bark, a big burn scar, a seriously thick side arm 50 feet up, and a double top. Continue downstream, with the riparian area to your left, passing in and out of groves of bigger trees and younger ones.

At about a mile, follow a big curve to the right, where giant logs have piled up in the channel. The flat landscape the river meanders through here was formed by a relatively recent lava flow, less than two thousand years ago. As you continue, you'll cross the channel on log bridges in a few places amid a sea of green (or red in the fall) vine maples and varied shrubs.

After about 2.5 miles, a pocket of forest takes on a unique configuration of ancient Douglas-fir, humongous incense cedar, and grand fir protected for millennia from fire by the river and the tall cliff to the east. Tall bigleaf maple and alder also line the more open areas. The cliff recedes to a distance after a half

mile, and you'll pass another stellar grove of ancient Douglas-firs—with all the requisite ancient forest structure—before crossing another bridge and approaching Blue Pool at about the 3.5-mile point.

When you emerge above the pool, you'll likely have company: it's a popular destination. Here the whole of the McKenzie River emerges

The wide base of a western redcedar along the McKenzie River Trail

from underground in the spectacularly blue pool, surrounded by tall trees. Resist the urge to get in the water unless it's a very warm day and you know what you're getting into—it can be dangerously cold.

If you are doing this as an out-and-back, this is your turnaround point. If you're doing the one-way option, the hike to the lower trailhead from here is another 2 miles. The first half of this stretch is narrow and rocky as it passes through rolling lava fields covered with sparse and stunted ancient Douglas-fir and incense cedar trees. The final mile is through a more classic, moist, old-growth Douglas-fir and redcedar forest, with a few crossings of crystal clear streams lined with ferns and moss-covered yew trees.

If you'd like to explore the beautiful and popular 2.5-mile McKenzie Waterfalls Loop, gaining 400 feet of elevation, turn right instead of left at the McKenzie River Trail junction. Head uphill, winding through a lush, layered forest atop the old lava flow. The first falls, Koosah Falls, plunges over a lava cliff into the McKenzie River canyon. The trail keeps you at river level for a bit, so you can gaze into the crystal clear, blue water, then it climbs to the top of Sahalie Falls.

Above Sahalie Falls, the trail rolls gently along the river, through patches of old-growth Douglas-firs, and past massive log jams. Cross the big footbridge at the 1.4-mile point and turn right to complete the loop. When you reach the Sahalie Falls parking area, turn right on the paved path to get to the main waterfall viewpoint. From here, follow the path and wooden steps downstream to pass Koosah Falls again. Stay on the downhill trails at the junctions, and then complete the loop by turning right when you emerge onto the road at Carmen Reservoir.

41. TIDBITS MOUNTAIN

DISTANCE: 4.5 miles round-trip
TRAILHEAD LOCATION: 44.2566°, -122.3004°
STARTING ELEVATION/ELEVATION GAIN: 4070 feet/1000 feet
DIFFICULTY: Moderate
SEASON: Best wildflowers in summer, access dependent on snow

FOREST TYPE: Douglas-fir, alpine and subalpine
PROTECTIONS: Unprotected roadless area with no specific protection from logging
MANAGEMENT: Willamette National Forest
NOTES: No restrooms at trailhead; no parking fee or permit required

GETTING THERE: From Eugene or Springfield, follow Oregon Route 126 east up the McKenzie River. About 44 miles past Springfield, and just past the Christmas Treasures store, turn left onto Blue River Road (Forest Road 15) at a sign for Blue River Reservoir. Drive 4.8 miles on this paved road, staying to the left where FR 1506 goes off to the right at the Lookout Boat Site. Just after a one-lane bridge, the road forks and turns to gravel. Stay to the left onto FR 1509. Follow this good gravel road a winding 8.4 miles into the Tidbits Creek basin, where you catch glimpses of Tidbits Mountain. Turn left onto very steep FR 877 at a hiker trailhead sign. Parking, but not much, is a quarter mile up this road.

Tidbits Mountain stands near the western edge of the Willamette National Forest, and its ancient ridgetop divides the South Santiam River drainage to the north and the McKenzie River

watershed to the south. Streams flow in both directions from this Old Cascades peak, some giving rise to the Calapooia River. The trail has something for everyone: huge trees, wildflowers, and grand views. It's part of a 5300-acre unprotected roadless area, an island (along with other nearby unroaded areas) in a fragmented landscape of roads and old clear-cuts.

The Tidbits Mountain Trail starts out in an old plantation for the first 100 yards but then passes into an unlogged forest with huge western hemlocks—an indicator of this stand's great age. As the trail traverses and climbs the southwestern slope toward the ridge of Tidbits Mountain, you'll pass through a primarily Douglas-fir forest, with trees five feet in diameter, over a multilayered understory of vine maple, Pacific yew, rhododendrons, huckleberries, and many woodland wildflowers. As you gain elevation, large snags and a mix of noble fir and silver fir enter the forest.

At the ridgetop junction at 1.5 miles, turn left. The trail switches aspect to follow the north side of the ridge here, and the forest is markedly different, with

The rocky crags of Tidbits Mountain's summit are framed by ancient trees.

silver fir and mountain hemlock. You can also expect to find remnant patches of snow and early spring wildflowers on this colder slope well into July, depending on the snow year. Small rocky openings showcase wildflowers, rocky mountain maple, and Alaska yellow-cedar. As the trail skirts below the crumbling peak of Tidbits Mountain, it crosses two large rocky debris fields where it is quite narrow. Watch your footing here, but also take in the views of Mount Jefferson and the interesting rock formations of this old volcano.

A half mile past the trail junction you'll come to another. Turn sharply left and uphill to complete the last, quite steep 0.2 mile to the rocky outcropping just below the proper summit of Tidbits Mountain. Up here, you'll find Alaska yellow-cedar, shrubby juniper, and alpine wildflowers, with views in every direction of Mount Jefferson, the Three Sisters, and Diamond Peak. If you're up for it, climb carefully to the very top of the eroding peak, where a lookout cabin once stood before returning the way you came.

42. LOOKOUT CREEK

DISTANCE: 6.5-mile loop
TRAILHEAD LOCATION: 44.2319°, -122.1624°
STARTING ELEVATION/ELEVATION GAIN:
2500 feet/1000 feet
DIFFICULTY: Difficult
SEASON: Late spring through fall, access
dependent on snow

FOREST TYPE: Douglas-fir
PROTECTIONS: Unprotected roadless area
with no specific protection from logging
MANAGEMENT: Willamette National Forest
NOTES: No restrooms at trailhead, no
parking fee or permit required; dogs not
allowed because of wildlife research

GETTING THERE: From Eugene or Springfield, follow Oregon Route 126 east up the McKenzie River. About 44 miles past Springfield and just past the Christmas Treasures store, turn left onto Blue River Road (Forest Road 15) at a sign for Blue River Reservoir. Follow the paved road for 4.3 miles and turn right onto FR 1506 opposite the Lookout Boat Site. Follow FR 1506 for a total of 6.8 miles (the first 2 miles are paved; then stay on FR 1506 at all intersections), finding the trailhead—on the right—a quarter mile past the intersection with FR 350. Parking is just a wide spot in the road. The upper trailhead is 2.8 miles farther up the road.

The Douglas-fir forest along the Lookout Creek Trail illustrates the classic ancient forest structure.

The wonderful Lookout Creek Trail and its namesake creek are located in the H. J. Andrews Experimental Forest. Scientists have learned a great deal about ancient forest ecology here, though unfortunately some of the research has been in how best to *log* ancient forests, leading to the destruction of some of this rare ecosystem.

Forest Road 1506 forms the northern boundary of a large but unprotected roadless area that encompasses Lookout Ridge and spills over the top to the south to form the backdrop for the town of McKenzie Bridge and the McKenzie River Scenic Byway (OR 126). Some recent logging has been carried out on the south slopes of Lookout Mountain, despite efforts by several groups to stop it. The north side, however, harbors a prime example of an ancient Douglas-fir forest accessible by the Lookout Creek Trail.

The trail begins by descending through a gorgeous Douglas-fir, western hemlock, Pacific yew, and western redcedar forest with a lot of down logs and shrubs. It seems like every inch of the flat area you reach on the way to Lookout Creek is covered in moss, including the four- and five-foot-diameter Douglas-firs and cedars. Stop to count the rings on a cut end of one of the logs along the trail to get a sense of the immense age of this forest. In a quarter mile, you'll cross Lookout Creek on a tall bridge. The creek pours over down logs and boulders where tall cedar snags stand sentry on either side and patches of beautiful but fierce devil's club are a feature of the riparian area.

Once across the creek, stay uphill at an old trail junction and then climb steadily—using the time you need to catch your breath to look around at the ferns, flowers, moss, trees, and other stunning forest structure. You might also notice colored flagging or other markers—indicators of the research being done in the forest and not to be disturbed.

At about 0.7 mile, the trail turns away from the creek as it continues to climb the slope of Lookout Mountain. Large redcedars and yew trees accompany you to and along the ridge as you approach the mile point. Larger hemlocks and patches of rhododendron become more noticeable as you continue, and views to the northeast of the Cascade foothills and high meadows can be caught between the trees. In 1.5 miles, you'll descend into a pocket of moister forest and cross a small stream, then switchback up to a rocky outcrop where you can perch for a rest.

From here, the trail rolls up and down (though still overall up) along the slope, through areas of moister and drier forest. At 2 miles begin a gradual descent, crossing a spring-seep area that can make the trail pretty wet, and a giant of a cedar as you approach a stream gushing through a narrow gully. Look for the smooth gray bark on some younger trees in this area—these are Pacific silver fir, found in a few places along the trail.

The crossing here is on a log and is only for the sure of foot and stout of heart. There's no shame in turning back now for a 4.4-mile round-trip hike. If you are able to cross safely, you'll pass another wet area and then switchback up through a grove of incredible redcedars, some with tapered trunks that reach seven feet at the base. Once out of this grove, you'll cross on the side slope through a few patches of snags and a more open canopy for a quarter mile.

Between 2.7 and 3.4 miles, you'll cross a few more streams and wet spots on logs and rocks—fairly easy unless there is high water. Surrounding this final crossing, you'll find some huge

Douglas-firs, and then descend toward Lookout Creek past a stellar example of a nurse log sprouting hemlocks. Cross Lookout Creek at 3.5 miles on a bridge and enjoy the final quarter mile through a towering forest of giant Douglas-firs and hemlocks, fat snags, and vine maples.

You'll reach the road (FR 1506) at about 3.7 miles. To return, the easiest way is to turn left and walk the 2.8 miles on the road (all downhill) to your car, but you can also return the way you came for a longer and more difficult overall hike with the benefit of walking through the stunning forest a second time. The road passes through some logged plantation stands—offering a good juxtaposition to the ancient forest trail—with a view of Lookout Mountain at about the mile point.

43. DELTA OLD GROWTH NATURE TRAIL

DISTANCE: 0.6-mile loop
TRAILHEAD LOCATION: 44.1642°, -122.2839°
STARTING ELEVATION/ELEVATION GAIN:
1280 feet/400 feet

DIFFICULTY: Easy
SEASON: Year-round
FOREST TYPE: Douglas-fir
PROTECTIONS: No specific protection but unlikely to be logged
MANAGEMENT: Willamette National Forest
NOTES: Restrooms nearby in campground; no parking fee or permit required

GETTING THERE: From Eugene or Springfield, follow Oregon Route 126 east up the McKenzie River. A quarter mile east of milepost 45 on OR 126, turn right (south) on Aufderheide Drive (Forest Road 19) at the sign for Cougar Reservoir. Just after crossing a bridge a quarter mile later, turn right at a sign for Delta Campground. Follow this paved road about a mile to the campground and continue to the back of the campground loop to find the day-use area—staying right at junctions—just after site 19 at a sign for a nature trail.

The Delta Nature Trail is a short, easy, showcase nature trail through a magnificent old-growth grove with year-round access. Located near the confluence of the McKenzie

A hiker is dwarfed by giant Douglas-fir trees and the forest understory on the Delta Old Growth Nature Trail.
(Photo by Mahogany Aulenbach)

Connecting the Forest Jigsaw Puzzle

As you travel around Oregon, you will no doubt notice that forests in general, and in particular ancient forests, are often fragmented across the landscape. Roads, private property, clear-cuts, mountain peaks, desert, and other natural and man-made landscape features divide forested areas into patches of various sizes.

Logging left some of these patches of old forests—islands or dissected puzzle pieces—along streams, in steep ravines, or in other small fragments. They can be beautiful, accessible examples of ancient forest (some are included in this book), with huge trees, snags and down wood, and diverse tree and shrub species—all the structural components of an ancient forest. But it is difficult for these islands to function like an ancient forest; they have lost their connection to the greater ecosystem.

Like islands in the ocean, these patches are more susceptible to disturbance in their isolated state. Without the larger, surrounding forest environment, they dry out faster and are more vulnerable to windstorms, and their soil network is cut off. They often aren't large enough to support wildlife species that depend on diverse structure, and if the islands are too far from each other, the offspring of wildlife that do survive in the small patch can't breed and interact with the offspring from other islands of habitat. This is a recipe for local extinction. The redundancy and diversity that help a forest function is eroded, making it less resilient to disturbance and outside forces.

In contrast, to provide the best wildlife habitat, water filtration, biodiversity, and other functions, forests need to be big or connected (preferably both). Today nearly 80 percent of our remaining ancient forest is in patches of less than a thousand acres because of past logging and a high density of logging roads that break up the landscape and act as barriers to wildlife and water flow.

That's why protecting the remaining ancient forests isn't enough. If we want our forests to function like a forest—with healthy soil; filtering water; sustaining a diversity of plants, fungi, and animals; and serving as the vital lungs of our planet—we need to restore forests that we have logged, simplified, and isolated. We need to fit the jigsaw pieces together into a landscape future generations will recognize as Oregon's ancient forest legacy.

A patchwork of clear-cuts and regrowing plantations fragment the natural forest landscape in the foothills of the Cascades. *(Photo by Doug Heiken)*

River and its South Fork, the fertile floodplain area has deposited rich soils for centuries, growing an especially lush forest.

If brochures are stocked at the trailhead, pick one up and follow along as you stroll. The loop trail starts to the right over a large wooden bridge. Pass through a riparian area with tall, moss-draped alders and bigleaf maples. Centuries-old Douglas-fir line the path, with western redcedar, Pacific yew, and bigleaf maple for company. A lush understory of hazelnut, vine maple, red huckleberry, and swordfern adds many colors of green to the forest.

Just before crossing a second bridge over Delta Creek you'll find an especially large group of Douglas-firs. Shade-tolerant western hemlocks, some quite large, are growing up below the Douglas-firs, biding their time for a patch of sunlight to open up where the giants fall. Just over the bridge is a Doug-fir with spectacular branch structure—look up to check it out before you complete the loop. Return your brochure at the trailhead.

44. SHALE RIDGE

DISTANCE: 6 miles round-trip
TRAILHEAD LOCATION: 43.8788°, -122.0718°
STARTING ELEVATION/ELEVATION GAIN:
2930 feet/400 feet
DIFFICULTY: Moderate
SEASON: Early summer through fall, access dependent on snow

FOREST TYPE: Douglas-fir
PROTECTIONS: Waldo Lake Wilderness
MANAGEMENT: Willamette National Forest
NOTES: No restrooms at trailhead; no parking fee or permit required

GETTING THERE: From Interstate 5 just south of Eugene, take exit 188 and follow Oregon Route 58 southeast. A half mile past milepost 31, turn left at signs for Westfir onto Aufderheide Drive (Forest Road 19), just before getting to the Middle Fork Ranger Station. Go a quarter mile, cross a bridge, and turn left at the stop sign. Travel 2 miles and go straight at the stop sign in Westfir. Continue on FR 19 for 30 miles (you can watch mileposts along the way) and, at a hairpin curve, turn right into the small trailhead parking area, marked by a hiker sign on the left.

The North Fork of the Middle Fork of the Willamette River (is there a river with a longer name in Oregon?) is the only outlet of pristine and massive Waldo Lake. The designated wild and scenic river flows due north out of the lake through the Waldo Lake Wilderness, then makes a hard turn to the west to begin its descent and southward flow to the Middle Fork.

At this curve, where Skookum Creek flows down off a high plateau of mountain lakes to join the North Fork, you'll find the lovely Shale Ridge Trail. The forest along this trail includes a spectacular western redcedar grove. Luckily, and thanks to the hard work of forest advocates over the years, the forest here is protected as wilderness and within the protected river corridor.

Vanilla leaf turns yellow at the base of giant trees along the Shale Ridge Trail.

At the trailhead, take the trail to the left and head south. The forest is on the young side, recovering from a fire that probably burned a century ago, but scattered remnant Douglas-firs with blackened bark are a reminder of the previous stand. Plenty of snags, down wood, wildflowers, vine maple, cedar, hemlock, dogwood, and Pacific yew fill the understory and forest floor. After about a mile, the forest transitions to bigger and older trees. Occasionally you can glimpse the green wall of vine maple to the right that indicates the river is nearby.

After 1.7 miles, you'll approach Skookum Creek through a grove of big cedars and pass a massive Douglas-fir. The creek flows over the forest floor in multiple channels, through exposed roots and rocks, and around a mixture of Douglas-fir, cedar, hemlock, Engelmann spruce, and cottonwoods. Crossing can be a bit tricky—it's helpful to find a walking stick for the balancing and hopping necessary to make it across with dry feet.

Just past Skookum Creek, the ridge to the left (with impressive Douglas-firs) flattens out, and the trail climbs onto its flank to follow the river from higher ground. The forest along this ridge loses the understory of the first 2 miles—the closed canopy blocks out the sunlight so little can grow. Large down logs, however, litter the forest floor. The trail gains a little elevation to stay on the ridge around the 2.5-mile mark, and then reaches a rocky stream corridor.

At 2.9 miles, cross the flowing creek and enter the first part of the cedar grove that is the highlight of this trail. Meander past these giants as the trail reaches the braided, mostly abandoned side channels of the North Fork Middle Fork at about 3 miles. In this floodplain area, tall bigleaf maples, yews, down logs, and giant cedars and Doug-firs—all draped in moss—thrive. The trail can become a bit hard to follow, but you can find your way to the river's bank to explore, rest, and soak in the forest before heading back.

45. GOODMAN CREEK

DISTANCE: 4 miles round-trip
TRAILHEAD LOCATION: 43.8511°, -122.6617°
STARTING ELEVATION/ELEVATION GAIN: 960 feet/300 feet
DIFFICULTY: Moderate
SEASON: Year-round; trail can be muddy in spring

FOREST TYPE: Douglas-fir
PROTECTIONS: Old forest reserved from logging in management plan
MANAGEMENT: Willamette National Forest
NOTES: Restrooms at trailhead; no parking fee or permit required but this may change; confirm with Willamette National Forest

GETTING THERE: From Interstate 5 just south of Eugene, take exit 188 and follow Oregon Route 58 southeast. Find the well-marked and heavily used Hardesty Trailhead parking area on the right, between mileposts 21 and 22.

The Hardesty Mountain–Mount June area—just 25 miles outside Eugene—was almost protected as wilderness in the early 1980s. Despite its rugged, wild character, large size, and the untouched forests at its core, politics interfered in this designation. Since then, logging has whittled away at some of the wild area's edges, though citizen defenders and conservation groups have managed to hold much of this at bay.

Today the extensive trail system that crisscrosses the area is popular with hikers, horseback riders, and mountain bikers, offering a unique opportunity to enjoy a wild forest in the backyard of a major population center.

Fire-scarred Douglas-fir trees and smaller western hemlocks are layered in the low-elevation forest on the Goodman Creek Trail.

Some of the oldest forests in the area are on the lower slopes of the ridge close to the highway, like along the Goodman Creek Trail. Lovely though it is, don't expect peace and quiet on this trail. Its accessibility and popularity mean you'll likely encounter other hikers and mountain bikers—especially on weekends. The trail can also be extremely muddy in the winter and spring. Walk gently, and be alert.

A forest of tall Douglas-fir, western hemlock, and western redcedar—the understory awash in shades of green shrubs and young trees—is the starting point for this trail. Over the first quarter mile, it gains a little elevation and offers views through the multilayered canopy before reaching a trail junction. Take the right fork to stay on the Goodman Creek Trail. Moss drapes the down logs, ground, and tree trunks as you pass giant Douglas-firs with twisted arms and furrowed bark, tall snags, and large cedars.

The trail winds in and out of small ravines within earshot of the highway for the first half mile, with a screen of green vine maples far below. After 0.7 mile, begin a descent toward an inlet of the Lookout Point Reservoir on a northwestern slope with a dense canopy and more sparse understory. Tall bigleaf maples dot the downhill slope,

and you reach a wide, shallow stream at 0.9 mile. Hop across on rocks and continue, keeping your ears and eyes open for ospreys and bald eagles that nest in the area.

The forest on the other side of the creek is a bit younger and more typical of the Hardesty Mountain–Mount June area: 150-year-old hemlocks that regenerated after the last major fire here, with scattered large Douglas-firs that survived that fire. Approach the Goodman Creek arm of the reservoir at 1.4 miles, where the trail descends steeply past a rock wall and some giant Doug-firs. It flattens out in a wonderfully moist forest, with towering bigleaf maple, furrowed Douglas-firs, large cedars, and yew trees dripping with moss. At the 1.8-mile point, cross a wetland area filled with salmonberry and ferns and then follow this flat, wide riparian area on the other side.

At about 1.9 miles, you'll come to a large clearing ringed with large firs, and a junction. Continue straight ahead a short way to find a lovely waterfall on a fork of Goodman Creek. Turn right to continue on the main trail, and go a few hundred feet to a bridge-crossing at 2 miles. This makes a good turnaround point. Return the way you came.

46. PATTERSON MOUNTAIN

DISTANCE: 5 miles round-trip
TRAILHEAD LOCATION: 43.7616°, -122.6190°
STARTING ELEVATION/ELEVATION GAIN: 4000 feet/500 feet
DIFFICULTY: Moderate
SEASON: Late spring through fall

FOREST TYPE: Douglas-fir
PROTECTIONS: Old forest reserved from logging in management plan
MANAGEMENT: Willamette National Forest
NOTES: No restrooms at trailhead; no parking fee or permit required

GETTING THERE: From Interstate 5 just south of Eugene, take exit 188 and follow Oregon Route 58 southeast. At about a half mile past milepost 24, turn right on Patterson Mountain Road (Forest Road 5840). Drive up (it's all uphill) this gravel road 5 miles. At the signed intersection, turn left onto FR 1714. Drive 3 miles, then left at FR 5847. Go a few hundred feet and turn left on FR 555. Go about a half mile and you'll see a roadside parking area on your right. The trail starts just up the road from here, on the left.

Patterson Mountain sits along the ridgetop separating the Coast Fork and Middle Fork Willamette watersheds. Ancient forests in this area south of the river and Lookout Point Reservoir aren't extensive, as they have been heavily logged in the past, but large, wild, natural forests do exist in the nearby Hardesty Mountain–Mount June wildlands to the west and the Desolation Creek drainage to the east. Patterson Mountain is less well known or visited than Hardesty and June and isn't large enough to be considered for wilderness protection (as Hardesty and June have been for years), but its forest is spectacular and generally older than the others in the area.

The first part of the trail skirts the edge of an old plantation, but it enters a maturing natural forest in about a third of a mile. Rhododendrons fill in the understory of this dense forest, and soon some big, five-foot-diameter Douglas-firs enter the stand. After about three-quarters of a mile, pass a junction with the Lawler Trail (stay to the left) and then pass Lone Wolf Meadow through the forest to the right. This flat area with big trees and a lot of down wood also has lovely woodland wildflowers in the spring and a diversity of mushrooms in the fall.

In a little over a mile you'll reach a spur trail to the right that leads a short way to the Lone Wolf shelter—a good place to have a snack. From here, the oxalis-lined trail gradually climbs through the really lovely forest of western hemlock, Douglas-fir, and silver fir, as it follows the ridge on a gentle north-facing slope. Be sure to look up into the old-growth trees for evidence of the storms that can batter the area.

The trail comes out into a meadow before summiting the mountain through a final half mile of Douglas-fir and grand fir. At the summit, 2.5 miles from the trailhead, you'll be treated to expansive views north and west over the Willamette Valley and the ground-hugging wildflowers that grow on this rocky soil. Retrace your steps to return to your car.

Oxalis covers the hillslope on the way to the Patterson Mountain summit.

47. LARISON CREEK

DISTANCE: 11.5 miles round-trip
TRAILHEAD LOCATION: 43.6878°, -122.4412°
STARTING ELEVATION/ELEVATION GAIN:
1550 feet/1150 feet
DIFFICULTY: Difficult
SEASON: Year-round
FOREST TYPE: Douglas-fir

PROTECTIONS: Unprotected roadless area where old forest reserved from logging in management plan
MANAGEMENT: Willamette National Forest
NOTES: No restrooms at trailhead; no parking fee or permit required

GETTING THERE: From Interstate 5 just south of Eugene, take exit 188 and follow Oregon Route 58 southeast to the town of Oakridge. Less than a mile past the east end of town and not far past milepost 37, turn right (south) onto Forest Road 23 at signs for Hills Creek Dam. In a half mile, turn right onto FR 21 and drive 3.3 miles to the trailhead parking area on the right, just before crossing Larison Cove.

Close to Oakridge, this low-elevation trail is popular with both hikers and mountain bikers, so be sure to keep your eyes and ears open for other users. It follows Larison Creek, which flows east out of the Cascade foothills toward the Middle Fork Willamette River, though its natural route is impeded when it hits the Hills Creek Reservoir, which dams the Middle Fork, in Larison Cove. This part of the Willamette National Forest has been heavily logged, and a mix of private timberlands in the area around Hills Creek Reservoir compounds the forest's fragmentation. The ancient forest in the small unprotected roadless area around Larison Creek offers an important island of habitat.

Mosses and Oregon grape line the forest floor among huge Douglas-firs and smaller hemlocks on the Larison Creek Trail.

The trail can be an out-and-back of any length, though some of the nicest ancient forest is found within a half mile of the recommended turn-around point, so if you have the time and stamina, hold out to the very end. Along the length of the trail, there are seven small stream-crossings wider than a hop (not all noted here), only one with a bridge, so be prepared to cross on rocks.

In a little under a half mile from the trailhead, cross the small stream the trail has been following and leave it behind as you head toward the main Larison Creek arm of the reservoir. The trail follows this inlet, the drowned remnants of Larison Creek, in and out of the open, where you have views of the exposed stumps that hint at the forest that was cut down when the dam was built. Some of the warmth-loving trees that sneak north from the Umpqua drainage into the Middle Fork in this area—incense cedar, madrone, and sugar pine—can be found on this exposed slope. Mossy, succulent-covered rock outcrops line the trail in places as it slowly descends toward creek level, in and out of a closed-canopy Douglas-fir, hemlock, and incense cedar forest—some of the trees quite large.

By the 1.5-mile mark, you've left the reservoir behind and are close to the creek, where western redcedar becomes more common. Over the next 2 miles, the trail rises and falls with the terrain, sometimes on flat benches, gradually gaining elevation as it follows the creek. The forest type is mostly classic Douglas-fir with Pacific yew, hemlock, redcedar, and some true firs, with scattered sugar pines and a shrubby understory. Where the trail crosses small streams, bigleaf maple, alder, and cottonwood thrive. Larison Creek gets wilder as you go up, with gravel bars, pools, and logjams adding structure and interest.

After crossing a creek at 3.5 miles, you'll enter a tall stand with big snags, bigleaf maple, and redcedar. Over the next half mile, the forest gets nicer still, with big, moss-covered boulders, huge Douglas-firs with deeply furrowed bark, down logs, and sugar pines (look for their long cones on the ground). The trail then climbs a drier ridge, skirting the edge of an old clear-cut, and descends again into a mossy stand with dogwood in the understory.

Climbing again, the trail passes a short distance through a young plantation. Just shy of 5 miles, cross another creek; then follow its ravine back to Larison Creek where the forest, flat here, takes on a beautiful cathedral-like feel and the creek tumbles over down logs through lush greenery. This half mile, up to a crossing on a rotting log bridge, is some of the nicest forest along the whole trail. Turning around at this crossing, a bit over 5.5 miles, is a good idea; the final mile of trail beyond this point simply leads steeply uphill to the western trailhead.

48. BLACK CANYON

DISTANCE: 8 miles round-trip
TRAILHEAD LOCATION: 43.7027°, -122.1112°
STARTING ELEVATION/ELEVATION GAIN: 3450 feet/2050 feet
DIFFICULTY: Difficult
SEASON: Late spring to late fall, access dependent on snow

FOREST TYPE: Douglas-fir, alpine and subalpine
PROTECTIONS: Waldo Lake Wilderness
MANAGEMENT: Willamette National Forest
NOTES: No restrooms at trailhead; no parking fee required but self-issued, free wilderness permit required at trailhead

A large fallen log gives scale to tall firs and a resprouting understory on the Black Creek Trail.

GETTING THERE: From Interstate 5 just south of Eugene, take exit 188 and follow Oregon Route 58 southeast to the town of Oakridge. Drive into Oakridge and turn left (north) at the only stop light in town. Cross the railroad tracks, turn right at the stop sign, and follow this road as it turns into Salmon Creek Road (Forest Road 24) just east of town. Go 10.5 miles on pavement; then keep right at a Y to follow FR 24 to the end of the pavement 3.1 miles later. From here, continue straight onto gravel FR 2421 for 8.2 miles along Black Creek. The trailhead and ample parking are at the end of this road.

This trail climbs from the western edge of the Waldo Lake Wilderness, which wraps around three sides of the lake, through a diverse ancient forest to the edge of the lake itself. The national forestlands west of the Waldo Lake Wilderness, including those along the road leading to this trailhead, have been heavily logged and roaded. The trail sets out through a plantation of trees with large stumps—an indicator of what might have become of the rest of the trail had it not been protected as wilderness.

From the trailhead, go a quarter mile and stop at the registration box before entering the wilderness. From here, a moist and beautiful forest of western hemlock, Douglas-fir, western redcedar, and Pacific yew beckons you onward as you cross multiple seeps and small creeks on the way to Lillian Falls. At about a mile and a quarter, there is a stretch of narrow trail (use caution) before it approaches Black Creek, turns up the cool streamside corridor, and reaches the waterfall at about 1.3 miles.

From here, the trail climbs away from the creek and starts to switchback up, entering a drier forest as you gain elevation, with a lot of down wood. At 2 miles, you reach a bench covered in mountain hemlock, with beargrass, rhododendrons, shrubby chinquapin, and Alaska yellow-cedar. This is a great spot to stop for lunch to gather strength for the climb ahead.

The forest from here gets more diverse as you climb into a subalpine zone above 4500 feet, with true fir and western white pine. The trail ambles through denser and sparser patches, some with very large trees, and crosses Nettie Creek at 2.7 miles. This crossing can be difficult if the water is high—look for a long stick to help you hop across on rocks and down wood, but huckleberries along the trail ahead in the late summer are good motivation.

At about 3 miles, traverse a rocky slope where a small fire burned, offering great views to the southwest of Bunchgrass Ridge and an understory of vine maple and ceanothus. Use care on this slope, as a misstep on the narrow, rocky trail could be dangerous. The trail then heads east up a creek channel, crosses it, and then switchbacks up through the dry, now higher-elevation forest with a beargrass and grouseberry understory.

As you continue to gain elevation (more gradually by about 3.8 miles), the forest gains western white pine, lodgepole pine, subalpine fir, and huckleberry—with some dense patches of young conifer reproduction. Finally, at just over 4 miles, the trail ends at the junction with the Waldo Lake Trail. A view of the lake from here is only through the trees, and there is not good access, so if you feel like walking a bit more, turn right for a little less than a quarter mile to the Klovdahl Bay area.

At Klovdahl Bay, you can get a better view of one lobe of the 6300-acre lake, which is among the purest in the world. The half-constructed dam you can see in the water here was a misguided attempt at tunneling through the mountain to create a new outlet. Luckily this effort failed, and thanks to the work of conservationists and wilderness lovers, the lake's water quality and the wild experience so many enjoy here remain intact. Return the way you came.

49. ISLAND LAKES BASIN

DISTANCE: 10-mile loop
TRAILHEAD LOCATION: 43.6328°, -122.0518°
STARTING ELEVATION/ELEVATION GAIN: 4900 feet/1300 feet
DIFFICULTY: Difficult
SEASON: Summer to fall, access dependent on snow; mosquitoes bad before late August

FOREST TYPE: Alpine and subalpine
PROTECTIONS: Inventoried roadless area; research natural area
MANAGEMENT: Willamette National Forest
NOTES: No restrooms at trailhead; no parking fee or permit required

GETTING THERE: From Interstate 5 just south of Eugene, take exit 188 and follow Oregon Route 58 southeast to the town of Oakridge. Continue another 22 miles, and just west of milepost 59 turn left (north) onto Waldo Lake Road (Forest Road 5897). Go exactly 2 miles to a wide shoulder on the right, which serves as trailhead parking for the Fuji Mountain Trail and this loop.

Views through the subalpine forest south of Waldo Lake offer a glimpse of Maiden Peak.

The Island Lakes loop, utilizing four different trails on the south end of Waldo Lake, highlights a rare high-elevation forest of mountain hemlock and firs. The growing season here is short, and even the oldest trees don't reach the great size of those at low elevations. Regardless, the forest has all the classic components of an ancient forest.

The area south of Waldo Lake includes many small lakes, carved by glaciers long ago, as well as two noticeable peaks—Fuji Mountain and Mount Ray. Both mountains lie outside the protected wilderness, a product of political wrangling when legislation was being considered for the 1984 wilderness bill that protected three sides of Waldo Lake.

Start the loop on the Fuji Mountain Trail and head uphill through a forest of Douglas-fir, silver fir, mountain hemlock, white pine, and some Engelmann spruce, all draped in lichen. As you gain altitude, lodgepole pine enters the forest stand, and there are patches of snags, blowdown, dense seedlings, and old-growth trees. Pass Birthday Lake and Verde Lake—green gems in the forest landscape—and in just over 3 miles, reach a trail junction with the South Waldo Trail.

Instead of turning left to continue up the Fuji Mountain Trail, turn right on the South Waldo

Trail. Pass the Island Lakes on either side of the trail and continue to climb past rocky outcrops, nice big trees, and views of Mount Ray to the north and Maiden Peak to the northeast. After 2 miles, at another junction, turn right and head downhill on the Mount Ray Trail. It descends rather steeply and then passes through Pothole Meadows—filled with wildflowers, tiny frogs, and the headwaters of Ray Creek. From here, it's another 1.5 miles back to road.

To complete the loop, cross the road and continue downhill a half mile to meet the Gold Lake Trail. The area around the Gold Lake bog is designated as a research natural area—the bog ecosystem and ancient Engelmann spruce make it unique. Turn right and enter the gorgeous spruce forest, noting the flaky gray bark of these half-millennium-old trees. The trail crosses springs that flow into the bog and lake and offers views over this wet expanse that is a popular winter destination for cross-country skiers. After 1.8 miles, turn right at a junction to head a short distance up to the road near where you began the loop.

50. ROSARY LAKES

DISTANCE: 6 miles round-trip
TRAILHEAD LOCATION: 43.5971°, -122.0316°
STARTING ELEVATION/ELEVATION GAIN:
5180 feet/630 feet
DIFFICULTY: Moderate
SEASON: Year-round, with ski or snowshoe access in winter; mosquitoes can be bad in early summer

FOREST TYPE: Douglas-fir, alpine and subalpine
PROTECTIONS: Inventoried roadless area
MANAGEMENT: Deschutes National Forest
NOTES: Restrooms at trailhead; no parking fee or permit required

GETTING THERE: From Interstate 5 just south of Eugene, take exit 188 and follow Oregon Route 58 southeast to the town of Oakridge. Continue another 27 miles to Willamette Pass. Just past the Willamette Pass Ski Area, turn left at a sign for the Pacific Crest Trail, then turn right just before a large building to find the trailhead and parking area.

The wild areas and forests surrounding Maiden Peak, southeast of Waldo Lake and north of OR 58 near Willamette Pass, are some of the wildest in the Cascades. The huge Maiden Peak roadless area is connected to the Three Sisters Wilderness on the north and just a hop across a road away from the roadless areas surrounding the Waldo Lake and Diamond Peak Wilderness areas.

Rosary Lakes (a string of three) are technically east of the Cascade Crest and not in the upper Willamette watershed (their outlet, Rosary Creek, flows into Odell Lake, which drains to the east), but they are so close to other hikes it makes sense to include them here.

Start out on the Pacific Crest Trail by heading right at the trail junction just into the forest from the trailhead. The trail rises slowly as it passes through an ancient forest of Douglas-fir, mountain hemlock, and Pacific silver fir, with smaller grand fir, western white pine, subalpine fir, and the odd Engelmann spruce. Down logs and snags add all the classic structure to the forest, and short plants like prince's pine cover the ground.

Around a half mile along the trail, you'll pass by some larger silver fir—look for the (you guessed it) silvery gray bark—and then some giant Douglas-firs. Look for the trunks that are four to five feet in diameter and follow them up. Many of these are now snags, and many others have had their tops broken off and lower limbs have taken over the role—resulting in some real character, cavities, and wildlife habitat. Some of these Douglas-firs have blackened bark and deep fissures, giving a clue to their past and great age—which at this elevation is likely over four hundred years.

About a mile along the trail, you might begin to catch glimpses of shimmering Odell Lake to the south, and possibly even Diamond Peak rising beyond it. Other than the other hikers you might encounter, the only sign of civilization along the trail is the rumble of a train as it follows Odell Lake's south shore. The forest at this point begins to include much more subalpine fir, some quite large, which stand out with their blue hue, geometric branch structure, and plated bark. The trunks of the dense forest between a mile and 2 miles are covered in wispy lime green lichen. At about 1.6 miles, you might notice something a bit strange along the trail—a three-foot-thick ponderosa pine, its orange plated bark giving it away.

The trail skirts the base of a ridge that rises to the north, passing patches of rock slides and thick seedling growth. Crest this ridge at 2.3 miles and curve around it to the left, still gaining some elevation. Lodgepole pines begin to appear in the forest, mixed more heavily with western white pine in sparser rockier areas, interspersed with pure mountain hemlock stands. At 2.8 miles, you'll pass a big rock outcrop and rocky slope of crumbling gray basalt and finally arrive at Lower Rosary Lake at 3 miles. Here you'll find a great view of the lake and Pulpit Rock, which rises above it, and down logs to sit on.

Feel free to explore farther along the PCT or around the lake before heading back the way you came. This trail can also be accessed in the winter to ski or snowshoe if you park at the Willamette Pass Resort and join the PCT from a connector trail on the east side of the parking lot.

The trail to Rosary Lakes is accessible in the winter on skis or snowshoes, a great way to take in this beautiful ancient forest trail.

Forest Soil—More Than Dirt

One thing that contributes to the complex and unique ecosystem of an ancient forest is under your feet wherever you go: soil! Soil is where a lot of a forest's magic happens—the water filtration and storage, the recycling of nutrients, the basis of the forest food web, and the birth of the next generation of plants.

The organisms and matter found in forest soil are a mostly unseen mixture of minerals derived from the underlying rocks, decomposing organic material, and a living network of roots, mycorrhizae, and billions of tiny organisms.

Wait. Back up. What on earth are mycorrhizae?

Mycorrhizae basically function as the roots of a fungus, just as a mushroom is the fruit. Mycorrhizae are unique in that they intertwine with the tiniest of tree and plant roots (on a microscopic scale) to create a truly vast network of water- and nutrient-gathering filaments throughout the soil. The increased surface area and unique properties of the mycorrhizae allow for greater uptake of water and nutrients—which is shared with trees and other plants in exchange for carbohydrates that fungi can't produce themselves. This fungal network also helps hold water and the physical structure of soil in place, preventing runoff of sediment and nutrients. Research has also shown that trees communicate through this network, sending signals about their health and resource needs, which the network responds to by sending more of what a neighbor needs to be healthy.

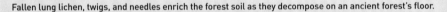

Fallen lung lichen, twigs, and needles enrich the forest soil as they decompose on an ancient forest's floor.

Other plants that root in the forest soil also tap into tree roots as parasites, and some called saprophytes live off decomposing materials in the soil (they don't have chlorophyll to make their own food, the little moochers).

As important as plant roots and fungi are, billions of other tiny organisms also make important contributions to forest soil. Many of them are bacteria and little arthropods (like insects, but technically not) that are actively shredding and decomposing the forest litter and wood that falls to the forest floor and turning it into soil humus. Humus is the organic part of soil that absorbs and holds on to water, slowly releases nutrients, nurtures seedlings and roots, and stores carbon.

Other special bacteria that live in symbiosis with certain plants (like lupines and alders) perform the vital task of turning nitrogen from the atmosphere into a form of the element that plants and animals can use for nutrition. Without this process of nitrogen fixation, life as we know it couldn't exist.

Unfortunately, like other ecosystem processes, the soil system can be drastically disrupted when roads are built, trees cut and removed, invasive plants and animals introduced, or big machines are driven over it. While quite resilient and adaptable, soil and the processes it supports can bounce back only if unnatural disturbances are limited and the earth is allowed to recover over time.

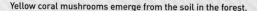

Yellow coral mushrooms emerge from the soil in the forest.

51. UPPER MIDDLE FORK WILLAMETTE: INDIGO SPRINGS

DISTANCE: 4.3 miles round-trip
TRAILHEAD LOCATION: 43.4971°, -122.2656°
STARTING ELEVATION/ELEVATION GAIN:
2800 feet/530 feet
DIFFICULTY: Moderate
SEASON: Late spring through late fall
FOREST TYPE: Douglas-fir

PROTECTIONS: Unprotected roadless area
with no specific protection from logging
MANAGEMENT: Willamette National Forest
NOTES: Restrooms at Indigo Springs
Campground; no parking fee or permit
required

GETTING THERE: From Interstate 5 just south of Eugene, take exit 188 and follow Oregon
Route 58 southeast to the town of Oakridge. Less than a mile past the east end of town and not
far past milepost 37, turn right (south) onto Forest Road 23 at signs for Hills Creek Dam. In a
half mile, turn right onto paved FR 21. In 28.5 miles (the mileposts make this easy) find Indigo
Springs Campground on the left to park.

Several stretches of the 30-mile designated national recreation trail along the Middle Fork
Willamette River are lined with wonderful ancient forest. On its upper end, the river carves
through a steep canyon below its source at Timpanogas Lake and then widens out to flow through
an ancient floodplain forest in Big Swamp. Farther downstream between Campers Flat and
Sacandaga Campgrounds, a drier forest dominated by ponderosa pine, incense cedar, and white
oak takes over. Other than the spectacular forest, the highlight of this stretch of the Middle Fork
Trail are the numerous springs that feed the river and provide the cold, clean water needed by
the threatened resident bull trout population. This incredibly dynamic upper river sees a lot of
natural disturbance, like floods rearranging its channels and fires but also logging and road-
building that have carved up this upper drainage so that only a few large blocks of intact ancient
forest remain.

To reach the trail, walk across the road and go left (upstream) along the shoulder a few hundred feet; then turn right on old FR 403. Go a short distance to the spur trail to arrive at the main Middle Fork Trail. Turn left to head upriver, and hike through a tall forest of hemlocks and Douglas-firs, with wildflowers popping out of the moss-covered ground. Big, charismatic western redcedar also line the trail as it follows the riparian forest near the river.

In about three-quarters of a mile, you'll come to the edge, gradual at first, of where the Tumblebug Fire burned in 2009. Charred snags tower above, along with scattered clumps and individual live trees that survived. Pressing on, note how seedlings, shrubs, and wildflowers are growing in the fertile soil, making for a dense thicket of brush and greenery in the understory. Stay to the left if you see a trail junction and continue uphill another quarter mile along small but raging Chuckle Springs to its source at 1.8 miles from the trailhead. Before the fire, the big trees and moist ground around the spring were covered in moss and draped with ferns—hopefully the forest's recovery from the fire will result in something similarly beautiful.

Hikers enjoy the towering trees along the upper Middle Fork Willamette River Trail. *(Photo by Janessa Dragovich)*

Head back the way you came on the trail from Chuckle Springs, but instead of turning onto the side trail to return to the road and your car, continue downstream. Cross a few spring-fed streams on bridges, and between 0.3 and 0.4 miles farther, pass along the base of a twenty-foot rock wall where water drips for much of the year, supporting mosses, lichens, and succulent wildflowers. Watch your footing here—it can be rocky and slick, but

it is well worth the side trip to get here. Along the way, you'll pass through a forest thick with five-foot-diameter Douglas-firs, towering bigleaf maples, and chinquapin trees. In the fall, the vine maples make the understory glow golden.

Head back to the trail junction, back up to the road, and at the Indigo Springs Campground, explore the short 0.2-mile loop around Indigo Springs if you're so inclined.

52. BRICE CREEK

DISTANCE: 4.6 miles one-way with shuttle or 8.6 miles round-trip
TRAILHEAD LOCATION: 43.6424°, -122.6588°
STARTING ELEVATION/ELEVATION GAIN: 1900 feet/700 feet
DIFFICULTY: Moderate
SEASON: Year-round; best swimming in summer months

FOREST TYPE: Douglas-fir
PROTECTIONS: Unprotected roadless area with no specific protection from logging
MANAGEMENT: Umpqua National Forest
NOTES: Restrooms at trailhead; no parking fee or permit required

GETTING THERE: From Eugene, drive Interstate 5 south to Cottage Grove exit 174. Head east on Row River Road, staying on the south side of Dorena Lake. About 18.5 miles from the freeway, stay right at a Y intersection onto Brice Creek Road (Forest Road 22) and proceed another 4.5 miles to the Cedar Creek Campground. Continue to the upper trailhead parking area on the left side of the road another 3.5 miles past Cedar Creek, just before the bridge over Brice Creek.

Brice Creek, easily accessible from Cottage Grove on the I-5 corridor, is a popular summer destination for those looking to swim in cold pools and bask on streamside rocks, but it's also accessible year-round for forest, wildflower, mushroom, and waterfall lovers. The easy access to the area and the forests surrounding it on this north end of the Umpqua National Forest mean that these surrounds have been heavily roaded and logged, but fortunately the ancient forests along this part of Brice Creek were spared.

It's great to do this hike as a shuttle—leaving one car at Cedar Creek and then continuing to the upper trailhead to begin the hike. This way, it's all downhill and the hike is just over 4.5 miles instead of 8. Alternatively, hike any shorter section as an out-and-back.

After parking at the upper trailhead, walk across the bridge on the road to find the trail on the left. Turn left to begin following Brice Creek downstream. This first part of the trail follows an old water pipe, so the trail is elevated and flat, but the forest is lush and lovely. After a third of a mile, you'll come to a bridge over Trestle Creek, with a view to its confluence with Brice Creek. Just past the bridge, take the side trail to the right to go to Lower Trestle Creek Falls. This 0.3-mile trail gains

a bit of elevation as it goes up a canyon lined with huge Douglas-firs, tall bigleaf maples, ferns, and mossy rocks. The hundred-foot waterfall sits at the end of the trail in the recesses of the canyon, with piles of fallen trees and a jumble of boulders barring access for all but the most sure-footed.

After returning to the main trail, continue downstream through a beautiful cathedral-like old-growth forest grove on a bench above Brice Creek. This stretch and a few others are among the few really old sections of forest. Most of the trail is through a younger (200- to 250-year-old) forest of Douglas-fir, western hemlock, western

OPPOSITE: Upper Trestle Creek Falls, part of a loop off the main Brice Creek Trail, keeps the forest moist and green.

redcedar, and Pacific yew, with scattered huge, fire-scarred Douglas-firs—remnants from the last iteration of this ancient forest. In a few places, you'll also spot incense cedar.

A half mile from the Lower Trestle Creek Trail, you'll intersect the Upper Trestle Creek Falls Trail, which loops up and above the lower falls to another enchanting waterfall and then descends back toward the upper trailhead. (This is a great hike, too. If done as a loop with the Brice Creek Trail, it's 3.5 miles.) Pass this trail and continue another half mile or so to another section of stellar old growth in the Lund Park area. This continues for a way, and the trail continues a total of 3 miles from the Upper Trestle Creek Falls Trail junction before approaching Cedar Creek Campground, where a bridge crosses to the main road. Along the way, there are places to view and also scramble off-trail down to Brice Creek where you can sit on the smooth rocks when the water is low enough and enjoy the scenery before returning the way you came.

53. FAIRVIEW CREEK

DISTANCE: 3.6 miles round-trip
TRAILHEAD LOCATION: 43.5833°, -122.7139°
STARTING ELEVATION/ELEVATION GAIN: 2000 feet/300 feet
DIFFICULTY: Easy
SEASON: Spring through fall

FOREST TYPE: Douglas-fir
PROTECTIONS: Inventoried roadless area
MANAGEMENT: Umpqua National Forest
NOTES: Restrooms at trailhead; no parking fee or permit required

GETTING THERE: From Eugene, drive Interstate 5 south to Cottage Grove exit 174. Head east on Row River Road, staying on the south side of Dorena Lake. After 16 miles turn right on Sharps Creek Road (Forest Road 2460). Go just over 10 miles, and about a half mile after entering the Umpqua National Forest turn left to stay on now-gravel FR 2460. The trailhead is 2 miles up this road on the left, across from Mineral Camp Campground and just after a bridge. Parking is at a wide spot in the road.

This low-elevation area on the western edge of the national forest abuts the heavily logged BLM–private land checkerboard that marches east out of the Willamette Valley toward the Calapooya foothills. This north end of the Umpqua National Forest more or less suffered the same fate. Somehow, ten thousand acres of nearly contiguous untouched forest remains in the area around Fairview Mountain.

The Fairview Mountain area is part of the Bohemia mining district—a hotbed of gold, silver, and other valuable metal mining beginning in the late 1860s, though not nearly as active today. Signs of this history are evident along the Fairview Creek Trail, with mining claim names posted near the creek and a rusted stove where there was once a homestead.

The Fairview Creek Trail follows this lovely rushing stream along the canyon bottom as it cuts its way from Fairview Peak around Hardscrabble Ridge to Sharps Creek. The classic

Tall bigleaf maple trees compete for sunlight with Douglas-firs near Fairview Creek.

low-elevation Douglas-fir forest that lines the steep hillsides and trailside features a mossy understory, big western redcedars, and Pacific yew. Along the creek, bigleaf maples reach for the sun. The narrow but well-maintained trail crosses the creek on a bridge shortly after it begins, near a giant Pacific yew. The trail gradually ascends along the babbling creek, with a few places to scramble to its edge if you're so inclined.

After crossing a rickety bridge over a small side channel, at about the 1.5-mile point be sure to look around for evidence of the fire that helped shape this forest: burn scars on the big Douglas-firs and western hemlock growing up in the understory. Those hemlocks date to the time just after the fire, when the biggest Doug-firs survived but the understory got a restart. The trail ends at a shallow, rocky crossing at about 1.8 miles. Turn around here to head back to your car.

UPPER UMPQUA HIKES

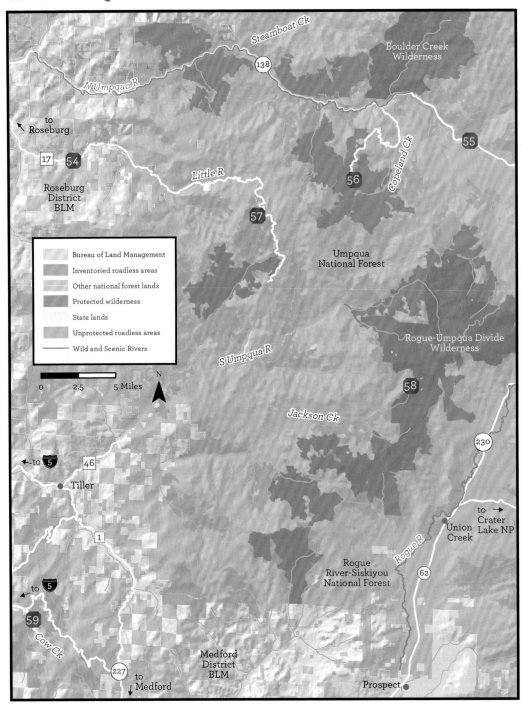

Steamboat Ck

Boulder Creek
Wilderness

N Umpqua R

138

to
Roseburg

Copeland Ck

55

17 54

Little R

56

Roseburg
District
BLM

57

Umpqua
National Forest

Bureau of Land Management
Inventoried roadless areas
Other national forest lands
Protected wilderness
State lands
Unprotected roadless areas
Wild and Scenic Rivers

Rogue-Umpqua Divide
Wilderness

0   2.5   5 Miles   N

58

S Umpqua R

Jackson Ck

230

to 5   46

Tiller

to
Crater
Lake NP

Union
Creek

1

Rogue R

to 5

Rogue
River-Siskiyou
National Forest

62

59

Cow Ck

227   to
Medford

Medford
District
BLM

Prospect

UPPER UMPQUA

The upper reaches of the Umpqua watershed—a massive river system that flows from the Cascades to the Pacific Ocean—can be found in the Umpqua National Forest and Roseburg District BLM lands. The forests here offer a gradual transition from the Willamette watershed's moister Douglas-fir forests into drier forest types as you move south. Still dominated by Douglas-fir, the forests in the Umpqua region contain more incense cedar and sugar pine, along with the still-typical true firs, yew, hemlock, alder, chinquapin, and maples.

The North Umpqua River begins in the High Cascades in the Mount Thielsen Wilderness north of Crater Lake and flows through incredible forests, cuts dramatically through basalt lava flows with dozens of waterfalls, and picks up famous fish-bearing tributaries like Steamboat Creek and Little River. Boulder Creek Wilderness, topped by a bench of ancient ponderosa pine, is in the North Umpqua watershed, and large roadless areas in the Calf and Copeland Creek drainages and others contain vast tracts of ancient forest.

The South Umpqua River begins as streams flowing from the Rogue–Umpqua Divide Wilderness. This little-visited wilderness area and its surroundings harbor higher-elevation forests, mountain lakes, and wildflower-filled meadows. Downstream, the watershed has been more extensively logged than the North

Umpqua, in part because of its lower elevation and more mixed private and BLM lands west of the Umpqua National Forest.

The remaining intact forests in this region are proposed for additional protections as part of the Crater Lake Wilderness. While the forests within Crater Lake National Park are mostly alpine and lodgepole pine, this proposal includes mixed conifer and Douglas-fir forests in large wild areas that stretch down the slopes into the

Maples add autumn color along the South Umpqua River. *(Photo by Greg Vaughn)*

Umpqua watershed. Advocates have fought for decades to stave off logging plans in these roadless areas—with some success—but permanent protection is still essential for the important wildlife habitat connections, water quality, and recreation here.

54. WOLF CREEK FALLS

DISTANCE: 2.6 miles round-trip
TRAILHEAD LOCATION: 43.2337°, -122.9512°
STARTING ELEVATION/ELEVATION GAIN:
1060 feet/250 feet
DIFFICULTY: Easy
SEASON: Year-round

FOREST TYPE: Douglas-fir
PROTECTIONS: Old forest reserved from logging in management plan
MANAGEMENT: Roseburg District BLM
NOTES: Restrooms in parking area near trailhead; no parking fee or permit required

GETTING THERE: From Interstate 5 in Roseburg take exit 124. Go through downtown Roseburg, following signs for Crater Lake/Diamond Lake and Oregon Route 138E, making first a left, then a right turn to get on Diamond Lake Boulevard. Travel a bit over 15 miles; then a quarter mile east of milepost 16, just before Colliding Rivers Viewpoint and North Umpqua Ranger Station in Glide, turn right (south) on Little River Road (County Road 17). Go 10.7 miles along the Little River to find the well-marked trailhead and parking at a large footbridge on the right. Additional parking and a restroom can be found on the left just past the trailhead.

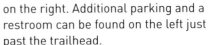

Traveling through the BLM–private land checkerboard along the lower reaches of the Little River, you might be forgiven for thinking there couldn't possibly be an ancient forest hike nearby—the Little River corridor, even as it continues into the Umpqua National Forest to the east, has been heavily logged. But Wolf Creek, barely west of the national forest border, does harbor an enchanting block of low-elevation, old-growth Douglas-fir and western redcedar forest on BLM lands.

A dramatic bridge over the Little River leads the way to the ancient Douglas-fir and western redcedar forest on the Wolf Creek Falls Trail.

The trail begins by crossing a substantial arched bridge over the Little River and heads into a lush, moss-draped forest of redcedar, Douglas-fir, bigleaf maple, vine maple, dogwood, and Pacific yew. At a second bridge, take in the view of the stunning ancient forest on the opposite hillside; then cross it to continue on the trail. Following this well-used, mostly level, and well-maintained trail, you'll see a side trail after a third of a mile next to a tall standing snag and big down log. This trail goes a short way to the edge of Wolf Creek and a picnic table.

Continuing, the trail follows the creek closely and skirts the base of a dripping rock wall for a short way. Tall alders line the creek, and the forest floor is alive in a mix of shrubs, wildflowers, and mosses. At 0.6 mile, cross a side channel on a bridge and go deeper into the ancient forest, where fire-scarred redcedars and Douglas-firs dominate the view.

At about three-quarters of a mile, climb steeply up for a short distance over a rockier section of trail and into a stand of giant Douglas-fir with deeply furrowed and plated bark. Descend again toward the creek into a riparian area with bigleaf maple and cedar, the crossing made easy on a boardwalk, then climb again at the 1.2-mile mark to finally reach views of Wolf Creek Falls. Pass the lower falls, seen through the trees, and continue past the chain-link fence to the upper falls viewpoint. The water streams down the face of the steep canyon wall into a lovely pool. Enjoy the view before retracing your steps to the trailhead.

55. TOKATEE AND WATSON FALLS

DISTANCE: Tokatee Falls, 0.9 mile round-trip; Watson Falls, 1-mile loop
TRAILHEAD LOCATION: Tokatee Falls, 43.2638°, -122.4274°; Watson Falls, 43.2455°, -122.3914°
STARTING ELEVATION/ELEVATION GAIN: Tokatee Falls, 2440 feet/Minimal; Watson Falls, 2690 feet/350 feet
DIFFICULTY: Easy

SEASON: Spring through fall, access dependent on snow
FOREST TYPE: Douglas-fir
PROTECTIONS: No specific protection but unlikely to be logged
MANAGEMENT: Umpqua National Forest
NOTES: Restrooms at trailheads; no parking fee or permit required

GETTING THERE: From Interstate 5 in Roseburg, take exit 124. Go through downtown Roseburg, following signs for Crater Lake/Diamond Lake and Oregon Route 138E, making first a left, then a right turn to get on Diamond Lake Boulevard. For Tokatee Falls, travel roughly 59 miles east of Roseburg, and turn left off of OR 138 at signs for Tokatee Falls/Tokatee Lake. Stay left at the junction in a few hundred feet to go over a bridge and left again on the other side of the bridge at a sign for the trailhead. Park in the lot to the left, opposite the large, leaking wooden water pipe.

For Watson Falls, travel another 2 miles past the Tokatee turn and turn right off of OR 138 a quarter mile past milepost 61 at a sign for Watson Falls. Then turn right into the large parking area.

The drive up the Wild and Scenic North Umpqua River is simply magnificent: ancient forests line its banks, and the river's clean, cold water helps steelhead and salmon thrive. Some segments of the forest along the river have experienced wildfire since the 1980s (and some just in the summer of 2017), offering an interesting mix of views as you head upstream.

Along the way, there are several trailheads for the nearly 80-mile-long North Umpqua Trail, and delightful ancient forests can be easily accessed from most of these points. The North Umpqua is better known for its waterfalls than anything else, though, so why not enjoy a few of these lovely features while getting a dose of ancient forest along with them?

The busy and popular trail to Tokatee Falls begins after you cross a small bridge at the far end of the parking area. The wide, level path beside the North Umpqua River lies below a tall canopy of Douglas-firs, redcedars, and bigleaf maples, with rhododendrons and vine maple filling in the understory. The path narrows and passes huge boulders sprouting a variety of plants before climbing up and down short stretches of stone steps to a viewpoint at a quarter mile where the river rushes into a narrow canyon, an ancient lava flow hollowed out into round chasms by millennia of the water's forces. Before continuing on, be sure to turn around to spot a giant sugar pine with its gray flaky bark and giant cones.

From here, the trail goes up and down both wooden and stone steps, with flat stretches between, passing tall shrubs—hazelnut, chinquapin, dogwood, and vine maple—high above the river's gorge. The last flight of stairs culminates at a viewing platform built around a four-foot-diameter Douglas-fir, just shy of a half mile. The river falls from the face of a lava cliff as Tokatee Falls and continues downstream through a spectacular canyon lined with ancient forest.

To reach Watson Falls, climb up some steps from the large parking area and cross the road at a crosswalk. In just a tenth of a mile, you'll reach Watson Creek as it pours over boulders on its way toward its

Tokatee Falls, on the North Umpqua River, pours over a basalt cliff.

confluence with the Clearwater River just west of the trailhead turnoff from OR 138. The trail then switchbacks up, passing Douglas-firs three to five feet in diameter, smaller hemlocks, and a mix of classic Douglas-fir forest shrubs: rhododendrons, salal, red huckleberry, swordferns, and Oregon grape.

In a quarter mile, get another view of the stream and cross it on a bridge that offers a view of the falls in the narrow canyon to the south. At a trail junction just beyond this point, turn left to climb another quarter mile. Along the way, Pacific yew trees, bigleaf maple, and vine maple line the trail and riparian area, covered in moss. As you approach the rock wall that Watson Falls pours over, tall Douglas-firs and hemlocks line its base, and thimbleberry and wildflowers are bathed in mist where the trail ends at an upper viewpoint near the base of the falls.

Heading back down, stay straight at the trail junction instead of turning right (the way you came from) to make a loop. This path descends steadily through an old forest with many layers of green. When you reach the road, turn right to walk a short distance down the shoulder to the crosswalk that takes you back to the parking area.

56. TWIN LAKES

DISTANCE: 5.6 miles round-trip
TRAILHEAD LOCATION: 43.2239°, -122.5788°
STARTING ELEVATION/ELEVATION GAIN: 4860 feet/800 feet
DIFFICULTY: Moderate
SEASON: Summer through fall, access dependent on snow

FOREST TYPE: Douglas-fir
PROTECTIONS: Inventoried roadless area
MANAGEMENT: Umpqua National Forest
NOTES: Restroom at trailhead; no parking fee or permit required

GETTING THERE: From Interstate 5 in Roseburg, take exit 124. Go through downtown Roseburg, following signs for Crater Lake/Diamond Lake and Oregon Route 138E, making first a left, then a right turn to get on Diamond Lake Boulevard. Travel roughly 50 miles east of Roseburg and turn left off of OR 138 onto Forest Road 4770 at a sign for the North Umpqua Trail and Twin Lakes just after crossing a bridge over the North Umpqua River. Follow gravel FR 4770 uphill 9.4 miles to the trailhead parking at the end of the road.

Twin Lakes are nestled in the heart of the large roadless area that encompasses the Calf and Copeland Creek drainages south of the North Umpqua River. The area offers a sampling of the best of the region: spectacular wildflower meadows, old-growth trees, mountain views, and ancient forests recovering from a 2017 fire.

The trail begins to the right of the parking area and passes a self-registration station where visitors should sign in. Right away you'll be surrounded by towering Douglas-firs and the green shades of lichen, vanilla leaf, and vine maple.

Fairly quickly the trail enters the burned area, where the big Douglas-firs sport blackened bark and fresh cavities from the fire—most still with green canopies. In a quarter mile, cross a little creek, piled high with burnt logs, flowing out

The view from the cliff above Twin Lakes offers a panorama of the Umpqua landscape.

of a meadow. In a little under a half mile, you'll find a clifftop view in a rocky meadow covered in clumps of beargrass. To the north the hills of the Boulder Creek Wilderness rise toward Diamond Peak, and to the east look for Mount Thielsen and Mount Bailey. Patches of burned forest are spread out below, showing the pattern of mixed severity that appears at a smaller scale all along the trail.

In three-quarters of a mile, cross a sloping meadow that offers another view of Diamond Peak and a multitude of wildflower blooms, including cornlily, larkspur, columbine, and valerian. At a signed junction just beyond this meadow, turn right toward Twin Lakes, and stay left at the next junction with the Deception Creek Trail. Continue through a meadow

with narrow bands of trees (both burned and unburned) and then descend to a wetter meadow filled with camas and alder shrubs, crossing part of it on a boardwalk before coming to a three-sided shelter on a ridge surrounding the larger of the twin lakes at just over a mile. Turn right to follow the trail on the ridge past a restroom and to join the lakeshore trail going counterclockwise.

An ancient forest of western hemlock, grand fir, and Douglas-fir lines the lakeshores, lichen clings to the tree trucks. As you continue around the lake, passing in and out of burned patches, you'll see some white pine, mountain hemlock, rhododendrons, and chinquapin. Cross an inlet creek and a giant boulder, and then intersect the trail that heads to the right to the smaller upper lake at the 1.4-mile point. Follow this trail up the outlet stream from the upper lake, and then again go counterclockwise around its shore. Fallen logs float along the lake's edge, and a tall cliff rises straight up to the south.

As you round the lake, a boardwalk leads across springs where Alaska yellow-cedar, silver fir, white pine, Douglas-fir, and western hemlocks thrive—where they haven't been scorched by the fire. The trail winds down past some huge rocks that long ago fell from the cliffs above and then reaches the larger lakeshore again. Continue to the right to reach the shrubby thicket that lines the lake's southeast corner—alder, vine maple, and mountain ash thrive in the wet area only partially covered by a boardwalk here. A healthy grove of Alaska yellow-cedar marks a split in the trail where you should head up to the right to return to the shelter (at 2.3 miles).

Head back through the meadow to the first of the two junctions you encountered on the way in, and go straight here for the second half of this recommended hike—to the top of the cliff that rises above the lakes. Just ahead, a huge, five-foot-diameter Shasta red fir looms, its lower branches drooping nearly to the ground. The trail climbs into the burned area and in and out of dry meadows with low-growing lupine and cat's ear mariposa lilies, ringed by singed incense cedar.

After about a quarter mile, enter a part of the forest more severely impacted by the 2017 fire—what was once a cool, shady forest has been opened up significantly, until the understory recovers. Tall Shasta red firs, many of which survived the fire, still shade the trail and offer impressive forest structure. After a half mile, the partly burned forest floor still harbors bunches of beargrass and rhododendrons, and huckleberries where the trail flattens out and follows the contour of the slope, passing a trickling spring.

At 1.2 miles into this segment of the hike, turn right at a trail junction on the ridgetop to reach the top of the cliff with white pines, subalpine firs, and stunning views to the north and east and down over the turquoise lakes below. A huge, gnarled Douglas-fir grows out of the rocks here, offering a shady spot to rest and take in the view before heading back down the hill. At 2.5 miles, be sure to turn right at the signed trail junction to hike the remaining 0.8 mile back to your car.

57. YELLOW JACKET GLADE

DISTANCE: 5.6-mile loop
TRAILHEAD LOCATION: 43.1878°, -122.7045°
STARTING ELEVATION/ELEVATION GAIN: 4410 feet/850 feet
DIFFICULTY: Moderate
SEASON: Early summer through late fall, access dependent on snow; best wildflowers in midsummer

FOREST TYPE: Douglas-fir
PROTECTIONS: Unprotected roadless area with no specific protection from logging
MANAGEMENT: Umpqua National Forest
NOTES: Restroom at trailhead; no parking fee or permit required

GETTING THERE: From Interstate 5 in Roseburg, take exit 124. Go through downtown Roseburg, following signs for Crater Lake/Diamond Lake and Oregon Route 138E, making first a left, then a right turn to get on Diamond Lake Boulevard. Travel a bit over 15 miles, and a quarter mile east of milepost 16, just before Colliding Rivers Viewpoint and North Umpqua

Ranger Station in Glide, turn right (south) on Little River Road (County Road 17), which becomes Forest Road 27 when it enters the Umpqua National Forest. Follow this road for 19.5 paved miles and an additional 11.2 on gravel, turning right after 8 miles to stay on FR 27 and otherwise staying on this main road at intersections.

After 30.7 miles on Little River Road, turn right onto an unmarked road and cross Hemlock Lake's dam in a half mile. The trailhead and campground are a quarter mile beyond the dam, with day-use parking and a picnic area to the left. If you miss the turn to the dam, you'll reach a turnoff for the Hemlock Lake boat launch a half mile farther on FR 27. Turn around here to go back to the correct trailhead.

The splendid forests and meadows of Yellow Jacket Glade are part of a series of high-elevation ridges and plateaus that lie near the dividing point between the North and South Umpqua drainages. Hemlock Creek feeds the Little River on the north side of this divide, and Hemlock Lake (actually a small reservoir) and this loop trail attract anglers, hikers, and mountain bikers and motorcyclists. Home to plenty of wildlife, unfortunately this area has no specific protections from logging, and in fact a portion of this loop trail was clear-cut at one time.

Start at the main signboard at the campground entrance near the restroom and go right to hike this loop counterclockwise. Tall Douglas-firs and silver fir covered with lichen dominate the forest trail as it passes behind the campground before coming to a large meadow in 0.2 mile. Cross this lovely field—rimmed by the tall forest and brimming with camas, buttercup, shooting stars, valerian, and cornlily—on a boardwalk and continue into the forest where serviceberry, mountain ash, huckleberry, and vanilla leaf fill in the understory along the trail.

Over the next nearly 2 miles, the trail climbs through a series of picturesque meadows, following small streams through the first few before switchbacking up a ridge to Yellow Jacket Glade, a high sloping plateau. Wildflowers and shrubs like elderberry and mountain ash fill the meadows, and the ancient forests interspersed with them vary from being dense with firs, to being more open with wildflower understories. Huge old Douglas-firs, silver firs, and Shasta red firs stand out in several areas, and big snags line some

of the meadows. On the forest floor, black and orange millipedes munch on detritus, breaking down and recycling nutrients needed to maintain the forest soil. At trail junctions with the Flat Rock Trail and Cavitt Mountain Tie Trail—at 1.3 and 2 miles respectively—stay to the left to continue the Yellow Jacket Loop.

At about 2.3 miles you'll finally reach a vast ridgetop meadow. The trail skirts the ridge on its north side, reentering the lovely ancient fir forest for a short distance before entering an area logged in the past. At 2.8 miles, pass back into the natural forest—messy with wildflowers, down wood, and snags—and climb up to a ridgetop that divides the Little River and North Umpqua drainage to the north from the Boulder Creek and South Umpqua watershed to the south. Follow this ridge, passing white pines and huge Douglas-firs, and catch periodic views over Hemlock Lake below as the trail meanders along or just below the ridge beyond the 3-mile point.

As you begin to descend off the ridge, note the clear lichen line, indicating how high the snow

Woodland wildflowers line the trail beneath towering silver fir and Douglas-fir along the Yellow Jacket Glade loop trail.

piles in the winter. The forest on this descent mirrors that of the trail before the high ridge began, with a lot of down logs and short snags, passing through open areas and a meadow that slopes away to the left. At 3.7 miles, skirt the edge of a logging road and a younger forest recovering from past logging; then reenter a dense native stand. At just over 4 miles, stay to the left at a sign for Hemlock Lake 1 mile and head more steeply downhill toward Dead Cow Lake (a small pond filled with down logs) and another junction with the Snowbird Shelter Trail.

Stay left and downhill again, descending along spring-fed Hemlock Creek and crossing part of the wet area on a boardwalk. Around the 4.5-mile point the forest is a dense, tall, and pleasing mix of younger trees that likely regrew after a fire a century ago. Just shy of 5 miles, stay to the left at a Y intersection, and cross a bridge over the creek you've been following. Follow Hemlock Lake's shore above a thicket of willow and alder, cross a bridge at an inlet stream, and enter an older, more diverse forest for the last quarter mile before reaching the parking area and completing the loop.

Forests as Carbon Machines

Considering the important role that they play in the global carbon cycle, ancient forests could be described as carbon capture machines (if you wanted to describe such a beautiful thing in such an industrial way).

Here's how it works. Trees in a forest naturally remove carbon dioxide from the air through photosynthesis and turn it into complex sugars that are used to build bark, wood, branches, roots, and leaves. When trees burn or decompose, CO_2 is released back into the atmosphere. In between, forests store massive amounts of carbon for long periods of time in the huge trunks and extensive root network of living trees and even in the slowly decomposing snags, down logs, and soil humus.

But vast areas of Oregon's forests aren't functioning naturally in this way. Logging has disrupted the natural cycle. This is a problem because logging kills trees, stops them from growing, and accelerates the transfer of carbon from the forest to the atmosphere. This disruption will intensify climate change because logged forests emit more carbon than they absorb, making them a source of greenhouse gases. In fact, over the past century, forest conversion and forest management have contributed a substantial fraction of the excess CO_2 observed in the atmosphere, and today, according to the Oregon Global Warming Commission, carbon emissions from logging are Oregon's single biggest source of climate pollution.

So what's the good news? The management choices we make today can continue to make forests a part of the problem of human-caused climate change or ensure they are part of the solution. It turns out that the ancient forests in western Oregon are particularly good at soaking up carbon, and the logging trend that has turned many forests into carbon sources can be reversed. When allowed to grow and absorb more carbon than they emit—becoming a carbon sink—forests help reduce excess greenhouse gas in the atmosphere. Studies have shown that policies and practices that protect ancient forests, allow plantations to grow, and reduce the rate of logging have been able to reverse the course of carbon emissions—turning northwest forest landscapes from carbon sources back into carbon sinks.

It's clear that global warming is going to impact Oregon's climate—with more winter precipitation falling as rain instead of snow, more frequent and prolonged droughts, and overall warmer temperatures (see Resources for the climate impacts assessments of M. M. Dalton and her colleagues for the Oregon Climate Change Research Institute). Forests, and the plants and wildlife that live in them, will have to adapt or they may be headed for extinction. They'll stand the best chance of being able to do this if there are more areas of ancient forest, which are best equipped to be resilient in the face of such changes. We can give them that chance by protecting our remaining ancient forests and by encouraging the recovery and restoration of forests in areas that have been logged, letting them grow into the carbon-storing and resilient forests they have the potential to be.

OPPOSITE: Ancient forests, with large trees living and dead, remove and store a tremendous amount of carbon from the atmosphere.

58. CRIPPLE CAMP

DISTANCE: 5.8 miles round-trip
TRAILHEAD LOCATION: 43.0329°, -122.4964°
STARTING ELEVATION/ELEVATION GAIN: 4770 feet/730 feet
DIFFICULTY: Moderate
SEASON: Summer, access dependent on snow

FOREST TYPE: Douglas-fir, alpine and subalpine
PROTECTIONS: Rogue–Umpqua Divide Wilderness
MANAGEMENT: Umpqua National Forest
NOTES: No restrooms at trailhead; no parking fee or permit required

GETTING THERE: From Interstate 5 south of Roseburg, take exit 98 for Canyonville and Days Creek. From Canyonville, take Tiller Trail Road (Douglas County Highway 1) east for 22 miles to a junction with Oregon Route 46 (South Umpqua Road) in Tiller. Turn left and drive 5 miles to Jackson Creek Road (Forest Road 29). Turn right on FR 29 and travel 14.5 miles on pavement and another 3 miles on gravel to a junction with FR 2947, where you'll turn right. Watch your odometer from here. Follow this streamside road for 2.3 miles and stay left on FR 2947 at a split with FR 300 at a sign for Cripple Camp.

At the 4-mile mark on FR 2947, turn right at a junction with FR 400, cross Jackson Creek, and climb another 4 miles on gravel FR 2947. At the 8-mile point you'll reach a curve on a ridgetop and find the trailhead pullout on the right, with a signboard nearby. (Along the way, consider stopping to see the World's Tallest Sugar Pine by turning right at a sign for it 10 miles up FR 29 onto FR 2829, then staying left at a split in a quarter mile.)

The aptly named Rogue–Umpqua Divide Wilderness, which separates these two major river drainages, offers numerous trails through ancient forests—luckily protected from the logging that is so evident on the way to the trailhead. In this southern part of the wilderness, the ridges connect a series of rocky peaks that generate streams flowing west to the South Umpqua River.

From the signboard for Cripple Camp Trailhead on the side of the road, enter a forest of Douglas-fir, western hemlock, and grand fir with plenty of lichen, down logs, patches of young hemlocks, and scattered incense cedars, some four feet in diameter. The dense canopy prevents much of an understory, but some wildflowers like vanilla leaf, wild strawberry, and prince's pine grow. Scan the bark of the surrounding trees to pick out the blocky, red-hued trunks of Shasta red fir, following them skyward to note the geometric pattern of the branches above. Look also for giant Douglas-firs, their five-foot-diameter trunks

broken at the top, with side branches assuming the role of the trees' new top.

At three-quarters of a mile, come to the junction with Trail 1437. Turn right, and a short distance later you'll find the Cripple Camp Shelter, just off the trail to the right—a cedar shake–covered structure on the edge of a sloping meadow, sheltered by a group of truly massive trees. Three- and four-foot-diameter incense cedars and Douglas-firs nearly ten feet in diameter make this spot one to linger in.

Back on the trail at the edge of the meadow, pass through a part of the forest freshly burned in

Ancient, huge, and diverse trees await hikers on the trail to Cripple Camp Shelter and beyond.

2017. The fire here mostly just burned the base of the big trees, scarring some and killing few. Hop across a small stream, continue into the unburned forest harboring some giant Douglas-firs, and then cross another creek pouring out of a meadow from the left.

From here, the forest takes on a wider spacing with some mixed sugar pine, Shasta red fir, and big hemlocks with low-swooping branches. Catch views of Highrock Mountain back to the northeast across the meadow through the trees. A drier area with a rocky outcrop sprouts white irises, patches of chinquapin, and incense cedars; the trail follows along a ridge with a steep drop-off to the right.

At about 1.5 miles, incense cedar becomes the dominant tree, young grand firs fill in parts of the understory, and lichen-covered snags line the trail before you reach a junction with the Rogue–Umpqua Divide Trail, which goes down and to the right at about 1.6 miles. Stay to the left instead and continue to cross the side of a steeply sloping ridge with a mix of forests and meadows, down logs, and big trees. Douglas squirrels, deer, and all manner of birds call this forest home. As you climb gradually, the forest gets denser and moister, with silver, grand, and Shasta red fir, and mountain hemlocks. At a pass at 2.3 miles, the trail swings to the left to head east across a gentle slope with tall, lichen-covered trees with a dry, brown understory.

At 2.6 miles, come to a meadow ringed by incense cedars and some large rocks, continue across this steep slope of mixed forests and meadows, and then begin to cross a large meadow ringed with trees singed by fire, continuing through a patch of big Shasta firs. Larkspur, waterleaf, bluebells, cornlily, and cow parsnip fill this meadow, making it hard to follow the path, and a series of trickling streams drain to Lonewoman Creek, lined with alder and Alaska yellow-cedar, to the right. The stream's edge, at 2.9 miles, marks the edge of a burned area and makes a good point to turn around.

For a much longer (15-mile) loop option, you can cross the creek, turn left at the junction with the Hershberger Mountain Trail, continue through Highrock Meadow and down Highrock Creek, left at a junction near Fish Lake, up Grasshopper Mountain's ridge to Grasshopper Meadow, and then back to the junction you find at the three-quarter-mile point of the Cripple Camp Trail.

59. UPPER COW CREEK

DISTANCE: 5 miles round-trip
TRAILHEAD LOCATION: 42.8031°, -122.9851°
STARTING ELEVATION/ELEVATION GAIN:
2500 feet/800 feet
DIFFICULTY: Moderate
SEASON: Early spring to late fall
FOREST TYPE: Douglas-fir

PROTECTIONS: Unprotected roadless area where old forest reserved from logging in management plan
MANAGEMENT: Umpqua National Forest
NOTES: Restrooms at trailhead; no parking fee or permit required

GETTING THERE: From Interstate 5, about 35 miles south of Roseburg or 32 miles north of Grants Pass, take exit 88 (for Azalea) to go east on Upper Cow Creek Road (County Road 36). Travel 20 miles, past Galesville Reservoir and into Umpqua National Forest. Just after the road crosses a cattle guard and turns to gravel, turn right on Forest Road 3232. Drive 1 mile on this good gravel road to the trailhead and parking area on the right, just after you cross a bridge over East Fork Cow Creek.

The southwest corner of Umpqua National Forest where this trail is located is surrounded by BLM checkerboard and is crisscrossed with roads and old clear-cuts. Three small roadless areas provide vital forest habitat in this bridge from the Klamath Mountains to the south into the Cascades. The stream, too, is wonderful habitat—its cold waters, pool-forming boulders, and down wood make it a haven for fish.

Though a bit out of the way, this trail through a streamside forest dominated by Douglas-fir and western hemlock is truly lovely and worth seeking out. Although little-used and narrow, the trail is well-maintained except for the fact that there are no bridges across the three stream-crossings along the route. Come prepared to step across on rocks or wade the stream at higher water.

The trail follows South Fork Cow Creek on its east side to start out, with vine and bigleaf maple, alder, and Douglas-fir in the bottomlands. Tall Douglas-firs, hemlocks, and some incense cedars line the canyon's slopes as you climb above the creek. A little over a quarter mile along the trail, the corner of a piece of clear-cut private property comes nearly up to the trail—a study in contrast to the unlogged forest the trail explores. Beyond this, the trail descends into a really wonderful example of the Douglas-fir and hemlock forest, with grand fir and incense cedar mixed in.

At 0.6 mile, the trail reaches the first stream-crossing. Just on the other side, it's worth exploring off the trail uphill to take a close look at some of the giant, five-hundred-year-old Douglas-firs, marked with blackened bark that indicates they survived long-ago fires. The trail continues along a beautiful riparian corridor with hemlock, Pacific yew, bigleaf maples, and plenty of greenery covering the ground before climbing a bit through the Douglas-fir and hemlock forest with large remnant trees.

The second stream-crossing, marked by an enormous yew tree, is at 1.2 miles. This is a good place to turn around if you're just out for a short hike. Otherwise, continue on through a forest of mixed conifers and deciduous trees to the

South Fork Cow Creek is lined with maples, hemlocks, Douglas-fir, and Pacific yew trees.

third crossing at 1.5 miles. Beyond this crossing, the forest becomes more open and the trail a bit more muddy and rutted. After a stretch of alder along the creek, the trail climbs above the creek to a drier slope of a generally younger stand with more incense cedars, chinquapin, and beargrass and an overgrown thicket of bracken ferns and berries. After about 1.8 miles, spot some bigger incense cedars, along with rhododendrons and salal. A particularly huge cedar with evidence of past fire stands at the 2-mile mark. Beyond this

and a small pond, the trail traverses a moister and densely forested slope far above the creek. It crosses White Creek at about 2.5 miles in the midst of this lovely forest—a good turnaround point for a moderate hike.

If you're up for a longer option, continue on until the trail eventually descends to the creek again at the 4-mile mark. The ancient forest doesn't continue far beyond this crossing, as the forest past this point was largely salvage logged and replanted after a fire in the late 1980s.

SOUTH CASCADES HIKES

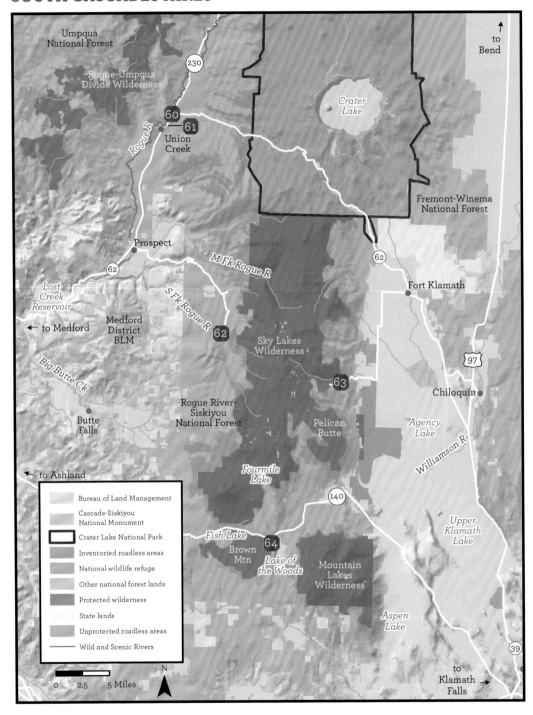

Umpqua
National Forest

Rogue-Umpqua
Divide Wilderness

230

Rogue R.

60
61
Union
Creek

Crater
Lake

Fremont-Winema
National Forest

to
Bend

Prospect

M Fk Rogue R

62

62

Fort Klamath

Lost
Creek
Reservoir

to Medford

Medford
District
BLM

S Fk Rogue R

62

Sky Lakes
Wilderness

97

Chiloquin

Big Butte Ck

Butte
Falls

Rogue River-
Siskiyou
National Forest

63

Pelican
Butte

Agency
Lake

to Ashland

Williamson R.

Fourmile
Lake

140

Upper
Klamath
Lake

Bureau of Land Management

Cascade-Siskiyou
National Monument

Crater Lake National Park

Inventoried roadless areas

National wildlife refuge

Other national forest lands

Protected wilderness

State lands

Unprotected roadless areas

Wild and Scenic Rivers

Fish Lake
Brown
Mtn

64

Lake of
the Woods

Mountain
Lakes
Wilderness

Aspen
Lake

39

0   2.5   5 Miles

N

to
Klamath
Falls

SOUTH CASCADES

The South Cascades region is among the wildest in western Oregon, spanning the crest of the Cascade Range from Crater Lake National Park south to the Mountain Lakes Wilderness. It includes the headwaters of the Rogue and Klamath Rivers—flowing opposite directions from the crest of the South Cascades—and innumerable mountain lakes. The former Mount Mazama, which blew its top nearly eight thousand years ago to form Crater Lake, helped shape and also illustrates the geology of this region, which is quite different from that of the Cascades to the north. The porous, pumicey soils allow water to seep belowground easily, and then spring up elsewhere to feed the many streams, lakes, and wetlands in this region.

The mighty Rogue River, which gushes from a spring out of the side of ancient Mount Mazama, is an example of this geology. The river cuts through lava flows and supports truly spectacular ancient forests of Douglas-fir, incense cedar, white pine, and hemlock as it descends

Crater Lake National Park lies at the heart of the South Cascades.

dramatically southwest on its way to its lower reaches and the Pacific Ocean.

This southern part of the Cascades is not just a bridge from west to east but also to the Klamath Mountains to the south. The trees and forests found here are a mix of what is found farther north throughout the Cascades and the drier forests of the Siskiyous and ponderosa pine zone. Species like Shasta red fir, sugar pine, and incense cedar mix with mountain and western hemlock, grand fir, and Douglas-fir.

The region's highest elevations are largely protected in the Sky Lakes and Mountain Lakes Wilderness areas or are contained within Crater Lake National Park, but most of the ancient forests lie at lower elevations outside of or on the edges of these protected areas. The Rogue River–Siskiyou National Forest on the west and Fremont-Winema National Forest on the eastern slope administer most of this region outside the national park. As elsewhere, these national forests have been heavily logged, in some cases right up to the border of the national park and wilderness areas. Proposals to expand the national park and add protections to the large wild areas adjacent to existing wilderness areas would help protect the remaining ancient forests in this region. Places like Pelican Butte, Brown Mountain, and the headwaters of the Rogue River would benefit from additional protections.

60. UPPER ROGUE RIVER TRAIL: TAKELMA AND ROGUE GORGES

DISTANCE: Takelma Gorge, 4–5 miles round-trip; Rogue Gorge, 2.5-mile loop
TRAILHEAD LOCATION: Takelma Gorge, 42.8623°, -122.5048°; Rogue Gorge, 42.9098°, -122.4436°
STARTING ELEVATION/ELEVATION GAIN: Takelma Gorge, 2980 feet/Minimal; Rogue Gorge, 3360 feet/Minimal
DIFFICULTY: Easy
SEASON: Spring through late fall, access dependent on snow

FOREST TYPE: Douglas-fir
PROTECTIONS: Wild and scenic river corridor
MANAGEMENT: Rogue River–Siskiyou National Forest
NOTES: Takelma Gorge, no restrooms at trailhead, no parking fee or permit required; Rogue Gorge, restrooms at trailhead, no parking fee or permit required

GETTING THERE: From Medford, travel 52 miles northeast on Oregon Route 62 toward Crater Lake National Park. Or from points north and east, travel to the junction of OR 138 and OR 230 at the northwest corner of Crater Lake National Park.

For the Takelma Gorge at the Woodruff Bridge Trailhead, turn west off of OR 62 between mileposts 51 and 52 (4.5 miles south of Union Creek) onto Forest Road 68. Drive 1.8 miles to the trailhead parking area on the left just before a bridge over the river.

For the Rogue Gorge, find the Rogue Gorge Day-Use Area and parking lot on the west side of OR 62, 4.5 miles north of the Takelma Gorge turnoff and just north of Union Creek Resort, or 25 miles south of the junction of OR 230 and OR 138.

The Upper Rogue River is designated as wild and scenic starting at the border of Crater Lake National Park and continuing to the little town of Prospect. The river actually starts just inside the park, from a spring at the base of a cliff. Along the way, the Upper Rogue is quite dramatic, passing through narrow canyons cut through lava rock, lava tubes where the whole river disappears, and gorgeous ancient forest in the quarter-mile strip the wild and scenic designation protects. Unfortunately, outside of that buffer, the national forest between OR 62 and the national park boundary has been logged. Even large trees in the scenic corridor along the highway haven't been entirely spared over the years.

While much of the Upper Rogue River trail has nice forests, the most accessible and spectacular stretch lies between the Rogue Gorge area near Union Creek and the River Bridge Campground 10 miles downstream. If you're not through-hiking, consider two specific sections for day hikes, starting at Woodruff Bridge to Takelma Gorge and then exploring the Rogue Gorge area.

For Takelma Gorge, from the Woodruff Bridge parking area, follow the trail downstream through a tunnel of vine maple. Gigantic Douglas-firs, six to seven feet in diameter, tower over this understory. The river takes a big bend where it is eroding the bank and offers views of the ancient forest on the other side as well. In about 1.5 miles, you'll come to the first view of Takelma Gorge, where the river has cut through

Giant trees line the banks of the upper reaches of the Wild and Scenic Rogue River. *(Photo by Sue Newman)*

the lava in a dramatic fashion. Continue down-stream up to a mile for more viewpoints of the gorge before heading back.

The Rogue Gorge area is a popular stop for travelers on OR 62. The paved path to the gorge viewpoint is a lovely little quarter-mile loop, but for a superb forest hike it's better to follow the river downstream on the unpaved trail once you've taken a look at the gorge. The trail passes cabins, accessed from the Union Creek area, so it doesn't feel very wild, but the views of the river and the huge Douglas-fir and pines make up for

that. Vine maple, western hemlock, Pacific yew, and chinquapin fill in the understory. As you follow the river, look for big logs that have fallen in, adding structure to the river that can be carried downstream or that hang up on the banks.

A little over a mile down the trail, cross Union Creek where it enters the Rogue. To loop back to your car, turn left and follow the trail through the Union Creek Campground toward OR 62; then turn left to follow the highway shoulder a short way past Union Creek resort and back to the Rogue Gorge parking area.

61. UNION CREEK

DISTANCE: 8.2 miles round-trip
TRAILHEAD LOCATION: 42.9062°, -122.4453°
STARTING ELEVATION/ELEVATION GAIN:
3350 feet/450 feet
DIFFICULTY: Difficult
SEASON: Spring through fall, access dependent on snow

FOREST TYPE: Douglas-fir
PROTECTIONS: No specific protection from logging
MANAGEMENT: Rogue River–Siskiyou National Forest
NOTES: Restrooms at trailhead; no parking fee or permit required

GETTING THERE: From Medford, travel 56 miles northeast on Oregon Route 62 toward Crater Lake National Park. Or from points north and east, travel to the junction of OR 138 and OR 230, on the northwest corner of Crater Lake National Park. Follow OR 230 for 25.5 miles south of this junction to Union Creek. At milepost 56, just south of the Union Creek Resort and a bridge, park in the large Union Creek Wayside parking area on the west side of the road, near the restroom.

To reach the upper (eastern) trailhead for a one-way shuttle hike, go 1.2 miles north of the Union Creek Resort and turn right to stay on OR 62. Continue 1.7 miles east on OR 62 and turn right on FR 610. A quarter mile later, turn left onto FR 700 to find the trailhead just ahead.

Union Creek springs from the west side of ancient Mount Mazama, just outside Crater Lake National Park. The forests on this west side of the national park have been heavily logged and roaded—right up to the park boundary—so this little watershed is far from pristine, but along the trail you'll find a spectacular forest set on the bank of a dynamic stream.

Cross OR 62, walk north to cross the bridge over Union Creek, and follow the creek east alongside the Union Creek Lodge and past Cabin 21 to find the trail. It starts out following the creek

through alder and dogwoods, with scattered five- to six-foot-diameter Douglas-fir trees. A messy understory of Oregon grape, bracken fern, thimbleberry, spirea, and shrubby chinquapin

Towering layers of Douglas-fir and hemlock trees, with lichen-encrusted bark, surround the Union Creek trail.

makes the thick trunks of Douglas-fir, incense cedar, and western white pine stand out. In a mile, the trail crosses a road near a big bridge that crosses the creek to the right, but keep going straight—the bridge isn't part of the trail. As you continue, look for burn scars on the gray scaly bark of the white pines and on the Douglas-firs from a long-ago fire.

At about 1.5 miles, prepare yourself to revel in some true giants—seven-foot-diameter Douglas-firs, with broken tops, deeply furrowed bark, and huge gnarled limbs. At about 2 miles, cross an area where lava once flowed and look for Engelmann spruce and Pacific yew (with its flaky red bark) on the streambank.

Over the next mile, the forest changes a bit to include more hemlock—grown in since the last fire—among the scattered giants. The canopy is fairly open, with a lot of snags and down wood—all the components of a truly ancient forest, likely six hundred years old. The big trees in this forest provide a lot of structure to the stream: logjams and root wads help slow and spread the water through the riparian area so that the water-loving trees, shrubs, and wildlife like river otters get the habitat they need.

Heading back at any point in this stretch between 2.5 and 3 miles makes for a nice hike, but if you want the full experience, continue a bit farther. The forest loses some of the old-growth feel, the creek runs more narrowly through a lava-constrained channel, and then, in just over 4 miles, you'll come to the 10-foot drop of Union Creek Falls. Unless you've arranged a shuttle to the far trailhead, this is the best place to turn around, before the trail climbs up another 0.4 mile through a younger forest to its end.

62. SOUTH FORK ROGUE RIVER

DISTANCE: 4 miles round-trip
TRAILHEAD LOCATION: 42.6476°, -122.3316°
STARTING ELEVATION/ELEVATION GAIN:
4000 feet/150 feet
DIFFICULTY: Easy
SEASON: Late spring through fall, access
dependent on snow

FOREST TYPE: Mixed conifer
PROTECTIONS: Old forest reserved from
logging in management plan
MANAGEMENT: Rogue River–Siskiyou
National Forest
NOTES: No restrooms at trailhead; no
parking fee or permit required

GETTING THERE: From Medford, travel northeast on Oregon Route 62 about 43 miles toward Crater Lake National Park to the town of Prospect. In Prospect, next to the hotel, turn left (east) onto Butte Falls–Prospect Road. In 3 miles, turn left on Bessie Creek Road (Forest Road 37). Staying to the right at 3 miles and 10.5 miles to stay on FR 37, go a total of 12.7 miles on this mostly paved road to the intersection with FR 34. You'll find the trailhead and parking area on the left past this intersection on FR 37.

To get to the upper trailhead, the easiest access point for the last mile of the trail with large, old trees, continue 5.4 miles farther on FR 37.

The orange-plated bark of an old ponderosa pine stands out among smaller firs and hemlocks along the South Fork Rogue River Trail.

Mosses and Lichens, Oh My!

A special thing about an ancient forest is how green and *messy* every surface can be. We can thank mosses and lichens for that.

Mosses and other bryophytes are ancient plants that depend on a moist environment to reproduce. You can find these dark, often olive green, plants on the forest floor, clinging to bark and branches and covering decaying down logs in moister forest types across Oregon. A mossy area in the forest almost seems a miniature forest unto itself. Look for their spore-carrying capsules on the end of thin stalks.

Lichens, often more of a gray green color, come in more shapes and sizes than you can probably imagine. While hundreds of species are found in ancient forests—with colorful names like old man's beard, devil's matchstick, lung lichen, and frog pelt—lichens are actually a symbiotic mixture of organisms: an alga and a fungus. Algae, a tiny plant form, are capable of photosynthesis so they can make their own food, but to take advantage of the many habitats of a forest they need to team up with a fungus that provides a more robust structure for this unique organism.

In forests lichens can be found crusted on tree trunks, hanging in long lacy ribbons from branches, or forming clumps in high branches. Some important varieties contain cyanobacteria— a type of blue-green algae that can fix nitrogen, removing it from the air and turning it into a form that trees and other forest life can use as nutrition. When these lichens fall to the ground in a windstorm, they provide food for wildlife and fertilize the forest in a way few other living things can.

Lichen, a symbiotic organism made up of algae and fungi, come in many shapes and sizes, like this devil's matchstick (top photo) and beard lichen (bottom photo).

The South Fork Rogue River springs to life out of the high lakes basin north of Mount McLoughlin. It flows north through the Sky Lakes Wilderness before reaching the more impacted parts of the Rogue River–Siskiyou National Forest. The South Fork Rogue River Trail begins well downstream of the wilderness, but along its length quite a bit is lovely ancient forest. The stretch described here is easy to access in two different places.

Starting at this middle trailhead along the length of the South Fork Rogue is a great option for hiking through a pretty and diverse forest. At the trailhead parking area, head south through the flat, fairly open forest, passing a huge ponderosa pine snag stripped of its bark in a few hundred feet. After going through a wire fence with an opening designed to let hikers through, you'll start to hear the South Fork to the right. On this plateau above the river, the forest includes a mix of maturing Douglas-fir, white fir, and western hemlock, with a smattering of bigger Douglas-firs and ponderosa pines. The dense canopy precludes there being much of an understory.

By about the half-mile point, the trail descends into the South Fork's ravine and follows the river upstream within a few hundred feet of its banks. Fewer pines grow here, but the views of the swiftly flowing river make up for that. The trail leads over a nice bridge at Big Ben Creek, to the right at 0.7 mile, and continues deeper into the forest, gaining scattered ponderosa pines again, passing a snag patch, and then, at 1.3 miles, entering an area with big western white pine, Pacific yew, and Engelmann spruce.

Just before the 1.5-mile point, enter a grove of five-foot-diameter Douglas-firs and a dense, spreading understory of yews. Cross Sam Creek on another nice bridge at 1.6 miles to continue in this wonderful forest for about another half mile. Turning around at about this 2-mile point is the best option for a shorter hike.

If you want a much longer (11-mile) hike, you can continue another 3.5 miles to the next trailhead. Some of the biggest trees along the trail are in the last mile before the trail's end, but they can be reached by driving to this upper trailhead and doing a short out-and-back hike for a little extra big-tree magic without the extra miles.

63. CHERRY CREEK

DISTANCE: 13 miles round-trip
TRAILHEAD LOCATION: 42.5889°, -122.1165°
STARTING ELEVATION/ELEVATION GAIN:
4630 feet/1700 feet
DIFFICULTY: Difficult
SEASON: Early summer through fall, access dependent on snow; mosquitoes can be bad in early summer

FOREST TYPE: Mixed conifer, alpine and subalpine
PROTECTIONS: Sky Lakes Wilderness
MANAGEMENT: Fremont-Winema National Forest
NOTES: No restrooms at trailhead; no parking fee or permit required

GETTING THERE: From Klamath Falls, head north on Oregon Route 140 for 25 miles toward Rocky Point. Turn right onto County Road 531 (West Side Road) and drive just under 11 miles to Forest Road 3450. Turn left at a sign for Cherry Creek Trail.

The second crossing of rocky Cherry Creek is framed by Engelmann spruce and younger firs in the floodplain.

From Bend, head south on US Highway 97 to the town of Chiloquin. Take exit 247 for OR 422. Turn right to follow OR 422 west. In 3 miles, turn right onto OR 62 (Crater Lake Highway), travel 5.3 miles, and turn left onto Loosley Road. A mile and a half later, turn right onto Weed Road, and in a half mile more, turn left onto Sevenmile Road. In 4.5 miles, the road curves to the left and heads south into the national forest. Six miles past the curve, turn right onto FR 3450 at a sign for Cherry Creek Trail. Park in the large wide area at the end of gravel FR 3450 in 1.8 miles.

Driving across the Wood River valley on the upper end of the Klamath Marsh National Wildlife Refuge affords a view of the South Cascades worth writing home about. To the north, the rim of Crater Lake stands out, and to the west and south the largely protected ancient forests surrounding Pelican Butte and pouring down the slopes from the high plateau of the Sky Lakes Wilderness rise

spectacularly above the basin. The edge of these two ecosystems offers an extensive area of ideal habitat for spotted owls, bald eagles, and a host of other critters large and small.

As you begin, you'll find the mixed conifer forest along this trail includes ponderosa and lodgepole pine, Douglas-fir, Engelmann spruce, and a variety of firs—all draped in lichen—among down logs and an understory of shrubs and wildflowers. Look for woodpecker and carpenter ant activity in the snags and down logs, wild strawberries, and the pink shades of phlox, wild rose, and orchids as you follow the south side of Cherry Creek's ravine.

After about a half mile, descend to a flat bench near the creek that supports large spruce trees and follow the creek's riparian area—lined with alder and some tall cottonwoods—more closely. Young mountain hemlocks create dense pockets in the understory while a smattering of forest wildflowers line the trail.

At three-quarters of a mile, enter the Sky Lakes Wilderness and continue through the forest of fir and spruce, straying alternately farther from and closer to the creek and passing a grouping of huge four- to five-foot-diameter Douglas-firs. At 1.5 miles, the forest thins out in a rocky, dry area where scattered ponderosa pines dominate for a quarter mile. As you approach the 2-mile point, a mixture of firs, spruce, and lodgepole pine takes over again, with huckleberry in the understory.

You'll arrive at the first crossing of Cherry Creek at 2.3 miles; if the water covers the stream's rocks, the easiest way to cross is to take off your shoes. Beyond that, cross two more small streams and continue through a mix of spruce, ponderosa pine, and big Douglas-firs, in and out of more moist, dense areas and more open forest. Cross a meadow filled with larkspur, lupine, sunflowers, and huckleberries at 2.9 miles, its edges ringed with pines, cottonwoods, and spruce.

Between 3.2 and 3.8 miles, when you approach the second crossing of Cherry Creek, the forest takes on some true old-growth characteristics: bigger trees, giant snags and decomposing down logs, and a diverse understory. Cross a smashed-up bridge in a grove of three-foot-diameter spruce trees and a wet area with down logs and shrubs before reaching Cherry Creek and finding rocks or logs to cross in the broad floodplain.

In a short distance, cross another bouldery creek flowing down from Trapper and Sonya Lakes on the plateau above, after which your climb begins in earnest. As you switchback up the ridge on the north side of the creek, the forest mix becomes dominated by Shasta red fir, spruce, and mountain hemlock, though giant Douglas-firs and a few ponderosa pines are scattered on the slope as well. Your hard work to get to the midpoint of this 2-mile climb is rewarded with a remarkable ancient forest stand, continuing for a half mile, with giant spruce and Shasta firs, tall mountain hemlocks, and Douglas-firs.

At about 6 miles, the grade flattens out near the edge of the creek and the forest takes on a decidedly more alpine feel: the trees are more stunted; lodgepole, white pine, and subalpine firs take over; and huckleberries line the trail. Cross the outlet stream from a small lake to the right and continue to climb past another small lake before reaching the edge of Trapper Lake at 6.5 miles. The junction with the Sky Lakes Trail here offers backpacking options, but for a day hike the edge of Trapper Lake, with a grand view of Luther Mountain, makes a great destination. Relax here for a while before retracing your steps to the trailhead.

64. BROWN MOUNTAIN

DISTANCE: 7.9 miles one way with shuttle or 9 miles round-trip
TRAILHEAD LOCATION: 42.3806°, -122.2329°
STARTING ELEVATION/ELEVATION GAIN: 4970 feet/800 feet
DIFFICULTY: Difficult
SEASON: Early summer through fall, access dependent on snow; mosquitoes can be bad in early summer

FOREST TYPE: Mixed conifer
PROTECTIONS: Inventoried roadless area
MANAGEMENT: Rogue River–Siskiyou and Fremont-Winema National Forests
NOTES: No restrooms at trailhead; no parking fee or permit required

GETTING THERE: From Medford, take Crater Lake Highway (Oregon Route 62) north for 6 miles; then turn right on OR 140. Follow OR 140 for 28 miles toward Lake of the Woods.

To leave a car at the South Brown Mountain Trailhead for a shuttle hike, turn right (south) on Big Elk Road (Forest Road 37) just before Fish Lake. Go 2 miles; then turn left on FR 3705. Follow this paved, one-lane road for 3.2 miles, ignoring side roads with signs for Brown Mountain Trail, to the trailhead at a large pullout on the right.

To drive to the main Brown Mountain Trailhead to begin the hike, continue east on OR 140 past Fish Lake, 7 miles past the FR 37 turnoff, and turn right (south) on FR 3601 between mileposts 35 and 36. Turn right on FR 3640 right away, and find the trailhead 0.4 mile down the road.

South of the Sky Lakes Wilderness and just west of the Mountain Lakes Wilderness, Brown Mountain and the ten-thousand-acre roadless area surrounding it sit unassumingly between Lake of the Woods and Fish Lake, two popular summer camping and recreation destinations. Better known for the section of the Pacific Crest Trail that crosses Brown Mountain's lava flow, the east and south flanks of the cinder cone actually support a tremendously diverse ancient forest teeming with wildlife.

Brown Mountain's forests straddle the high divide of the south Cascades from west to east, but they also sit on the divide between the Cascades and the Klamath Mountains to the south, bringing an array of conifers and wildflowers together along this beautiful trail.

Start out by going left on the joined Brown Mountain and High Lakes Trail, paralleling the road at first and then crossing a creek surrounded by yew trees just before a trail junction at 0.6 mile. Here, a sign directs you to turn left to follow the Brown Mountain Trail. For the first mile and a quarter, the forest is impressively diverse with Shasta red fir, Douglas-fir, western white pine, grand fir, mountain hemlock, Pacific yew, and Engelmann spruce all mixed in at this elevation of 5000 feet. Look for the reddish, mosaic, and furrowed bark of the Shasta red fir, the bark's character belying the trees' great age. Shrubby chinquapin and huckleberries fill in the understory.

At about 1.3 miles, there is a springy area with particularly big trees, more yews and spruce, and more of a lush green understory. Beyond that, the trail ascends and goes in and out of a more open

forest with snags for three-quarters of a mile, skirting an old clear-cut.

As the trail continues to go up, some of the tree diversity falls away, and mountain hemlock and red fir begin to dominate. A trail junction at 2.4 miles accesses FR 3640, and beyond the junction, the towering forest affords you a good glimpse of Brown Mountain's lava flow to the right.

After 3.3 miles, the trail descends, eventually crosses a creek, and follows a wet drainage with riparian vegetation for three-quarters of a mile. Huckleberries line the trail, and just past the 3.8-mile mark you catch a glimpse of Brown Mountain itself across the riparian zone.

At about 4 miles, the trail begins to be marked with blue diamonds (for winter trails), and it crosses the Pacific Crest Trail at about 4.5 miles. Huckleberry and yew fill the understory. If you haven't arranged a car shuttle, this is a good destination for an out-and-back day hike.

If you have arranged a shuttle at the south trailhead, continue across the PCT. At about 5.2 miles, the trail crosses a small road—turn right to find the trail on the other side—and enters an area with really impressive Douglas-fir as you follow an alder-rich riparian area. Just over 6 miles, enter an open riparian area with diverse shrubs and wildflowers. Turn right on a road to cross this small creek, and then find the trail again on the left. For the next 1.5 miles, this tributary of Butte Creek is on the left and you can hear, though not see, the flowing water. Large Douglas-firs, yews, and diverse riparian vegetation including Douglas maple and aspen continue, and a rock outcropping at a little over 7 miles adds interest.

The last half to three-quarters of a mile of the trail has some spectacular Douglas-fir and yew stands, with noteworthy pine mixed in. Many of these giants are scarred by previous fires. The trail ends just shy of the 8-mile mark at FR 3640.

OPPOSITE: Western white pines are just one of the diverse species of trees growing on the slopes of Brown Mountain.

CENTRAL OREGON HIKES

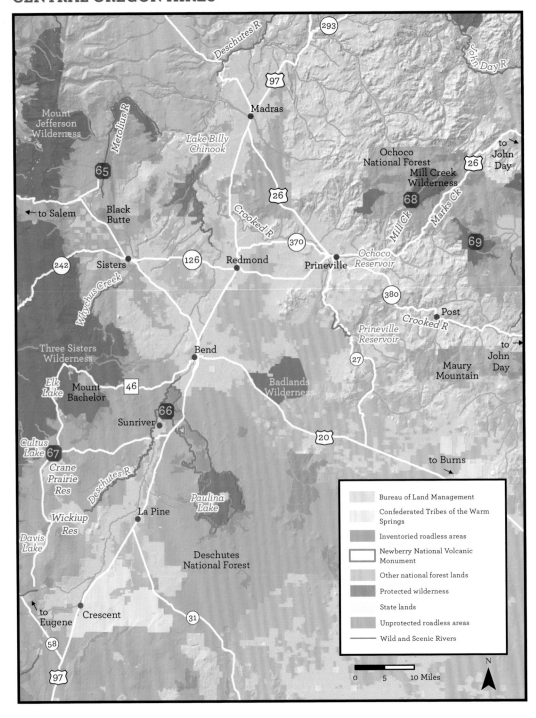

Mount Jefferson Wilderness

Deschutes R

293

97

Madras

Metolius R

65

← to Salem

Black Butte

Lake Billy Chinook

Crooked R

26

Ochoco National Forest

Mill Creek Wilderness

68

to John Day

26

Marks Ck

Mill Ck

69

370

Sisters

126

Redmond

Prineville

Ochoco Reservoir

Whychus Creek

242

380

Post

Crooked R

to John Day

27

Prineville Reservoir

Three Sisters Wilderness

Bend

Badlands Wilderness

Maury Mountain

Elk Lake

Mount Bachelor

46

Sunriver

66

20

to Burns

Cultus Lake

67

Crane Prairie Res

Deschutes R

La Pine

Paulina Lake

Wickiup Res

Davis Lake

Deschutes National Forest

to Eugene

Crescent

31

58

97

	Bureau of Land Management
	Confederated Tribes of the Warm Springs
	Inventoried roadless areas
	Newberry National Volcanic Monument
	Other national forest lands
	Protected wilderness
	State lands
	Unprotected roadless areas
	Wild and Scenic Rivers

N

0   5   10 Miles

CENTRAL OREGON

The forests of Central Oregon stretch from just east of the Cascade Crest from Mount Jefferson on the north to Maiden Peak on the south, and head east of Prineville through the Ochoco Mountains. This area, in the rain shadow of the High Cascades, is generally much drier than the western slopes. Depending on elevation, slope, and local moisture, you might find mixed conifer, lodgepole pine, or ponderosa pine forests, as well as high desert with sagebrush and juniper.

The ponderosa forests of the Deschutes and Ochoco National Forests in this region have been heavily impacted by human management—from the obvious effects of logging to the less obvious results of livestock grazing and suppression of natural fire cycles. Logging here included "high-grading," which removed the biggest, oldest trees across the landscape, leaving true ancient forests with all of their components as a rare feature in Central Oregon.

Fortunately, some large tracts of unlogged forests are still protected on the eastern slopes of Cascade wilderness areas like Mount Jefferson and Three Sisters, though many of these are high-elevation lodgepole pine types that don't naturally grow to great age or diversity. Farther east in the Ochoco Mountains, the Mill Creek Wilderness and Lookout Mountain roadless areas hold beautiful old forests, and other large wildlands remain, though few have trails.

The headwaters of the Deschutes and Metolius Rivers spring from the base of the Cascades—through the porous lava rock—and flow north to the Columbia through the dry plateaus on the eastern slope of the mountains. These designated wild and scenic rivers are lined with stunning ancient ponderosa pines and accessible trails. The Crooked River flows in from the east, picking up tributaries flowing off the Ochoco Mountains before joining the Deschutes north of Bend.

Stately ponderosa pines mark many of the Central Oregon region's forests, like these near the Ochoco Divide along US Highway 26.

These rivers have helped fuel the huge shift in Central Oregon's economy from timber to tourism, outdoor recreation, and high tech. Bend and other nearby towns have grown at a high rate for the past few decades, as people move to and visit them for the quality of life afforded by accessible recreational opportunities like skiing, hiking, boating, and fishing. This growth has also led to new challenges for forest management. Fire suppression has led to unnaturally dense forest stands in some places, and as development creeps farther into the forests, fire risk to homes in this forest interface increases. Homeowners here need to be "fire wise" as forest managers work to restore the role of fire and a more natural forest structure.

65. METOLIUS RIVER

DISTANCE: 5.5 miles round-trip or 3 miles one way with shuttle
TRAILHEAD LOCATION: 44.5006°, -121.6397°
STARTING ELEVATION/ELEVATION GAIN: 2900 feet/Minimal
DIFFICULTY: Moderate
SEASON: Early spring through late fall, access dependent on snow

FOREST TYPE: Ponderosa pine
PROTECTIONS: Wild and scenic river corridor; unprotected roadless area
MANAGEMENT: Deschutes National Forest
NOTES: Restrooms at Wizard Falls; no parking fee or permit required

GETTING THERE: To reach Lower Canyon Creek Campground from Sisters, travel west on Oregon Route 126 and US Highway 20 for 10 miles (or east from Santiam Pass for 10 miles). Turn right on Camp Sherman Road (which becomes Forest Road 14). In 2.5 miles, stay straight at a junction onto FR 1419, then continue straight after a stop sign onto FR 1420. In another 2.9 miles, turn right on FR 400 to find the campground and trailhead at the end of the road in 1 mile.

For the Wizard Falls Hatchery, instead of taking FR 1419, stay to the right at that junction to stay on FR 14 for another 7.7 miles. The hatchery and parking are on the left. To leave a car shuttle at the Lower Bridge Trailhead, continue past Wizard Falls another 2.5 miles, cross the bridge, and park on the left to find the trailhead.

The Metolius River is world-famous for its stunning, clear blue water, which springs from the base of Black Butte at full force. Its ponderosa pine–lined banks are protected for many miles—from its source to where it is constrained by Lake Billy Chinook—as a wild and scenic river, though some high grading of these forests has occurred over the years. Fires that burned many of the forests in the area here on the eastern edge of the Mount Jefferson Wilderness didn't reach the river or these giant pines, though some of the forest stands along the Metolius could use fire restoration.

The West Metolius River Trail follows the river for 6 miles, but for a reasonable day hike, the stretch between Lower Canyon Creek Campground and Wizard Falls Hatchery is the nicest. Many visitors are drawn to this lovely trail, where the ice cold water creates cool breezes on a hot summer day.

From the trailhead at the Lower Canyon Creek Campground, follow the swift, wide river through a riparian area with shrubby maples, oceanspray, and wild roses under a canopy of ponderosa pines, Douglas-firs, and incense cedars. Just over a third of a mile along the trail, pause to notice the water gushing out of the forest-covered hillside across the river. The riverbanks and some wet spots in the trail come with vine maples, ninebark, other shrubs, and a lot of wildflowers. Over this first mile, the trail passes in and out of sun and shade—denser areas with young firs, large Douglas-firs, and a mix of incense cedars and ponderosa pines. In the more open patches, lupine and balsamroot add color.

In the second mile, there are more warm, dry openings where the pines take over (including some big, fire-scarred snags), and there are views of the rocky canyon. The river is at its loveliest between 2 and 2.3 miles, where the trail brings you right to its edge—a good distraction from a stretch of younger forest with few large trees. Notice the log islands made of fallen trees in the river, where wildflowers and small shrubs have found a foothold.

As you approach Wizard Falls, the trail widens, passes through more incense cedars, and crosses three small bridges between 2.5 and 2.7 miles. At the hatchery, you'll find restrooms, picnic areas, and information about the area. If you're doing an out-and-back hike, return to the trailhead from here.

If you've arranged a shuttle, continue along the trail, following the river past more big pines and cedars and skirting the edge of dense young forest on private property. In 3 miles you'll arrive at the Lower Bridge Trailhead and your shuttle vehicle.

A forest of ponderosa pines lines the spectacular Wild and Scenic Metolius River. *(Photo by Brizz Meddings)*

66. BENHAM FALLS

DISTANCE: 1.4 miles round-trip
TRAILHEAD LOCATION: 43.9309°, -121.4131°
STARTING ELEVATION/ELEVATION GAIN: 4150 feet/Minimal
DIFFICULTY: Easy
SEASON: Late spring through fall, access dependent on snow

FOREST TYPE: Ponderosa pine
PROTECTIONS: Wild and scenic river corridor
MANAGEMENT: Deschutes National Forest
NOTES: Restrooms at trailhead; $5 fee or permit required to park

GETTING THERE: From Bend, take US Highway 97 south about 10 miles. Turn right between mileposts 149 and 150 at signs for the Lava Lands Visitor Center. Continue past the entrance to the visitor center, staying to the left, and follow Forest Road 2702 for 4 miles to the large and well-marked Benham Falls Picnic Area and East Trailhead.

Several sections of the upper Deschutes River, designated as a wild and scenic river from where it flows out of Wickiup Reservoir to the Bend city limits, are lined with beautiful old ponderosa pines, but there are few official trails. The easily accessible trail system between Bend and Sunriver, however, highlights some of these forests as the river meanders lazily through meadows and lava flows, and where it rages through narrow areas in places like Benham Falls.

Benham Falls, on the Wild and Scenic Deschutes River, is reached via an easy hike through giant ponderosa pines. *(Photo by Rick Seymour)*

Protected today as part of the wild and scenic river corridor, the giant pines near Benham Falls are still there only because the area was used for company picnics by the timber company that once owned it; they logged many other ancient forests in the area long ago.

The trail starts out by following the wide river downstream. In a short way, the trail intersects the Sun-Lava Bike Path at a big bridge at a bend in the river. Turn left to cross the bridge and continue on the wide, well-used dirt trail, watching out for the many other trail users on foot and bicycle. The trail passes through a nice riparian zone with willows and other shrubs as the river flows wide and fast past a wet meadow on the opposite bank. Big ponderosa pines line the trail and cover the slopes to the left. Unofficial trails paralleling the main path lead you to the bluff overlooking the river.

In 0.7 mile, you'll reach another developed trailhead. From here, the trail switchbacks a short way down to viewpoints of the raging rapids where the river squeezes through the lava flow. Retrace your steps to return to the parking area.

67. CULTUS RIVER AND BENCHMARK BUTTE

DISTANCE: 1.5 miles round-trip
TRAILHEAD LOCATION: 43.8264°, -121.7969°
STARTING ELEVATION/ELEVATION GAIN:
4450 feet/Minimal
DIFFICULTY: Moderate
SEASON: Late summer through fall, access dependent on snow

FOREST TYPE: Lodgepole pine
PROTECTIONS: Research natural area
MANAGEMENT: Deschutes National Forest
NOTES: No restrooms at trailhead; no parking fee or permit required

GETTING THERE: Follow Cascade Lakes Highway (Forest Road 46) either north from Crescent Cutoff Road or south from Mount Bachelor. From Crescent Cutoff Road, travel north 25.5 miles (about 1 mile north of the turn to Cultus Lake Resort) and turn left (west) on FR 4645. From Bend, travel west on Cascade Lakes Highway around Mount Bachelor and then south for a total of 45 miles. About 1 mile north of the turn for Cultus Lake Resort, turn right (west) on FR 4645. (FR 4645 is not marked going west, but it is signed on the east side of FR 46.) The road ends in about a quarter mile at the river, where you can park on the side of the road.

The little-known (and very short) Cultus River is one of Oregon's instant rivers—springing out of the base of a volcanic butte. About three hundred acres of the broad, shallow river and its surrounds are designated a research natural area for their cold springs origin and unique bottomland forest of Engelmann spruce and lodgepole pine. While not an official trail, this route to the headwaters of the Cultus River is a fun hike through a unique forest for the adventurous and agile explorer.

To begin, follow a faint trail along the river upstream. Staying close to the riverbank allows you to enjoy the amazing array of summer wildflowers in this cool, moist area and also lets you admire the large Engelmann spruce trees that grow within 20 or 30 feet of the wide, shallow

Lodgepole pines and Engelmann spruce make up the dense, moist forest along the Cultus River.

flowers and grasses. There is ample evidence that deer and beaver use this area, so keep an eye out for prints, scat, and gnawed trees.

As you get closer to the base of Benchmark Butte and the river's head, a few spring-fed streams cross the path, and these streams and wetlands have to be crossed on logs and bypassed through the jumble of downed lodgepole. If you stray too far from the river, just head back toward the river's edge when you have the opportunity. The springs that form the river at the base of Benchmark Butte come out of a pile of lava rocks at about three-quarters of a mile from the start of the hike and your turnaround point.

Notice that the forest on the butte is completely different from the one you walked through to get here—huge ponderosa pines cover the hill. These are great to look at from below, but if you're up for a careful climb, scramble up the lava rocks to see these ancient beauties up close and personal. They have tons of character—black fire scars and giant twisted limbs high overhead. The view from the top features Odell Butte, Diamond Peak, and the whole river laid out below.

stream. Inland from the river, the forest is a thicket of lodgepole pine, with an obstacle course of down logs. As you head upstream, you'll pass some large root balls from trees that have tipped over in the inland direction and it's best to skirt those on the river side. Many other trees have fallen toward the river, and because the river's level does not fluctuate, these logs form floating gardens covered in

68. MILL CREEK WILDERNESS

DISTANCE: 11.5 miles round-trip
TRAILHEAD LOCATION: 44.4397°, -120.5806°
STARTING ELEVATION/ELEVATION GAIN:
3700 feet/1900 feet
DIFFICULTY: Difficult
SEASON: Late spring through fall; best wildflowers in midsummer

FOREST TYPE: Ponderosa pine
PROTECTIONS: Mill Creek Wilderness
MANAGEMENT: Ochoco National Forest
NOTES: Restrooms at Wildcat Campground near trailhead; no parking fee required but self-issued, free wilderness permit required at trailhead

GETTING THERE: From Bend, head north on US Highway 97 toward Redmond/Portland for about 15 miles. In Redmond, turn right to follow Oregon Route 126 east for about 17 miles toward Prineville. In Prineville, OR 126 becomes NW 3rd Street and US 26E. Continue on US 26E for about 9 miles and turn left onto Mill Creek Road (Forest Road 33) just past milepost 28. Travel just under 11 miles on FR 33 (half of it paved) to find the Twin Pillars South Trailhead on the right, just before Wildcat Campground.

The Mill Creek Wilderness, protected in 1984 after years of efforts by conservationists, includes everything you'd want out of Central Oregon's landscape: stands of huge ponderosa pines, wild streams, and striking rock formations. The 17,400-acre wilderness is the source of Mill Creek, one of several large streams that tumble out of the Ochoco Mountains to feed the Crooked River. Though Mill Creek Wilderness is protected from logging, the Forest Service allows livestock grazing there, which can change the natural forest structure. Fires have burned in the area since it was protected, too, offering expansive views and a great example of a naturally recovering forest landscape.

The trail, lined with wildflowers in the summer, begins on the west side of the canyon in a stand of ponderosa pine before coming to the first of eight stream-crossings along East Fork Mill Creek: be prepared to hop across on rocks and wood as there are no bridges and water levels vary throughout the year.

After the first creek-crossing, the trail enters a dense canopy of Douglas-fir and ponderosa pine. It then drops back along the creek, where the riparian area is dominated by alder and willow trees. As the trail gradually ascends into the wilderness, note that the hillslopes outside of the riparian area are covered in a ponderosa pine and fir forest with a much sparser understory—a classic example of Oregon's eastside forests where the vegetation varies wildly based on moisture, slope, soil, and aspect. Fire scars on old-growth ponderosa pines are visible around the fourth and fifth creek-crossings, demonstrating the species' fire-resistant nature. By the time the trail reaches the sixth and seventh crossings, there is hardly any understory beneath the fir and pine forest. This allows for a view through the trees of an extensive burned area with many standing snags and dense shrubs. The trail ascends on the way to the eighth crossing where larch and ponderosa pine coexist in an open canopy structure. Then

the trail heads down and across Belknap Creek before the final Mill Creek crossing at just over the 3-mile mark.

Leaving the moist soils of the riparian area behind, the trail takes a steep western turn out of the Mill Creek drainage and across the rolling landscape of the wilderness. As the trail enters the area that burned in 2000, there are sprawling views of the landscape covered in charred snags and a few pockets of living larch trees in protected ravines. Half a mile into the burned area, the trail crosses Brogan Creek before gaining 1400 feet of elevation in the next 2 miles.

After a series of steep and sharp switchbacks, you will reach the base of the two-hundred-foot-tall Twin Pillars rock formations. The view from the pillars into the Mill Creek Wilderness is breathtaking, with glimpses of the Cascades on a clear day. Head back the way you came after soaking in the beauty of the wilderness and listening to the howling wind.

A sign on one of the Twin Pillars Trail's ancient ponderosa pines greets visitors to the Mill Creek Wilderness.
(Photo by Melissa Hubler)

69. LOOKOUT MOUNTAIN

DISTANCE: 7-mile loop
TRAILHEAD LOCATION: 44.3397°, -120.3592°
STARTING ELEVATION/ELEVATION GAIN:
5600 feet/1300 feet
DIFFICULTY: Difficult
SEASON: Summer through fall, access
dependent on snow

FOREST TYPE: Ponderosa pine, western
juniper
PROTECTIONS: Inventoried roadless area
MANAGEMENT: Ochoco National Forest
NOTES: No restrooms at trailhead; no parking
fee or permit required. Be aware of hunters,
mountain bikers, and other trail users.

GETTING THERE: From Bend, head north on US Highway 97 toward Redmond for about 15
miles. In Redmond, turn right to follow Oregon Route 126 east for about 17 miles toward
Prineville. In Prineville, OR 126 becomes NW 3rd Street and US 26E. Continue on US 26E for
about 13 miles. Turn right onto County Road 123 and go about 7.5 miles. Stay right at the
junction of Forest Roads 22 and 42, and continue on FR 42 for 7 miles. Turn right on FR 4205,
pass the Round Mountain Trailhead, and continue on this rough (but drivable) road until it ends
in about 1.5 miles at the Mother Lode Mine Trailhead. The trailhead for Independent Mine Trail
808 is on the far left out of the parking area at the end of the road.

**Lookout Mountain lies at the heart of a vast wild landscape of ponderosa pine and mixed
conifer forests, grasslands and meadows, and streams that is ideal for all forms of backcountry
recreation. Conservationists have long sought to codify the protections for the designated
roadless area and are currently seeking to designate over three hundred thousand acres of the
Ochoco Mountains as a national recreation area, including wilderness protections for twenty-six
thousand acres. (Learn more at www.friendsoftheochocos.org.)**

This hike follows Independent Mine Trail 808
for about 3.5 miles up to the summit of Lookout
Mountain, followed by a 3.5-mile descent. While
the view at the top is stunning, spring and summer also bring an abundance of wildflowers to
enjoy along the way. Keep an eye out for tracks
of deer, elk, and coyote.

Follow the Independent Mine Trail out of the
parking lot to the left and hike through a forest
of Douglas-fir and old-growth ponderosa pine.
As you gradually ascend you start to see more
larch, grand and white fir, and Douglas-fir and
less ponderosa. Baneberry, gooseberry, and cur-
rant are other common understory plants during
the first several miles as well as in the densely

forested patches as the trail climbs up to Lookout
Mountain's wide plateau. Here, open mountain
meadows full of cornlily and other wildflowers are
slowly shrinking over time as fir trees, without the
frequent fires that once burned the area, encroach.
Giant Douglas-fir trees are sprinkled along the
trail, among abundant snags and down wood.

After 1.5 miles, openings become more common, with views to the north and east; and in
2 miles, views to the northwest showcase the
Cascade peaks. The trail descends toward Brush
Creek, where water-loving alders and aspen are
found in the riparian area. From here, it's about
another mile and half to the summit, with some
steep stretches to tackle on your way up.

The last half mile is right along Lookout Mountain's ridgetop through a field of sagebrush and wildflowers, with gnarled ancient juniper scattered about. On a clear day, the summit offers views of the entire Cascade Range, from Mount Shasta in California to Mount Rainier in Washington. The sometimes windy summit offers rocky outcrops and an old fire lookout to explore before beginning the descent.

To complete the loop, descend from the ridgeline to the northeast, being careful to stay on Lookout Mountain Trail 808, and *not* following Trail 804 to the northwest. As you cross the broad basalt flow of Lookout Mountain's plateau, you'll hike through sagebrush and pockets of fir, and at about a half mile into the descent, you'll reach a junction with Trail 808A. Take a left onto Lookout Mountain Trail 804 here. Now the trail becomes shadier as you hike through dense pockets of old-growth trees and traverse the lush headwater springs of Canyon Creek where moisture-loving wildflowers thrive. About 3 miles into the descent, you'll see the remains of Independent Mine, an old cinnabar mine and an interesting exploration, to the right of the trail. The parking lot is just another half mile from the mine.

Blooming balsamroot, sagebrush, and scattered trees mark the summit plateau of Lookout Mountain. *(Photo by Sarah Cuddy)*

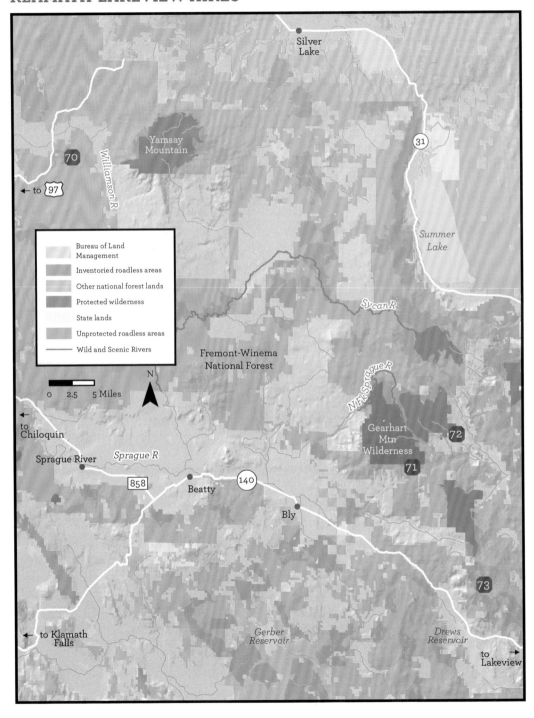

Silver
Lake

Yamsay
Mountain

Williamson R

70

← to 97

31

Summer
Lake

Bureau of Land
Management

Inventoried roadless areas

Other national forest lands

Protected wilderness

State lands

Unprotected roadless areas

Wild and Scenic Rivers

Sycan R

NF Sprague R

Fremont-Winema
National Forest

Gearhart
Mtn
Wilderness

72

0   2.5   5 Miles

N

71

to
Chiloquin

Sprague R

Sprague River

858

Beatty

140

Bly

73

to Klamath
Falls

Gerber
Reservoir

Drews
Reservoir

to
Lakeview →

KLAMATH-LAKEVIEW

Tucked away in the south-central part of the state far from most of Oregon's population centers, the Klamath-Lakeview region, as defined here, lies east of the Cascades and west of US Highway 395 and the town of Lakeview. The region is an interesting mix of spring-fed rivers and wetlands, forests, high-desert rims and plateaus, and the northern extent of the Warner Mountains.

The Williamson, Sycan, Sprague, and Che-waucan Rivers flow here, feeding wetlands, aspen groves, and ponderosa pine forests before they encounter Klamath Lake and feed that mighty river system. In cooler, moister areas on the slopes

of Yamsay Mountain and other hills, lodgepole pine and mixed conifer forests thrive. High rims and plateaus offer drier slopes with mountain mahogany and juniper among the sagebrush.

Remote as this area is, it has not been spared the chainsaws that have reduced ancient forests everywhere else in the state. Intermixed with high desert and other less "productive" lands, the forested areas of the Fremont-Winema National Forest were the focus of timber cutting that fed mills in the area, concentrating the destruction of ancient forests here. The Winema half of the Fremont-Winema National Forest that was once

Spring-fed streams and wetlands lined with ponderosa pines, as here along the Sycan River, are a highlight of the Klamath-Lakeview region.

part of the Klamath Indian Reservation was heavily logged. Now that the forest and watersheds in the area are part of the national forest system, the Forest Service and Klamath Tribes work together to manage them.

Despite the history of logging, some stunning groves of ponderosa pine forests and large wild areas around Gearhart Mountain, Yamsay Mountain, and Coleman and Deadhorse Rims remain, though few of these forests have been protected.

70. BLUE JAY SPRING

DISTANCE: 2 miles round-trip
TRAILHEAD LOCATION: 42.9315°, -121.5369°
STARTING ELEVATION/ELEVATION GAIN: 4760 feet/250 feet
DIFFICULTY: Easy
SEASON: Spring through fall, access dependent on snow

FOREST TYPE: Ponderosa pine
PROTECTIONS: Research natural area
MANAGEMENT: Fremont-Winema National Forest
NOTES: No restrooms at trailhead; no parking fee or permit required

GETTING THERE: Take US Highway 97 about 26 miles south of Chemult or 48 miles north of Klamath Falls. Turn east onto Silver Lake Road (County Road 676) and cross part of the Klamath Marsh National Wildlife Refuge. A quarter mile north of milepost 13, turn right onto Forest Road 7640. Follow this gravel road for just under a half mile, then turn left onto FR 7642. Follow this narrow, brushy road, with a high center and some bumps, for 2.2 miles, then turn left to rejoin FR 7640. One mile up this bumpy road (a high-clearance vehicle is ideal), turn left onto FR 7640-440 and head downhill a quarter mile to find a parking area and Blue Jay Spring at a wooden fence.

Blue Jay Spring pops out of the pumice-rich soil laid down by Mount Mazama's explosion, the only water source for miles and thus an oasis for birds and other forest wildlife. The two-hundred-acre research natural area (RNA) was designated in 1971 to exemplify the ponderosa pine and lodgepole pine forest types. The designation has protected these impressive pine groves from most management, a rarity in this region. While there is no real trail here, an old road into the area makes for fairly easy hiking, but keep in mind that it is not maintained as a trail would be.

A dilapidated wooden fence and sign marking Blue Jay Spring sits at the parking area, a grove of aspens shimmering in the breeze. Check out the spring and then, to hike through the RNA, start down an old jeep track that begins from the left side of the parking area and fence. The road descends steadily, heading roughly west, passing clumps of large snags and young ponderosa pines. Sagebrush and grass make up the understory.

Many large pines here have recently died, possibly victims of a pandora moth outbreak combined with drought and competition.

After a half mile, look to the left for a view into a healthier-looking stand of trees, and at 0.7 mile, the trail has leveled out in an open pine stand with trees two to three feet in diameter. Look for burn scars at the bases of trees, indicating that low-intensity fires have impacted the area

No official trail leads into the Blue Jay Spring Research Natural Area, but the open ponderosa pine stand is easy to walk through and enjoy.

in a way that benefits this classic ponderosa pine forest structure. Keep following the faint road as it turns to the right and into a small loop at about the mile point.

From here, it's easy to continue exploring the park-like stands of pines in any direction, looking for interesting branch structures, groupings of giant trees, wildlife, and down logs. If you have a good sense of direction or a GPS unit, you can pick your way through the forest and up the slope cross-country to the spring, but the easiest way to return is to follow the jeep track back up when you're done taking in the beauty of this area.

71. GEARHART MOUNTAIN WILDERNESS

DISTANCE: 9.5 miles round-trip
TRAILHEAD LOCATION: 42.4611°, -120.8014°
STARTING ELEVATION/ELEVATION GAIN: 6340 feet/1920 feet
DIFFICULTY: Difficult
SEASON: Summer through October, access dependent on snow; mosquitoes can be bad through August
FOREST TYPE: Ponderosa pine, mixed conifer

PROTECTIONS: Gearhart Mountain Wilderness
MANAGEMENT: Fremont-Winema National Forest
NOTES: No restrooms at trailhead, but they are available at nearby Coral Creek Campground; no parking fee or permit required

GETTING THERE: From the town of Bly, head southeast on Oregon Route 140. In just over a mile, turn left on Campbell Road. In just under a half mile, turn right onto Forest Road 34 at signs for Gearhart Mountain Wilderness and Mitchell Monument. Follow this paved but bumpy road across the Sprague River valley, passing Campbell Reservoir and, in 10 miles, Mitchell Monument—keeping an eye out for cows that might be on the road. In 15 miles, turn left at a sign for Coral Creek Campground and Gearhart Mountain Trail onto FR 12. Pass the campground in less than a half mile and continue another mile and a half up this steep, rough road to the trailhead with parking in the turnaround area.

Designated in 1964 as one of the original wilderness areas and expanded to its current 22,684 acres in 1984, the Gearhart Mountain Wilderness is among the most beautiful and least known places in Oregon. Its rugged peaks and glacial-carved valleys are the source of both the North Fork and South Fork of the Sprague River, the former designated as a wild and scenic river and wrapping around the north end of the wilderness.

Gearhart Mountain isn't often thought of for its forests (if thought of at all) because its unique rock formations dominate much of the landscape, but forests it has. Much of the wilderness is covered in lodgepole pine, but on the south end of the wilderness, the Lookout Rock Trailhead grants access to miles of ponderosa pine and mixed conifer forest well worth exploring.

The rocky "Palisades," scattered with ponderosa pines, are just one interesting feature of the Gearhart Mountain Trail. *(Photo by Jonathan Jelen)*

The trail starts out by climbing gradually through a dry ponderosa-pine forest with sizable orange-barked beauties and big white firs. After just under a mile, the forest will open up and give way to a fascinating geologic spot, the Palisades. Passing through this unique rock garden featuring dozens of thirty-foot spires and rock mazes, look for wildflowers like paintbrush and fireweed in the early summer months.

The trail then reenters the mixed conifer, high-elevation forest with a regular smattering of big old trees as it climbs a bit more steeply.

Views of fortress-like Gearhart Mountain in the distance and of the Dome monolith, a bit closer, are highlights as you climb for a few miles past a mix of alpine meadows, lodgepole pine forest, and gnarled old snags. At just over 4.7 miles from the trailhead, you'll reach the Saddle, which offers tremendous views of the wilderness and a head-on view of its namesake mountain.

If you love rocky climbs and alpine meadows and feel the need for more views, you can continue for another 1.3 miles to the Notch for a 12-mile round-trip hike.

72. AUGUR CREEK

DISTANCE: 2 miles round-trip
TRAILHEAD LOCATION: 42.5131°, -120.7076°
STARTING ELEVATION/ELEVATION GAIN: 5930 feet/250 feet
DIFFICULTY: Easy
SEASON: Early summer through fall, access dependent on snow; best wildflowers in early July

FOREST TYPE: Ponderosa pine, quaking aspen, lodgepole pine
PROTECTIONS: Inventoried roadless area
MANAGEMENT: Fremont-Winema National Forest
NOTES: No restrooms at trailhead; no parking fee or permit required

GETTING THERE: From the town of Bly, head southeast on Oregon Route 140. In just over a mile, turn left on Campbell Road. In just under a half mile, turn right onto Forest Road 34 at signs for Gearhart Mountain Wilderness and Mitchell Monument. Follow this paved but bumpy road across the Sprague River valley, passing Campbell Reservoir and, in 10 miles, Mitchell Monument—keeping an eye out for cows that might be on the road. In a little over 15 miles, stay left at a Y intersection, and in 19 miles, continue straight at a four-way intersection just past Dairy Creek to stay on FR 34 both times. At 4.5 miles past this intersection, turn left at a trailhead sign for Dead Horse Rim Trail. Turn onto this jeep track to find the trailhead in a few hundred feet in the road's wide turnaround loop.

Augur Creek and its tributaries flow south off of Dead Horse Rim, one of a series of ridges that characterize the Klamath-Lakeview region's geography. Much of the area here to the east of Gearhart Mountain has been heavily impacted by beetle outbreaks that killed vast swaths of lodgepole pine forests in recent years (you can see how the Forest Service responded to this outbreak if you drive up to Deadhorse and Campbell Lakes—it's not pretty). But the lower slopes of this large unroaded area include extensive swaths of healthy ancient ponderosa pine forests.

A Million Ways to Die in an Ancient Forest

While some trees in an ancient forest may live several hundred years, this is not the norm. Trees of various species are constantly growing, but also dying. There are so many ways and reasons why trees die—and these all contribute to the diversity of structure and habitats in ancient forests. Most of the time, a complex combination of factors contributes to a tree's ultimate demise. Some common (natural) contributors to a tree's death include:

- Beetle infestations
- Competition
- Drought stress
- Fire
- Fungal and bacterial infection (rot)
- Mistletoe
- Physical damage
- Windstorms

How do these factors work together? Let's say a windstorm blows down a small patch of trees in the forest, leaving just a few big, tall trees and opening up the canopy around them to more sunlight. One of those remaining two-hundred-year-old trees thrives for years afterward, but many young trees fill in the gap in the forest and start growing quickly in the sunlight.

The added stress of that competition for water and nutrients is compounded by a series of drought years, and the tree's growth slows down. Bark beetles (which are constantly drilling into trees to lay their eggs) are able to gain a foothold within the tree's cambium because the tree doesn't have enough energy to respond with its sappy natural defense system, and the hungry larvae further weaken the tree. Fungal and bacterial

spores brought into the tree on the beetles' backs start decomposing the tree from the inside out. In its weakened state, many years after the initial windstorm, the tree finally succumbs to the multitude of factors. It dies, becomes a snag, and the cycle continues.

Forest management (logging, grazing, and fire suppression) and climate change are changing the way these death factors interact, accelerating some of them from normal to epidemic levels. Added stress from prolonged droughts, more severe fires from fire suppression and heat waves, more beetles from warmer winters, and large areas converted to a simplified forest structure with just one or two tree species all mean our forests are more susceptible to large-scale epidemics and unnaturally severe disturbances. Restoration of natural fires—and of forest diversity and structure—will hopefully help keep death in the forest in balance.

Evidence of bark beetles scars this snag in central Oregon.

The trail starts out from the parking area traveling through a stand of impressive ponderosa pines three feet in diameter with furrowed orange bark and thick twisted arms. It skirts the edge of logged private land to the right and can be quite faint—look for silver markers on the trees if you lose track. The ground below this open canopy bursts with sunflowers, larkspur, and a ceanothus groundcover. Large Douglas-firs are mixed in, wearing colorful lichen on their trunks.

In 0.3 mile, you'll pass the first of a series of moist meadows filled with cornlily and aspen, and in 0.4 mile reach the edge of North Fork Augur Creek. The pines here on the meadow edge are smaller and more dense than on the first part of the trail, but some giants dot the forest as you continue through a mix of dense and more open, wetter, and drier areas paralleling the North Fork as it meanders through the forest edge. A grove of aspen at three-quarters of a mile highlights this tree's tendency to sprout clones around an ancient individual.

At 0.9 mile, an unmarked but obvious trail junction poses a dilemma: continue ahead on the trail through an obstacle course of fallen lodgepole pines (making it nearly impossible to follow) or chart a different course. I recommend that you turn right at this junction to where the track quickly ends in a large meadow containing North Fork Augur Creek. This lovely wide-open area ringed in aspen affords views of the surrounding low ridges covered in giant pines and is filled with the colorful blooms of larkspur, camas, buttercup, and other flowers. The oasis attracts deer and elk, songbirds, raptors, and even sandhill cranes.

A wildflower-filled meadow along North Fork Augur Creek draws wildlife and offers views of Deadhorse Rim.

Explore and enjoy the edges of this unique and beautiful place before heading back the way you came.

If you choose instead to attempt to continue on the trail before turning around, the junction of the Dead Horse Rim Trail and Cache Creek Trail (which follows Augur Creek) can be reached in another third of a mile. The large pines continue up the slope along both of these trails for a while as they climb toward the rim, but as you gain elevation the skeletal ghosts of lodgepole pines take over.

73. COTTONWOOD MEADOW LAKE

DISTANCE: 3.5-mile loop
TRAILHEAD LOCATION: 42.2811°, -120.6486°
STARTING ELEVATION/ELEVATION GAIN: 6200 feet/420 feet
DIFFICULTY: Easy
SEASON: Summer through early fall, access dependent on snow
FOREST TYPE: Mixed conifer, quaking aspen

PROTECTIONS: No specific protection from logging
MANAGEMENT: Fremont-Winema National Forest
NOTES: No restrooms at trailhead but available at nearby recreation day-use area; no parking fee or permit required

GETTING THERE: From the town of Bly, head southeast for 20 miles and turn left onto paved Forest Road 3870. Drive 5.6 miles on FR 3870 to the entrance of the Cottonwood Meadow Lake Recreation Area. Just before the entrance sign and where FR 3870 turns to the right, turn left into the trailhead parking area.

The drive into the mountains from the Sprague River valley toward Cougar Peak and Cottonwood Meadow Lake winds up the Howard Creek drainage and offers views of the rocky ridges characteristic of the area. The lake sits in a depression at the base of Cougar Peak and offers quiet camping among giant ponderosa pines; an abundance of waterfowl, bald eagles, ospreys, and elk; and aspen-filled meadows. An outbreak of pine beetles led to the mortality of some of the landscape's lodgepole pines and to subsequent "salvage" logging of their remains along the entrance road to the campground.

The loop trail around Cottonwood Meadow Lake begins by climbing through a mixed conifer forest of grand fir, Douglas-fir, and ponderosa pine without many big old trees, a result of past high-grade logging. Hop across a small, boulder-filled stream lined with greenery and continue on, traversing the side of a hill that drops off steeply to the right. Wildflowers—including paintbrush and sunflowers—grow among scattered boulders and pines, and you can catch glimpses of the lake and surrounding peaks.

Between half and three-quarters of a mile, the trail passes in and out of cool, shady fir forest patches and more open ponderosa stands, some large Douglas-fir and pine specimens standing out among the younger trees.

At 0.8 mile, cross a wildflower-filled meadow, with aspen and large ponderosa pines, and then descend toward Cougar Creek, lined with aspen and willow. Hop across and continue through a forest with some stately pines, the understory crowded with young grand fir. Not far before

Pine- and aspen-lined Cottonwood Meadow Lake offers quiet camping and a pleasant loop hike.

the 1-mile mark, cross an old road and pass a trail junction where a left turn would take you up Cougar Peak. Continue straight ahead and climb again through a younger mix of trees (the big pines were logged here too), then gradually descend again, passing some white and lodgepole pines before reaching an old roadbed that parallels a fence enclosing a large aspen meadow.

At about 1.4 miles, leave the road to take the trail to the left and climb through lodgepole pines past another junction (this one leads to the right and to a campground area near the lake), where you stay to the left. Crest a ridge far above Cottonwood Creek, with young grand firs and tall Douglas-firs and ponderosas, and then descend to the creek for a quarter mile. Just shy of 2 miles, you'll reach another old road: the Cottonwood Creek Trail that heads to the left. Don't turn, but find a place to cross the fast-flowing creek here—a log may be required at high water—and

continue through white, lodgepole, and ponderosa pines beginning to reach maturity.

At 2.3 miles, a long narrow meadow stretches ahead, with flowers blooming in early summer, young firs filling in the edges, and a few fat ponderosas. At the far side of the meadow, cross a wet area and enter a forest with bigger trees. Cross another old road to stay on the trail and traverse a dry bench with nice big pines and an open understory, then follow a riparian area to the left and switchback down to reach a trickling creek that drains a series of wet meadows, crossing on rocks and logs.

Switchback up on the other side, parallel a road, and then at just under 3 miles, the trail meets the side road that enters a group camp area to the right. Turn left on the side road and then right to follow FR 3870, cross Grizzly Creek, and hike about half a mile to reach the road you drove in on. Turn left, and then right into the parking area to complete the loop.

NORTHERN BLUE MOUNTAINS HIKES

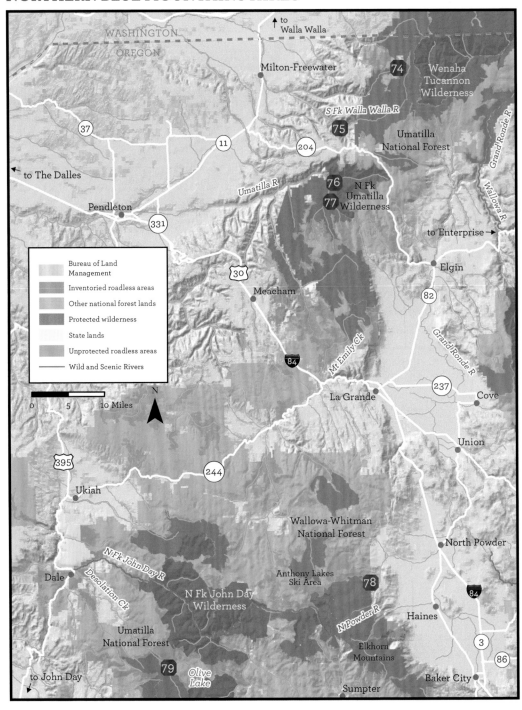

WASHINGTON
OREGON

to
Walla Walla

Milton-Freewater

74

Wenaha
Tucannon
Wilderness

S Fk Walla Walla R

37

11

204

75

Umatilla
National Forest

Grand Ronde R

to The Dalles

Umatilla R

76
77

N Fk
Umatilla
Wilderness

Wallowa R

Pendleton

331

to Enterprise

Elgin

30

82

Meacham

Mt Emily Ck

84

La Grande

237

Cove

Union

395

244

Ukiah

Wallowa-Whitman
National Forest

North Powder

Dale

N Fk John Day R

Desolation Ck

N Fk John Day
Wilderness

Anthony Lakes
Ski Area

78

N Powder R

84

Haines

Umatilla
National Forest

79

Olive
Lake

Elkhorn
Mountains

3

86

to John Day

Sumpter

Baker City

Legend:
- Bureau of Land Management
- Inventoried roadless areas
- Other national forest lands
- Protected wilderness
- State lands
- Unprotected roadless areas
- Wild and Scenic Rivers

0   5   10 Miles

N

NORTHERN BLUE MOUNTAINS

Remote and largely unknown even to Oregonians, the Northern Blues—the northernmost region of the Blue Mountains—stretch into Washington within the Walla Walla and Wenaha River drainages. The region, as defined here, includes parts of the Wallowa-Whitman and Umatilla National Forests from the Oregon-Washington border south roughly to west of Baker City. Interstate 84 runs diagonally through the middle in the Grand Ronde Valley. Rivers here all flow to the Columbia, some like the Umatilla and Walla Walla more directly and others like the Grande Ronde via the Snake River.

Forests in the Northern Blues vary dramatically based on soil, aspect, slope, and moisture. The deeply dissected ravines and dry plateaus characteristic of the landscape mean that forests are generally found in the bottoms of ravines where streams harbor moisture and in stringers where seasonal moisture is captured. A warm south-facing slope might be nearly barren, with grasses and a few scattered ponderosa pines, while a north-facing slope on the other side of the ravine and along a stream might be a closed canopy of Douglas-fir, white fir, and larch. At higher elevations, lodgepole pine are found in mixed conifer forests too.

This region has some of the wildest areas left in Oregon, with vast intact forests in and surrounding the protected wilderness of the Wenaha-Tucannon,

The Elkhorn Mountains form a rugged portion of the Northern Blues.

North Fork Umatilla, and North Fork John Day. Few roads penetrate these strongholds, and the human population is low. The secluded nature of this region means there is an abundance of wildlife. Deer and elk thrive, Oregon's small population of moose can be found northwest of La Grande, and it is here that wolves are expanding from their original repopulated area in the Wallowas.

The forests north of I-84 in this region are generally more moist, as they capture wet air that flows up the Columbia River. Outside of designated roadless areas and wilderness, these moister, more productive forests have been heavily logged, and a fair amount of privately owned timberland adjacent to the national forests continues to be clear-cut. To the south, the Greenhorn and Elkhorn Mountains—subsets of the Blues—dominate the landscape. The heart of these wild, glacier-carved mountains is protected in the North Fork John Day Wilderness, and additional wild forestlands march across Elkhorn Ridge and to the south.

74. NORTH FORK WALLA WALLA RIVER

DISTANCE: 4.4 miles round-trip
TRAILHEAD LOCATION: 45.9416°, -118.0016°
STARTING ELEVATION/ELEVATION GAIN:
4700 feet/1100 feet
DIFFICULTY: Difficult
SEASON: Early summer through fall, access dependent on snow
FOREST TYPE: Mixed conifer
PROTECTIONS: Inventoried roadless area
MANAGEMENT: Umatilla National Forest
NOTES: No restroom at trailhead; no parking fee or permit required

GETTING THERE: From downtown Walla Walla, Washington, follow Mill Creek Road east out of town to the junction with US Highway 12. From here, continue on Mill Creek Road 11 miles to where the pavement ends; then at 14 miles turn right at Tiger Creek Road (Forest Road 65). Cross Mill Creek and start to climb, entering the Umatilla National Forest in 1 mile and getting spectacular views across Tiger Creek's canyon and of roadside wildflowers as you go up.

Seven miles up Tiger Creek Road, you'll find a convergence of forest roads; continue on FR 65

A mix of tree species lines the trail leading down the North Fork Walla Walla River. *(Photo by Jean Jancaitis)*

over the crest of the ridge and then take the first right onto FR 6512. Travel 1 mile on this rough road (high-clearance vehicles recommended) and park in a wide gravel pullout where the road makes a sharp turn to the right. There is more parking at the gate to FR 6520 just past this point as well.

Out of the way and far from large population centers, the trail that follows the upper reaches of the North Fork Walla Walla River is a great way to experience an ancient mixed conifer forest that supports thriving populations of elk, small carnivores, and even moose. The forest here hasn't seen a large-scale disturbance in a few hundred years—neither fire nor logging—as it is part of a large protected roadless area. It is used by motorized vehicles, so be aware.

The trail begins by descending the northwest-facing slope, with the river on the right below it—you'll catch occasional views of the stream but mostly just hear it burbling through the trees. A mix of large grand fir, Engelmann spruce, and Douglas-fir trees forms a discontinuous, fairly open canopy, with old rotting snags throughout the forest. Look for occasional giants—five to six feet in diameter—survivors of a long-ago disturbance that led to the establishment of the younger generation of trees. Areas of dense young fir sprouts; shrubs like salmonberry, elderberry, and oceanspray; oodles of down logs; and forest wildflowers form the complex layers of the lower canopy and forest floor.

After a little less than a mile, the trail crosses the river—use a log, or rocks at lower water, as there is no bridge. Climb to the slope on the opposite side of the river, taking in views of the narrow riparian area and floodplain below to the left down a mellow slope. Above to the right, the hill rises more steeply and the trail skirts the edge of this drier forest type with a more open canopy and meadow wildflowers. At the 2.2-mile point the trail comes out at a well-used unofficial campsite—a clear turnaround point.

75. SOUTH FORK WALLA WALLA RIVER

DISTANCE: 9 miles round-trip
TRAILHEAD LOCATION: 45.8306°, -118.1687°
STARTING ELEVATION/ELEVATION GAIN: 2100 feet/400 feet
DIFFICULTY: Moderate
SEASON: Early spring through late fall
FOREST TYPE: Mixed conifer

PROTECTIONS: Area of critical environmental concern; inventoried roadless area
MANAGEMENT: Vale District BLM, Umatilla National Forest
NOTES: Restrooms at trailhead; no parking fee or permit required. Motorcycle and horse use can be heavy, especially on weekends in the fall during hunting season.

GETTING THERE: From Oregon Route 11 in the town of Milton-Freewater, follow signs for Harris County Park, turning east on Main Street and then left (east) on 15th Avenue. This turns into Walla Walla River Road for 4.5 miles until it forks; then turn right to follow South Fork Walla Walla Road for a total of just over 12 miles to Harris Park. About three-quarters of a mile past the park, the road turns to gravel and then ends at a BLM parking area by a bathroom after a total of 13 miles.

The South and North Forks of the Walla Walla River originate just south of the Washington border and west of the vast Wenaha-Tucannon Wilderness. In fact, these headwaters are part of a large roadless forest complex adjacent to the wilderness, including the Mill Creek watershed to the north and the majority of both forks of the Walla Walla. Just below the confluence of the south and north forks lies a two-thousand-acre designated area of critical environmental concern managed by the Vale District BLM. The trail—heavily used by motorcycles and horses—heads 3 miles through this area, a mix of private lands, and into the Umatilla National Forest.

The trail begins by following the riverside road through a gate and then crosses a bridge. The trail (really more like a road in many places, with heavy rock and muddy ruts) follows the river, going up and down a bit from open hill slopes to the riparian area. The forest is mixed in age and species, with ponderosa pine, Douglas-fir and white fir, and riparian hardwoods. This walk up the South Fork Walla Walla perfectly illustrates how warmer, south-facing slopes are more open and dominated by pines, while cooler, north-facing slopes support denser, more mixed conifer forests.

While many trees in this forest are on the small side, big Douglas-firs and ponderosa pines appear periodically along the way. The fast-moving river itself is quite lovely as well—with braided channels, big gravel, and down wood. The banks are lined with shrubs, water birch, and scattered tall cottonwoods.

Water birch trees, rare in Oregon, can be found along the South Fork Walla Walla River.

At about 2.5 miles, cross a bridge and continue into an area with more pine. In general, the forest gets older, more structure-rich, and more diverse as you progress along the trail. At 2.8 miles, climb to a nice view and then reach an old, busted-up cabin at a trail junction near some big firs. The trail then passes through a stretch of private land, with some evidence of logging, and a series of houses and cabins where it can be quite muddy.

After about the 3.5-mile point when you've passed the last cabin, you'll enter Umatilla National Forest and the forest and trail become wilder again. A mix of fir, Engelmann spruce, yews, and tall shrubs makes for a diverse natural (though not incredibly old) forest. At 4 miles, ponderosa pines march down the hillside from the left into this stand. Towering cottonwoods line the riverbank here.

At about 4.4 miles, you'll reach a junction with the Bear Creek Trail. On your return, it's worth exploring up Bear Creek a short way. For now, continue on the South Fork Trail. You'll pass through a dense riparian area dominated by alder and get views of the deepening canyon

before reaching the river's edge at 4.5 miles. Turn around here and retrace your steps.

When you arrive back at the junction with the Bear Creek Trail, you can extend your hike by heading up Bear Creek. You'll be treated to a really wonderful forest of tall pines and shrubs, with a mix of younger developing forest stands as well. This trail goes fairly steeply uphill, and unless you are planning a multiday trip, it's best to turn back after a third of a mile or so. Return to the South Fork Trail and turn right to return to the trailhead.

76. NORTH FORK UMATILLA

DISTANCE: 5.8 miles round-trip
TRAILHEAD LOCATION: 45.7267°, -118.1857°
STARTING ELEVATION/ELEVATION GAIN:
2420 feet/480 feet
DIFFICULTY: Moderate
SEASON: Spring through late fall, access dependent on snow

FOREST TYPE: Mixed conifer, ponderosa pine
PROTECTIONS: North Fork Umatilla Wilderness
MANAGEMENT: Umatilla National Forest
NOTES: Restrooms at trailhead; no parking fee or permit required

GETTING THERE: From Pendleton, drive east 7 miles on Interstate 84 and take exit 216. Go left (north) for 2 miles to the blinking stoplight and turn right at this intersection onto Mission Road. After 1.7 miles turn left onto Cayuse Road, following signs for Bar M Ranch. Travel just under 16 miles and turn right onto Bingham Road (County Road 900).

From Walla Walla, Washington, or Milton-Freewater, Oregon, take Oregon Route 11 south of Milton-Freewater about 12 miles to just past the Athena junction and turn left on Pambrum Road. Travel 5 miles to the road's end, turn left onto Spring Hollow Road, and go 6 miles. Turn left onto Bingham Road (CR 900).

Cross the railroad tracks on Bingham Road and follow it for 12 miles of paved and another 2.6 miles of gravel road, following first the railroad tracks and then the North Fork Umatilla River. At the national forest boundary, the road becomes Forest Road 32, which you follow for another half mile and then bear left (don't cross the bridge to the right) into the Umatilla Forks Day-Use Area. Pass a restroom and continue to the trailhead with plenty of parking at the end of the road.

The North Fork Umatilla Wilderness, protected in 1984, is twenty thousand acres of steep rugged canyons carved by the North Fork Umatilla River, Buck Creek, and many side drainages that meander to a plateau at 5000 feet. This area typifies northeast Oregon's canyon country in many ways: the cooler, moister north slopes are heavily forested with a mix of conifers, while warmer, drier south slopes support grasslands and ponderosa pine. Giant trees are often found concentrated in the canyon bottoms—which is why the North Fork Umatilla River and Buck Creek Trails are so delightful.

The North Fork Umatilla River Trail starts out in a healthy, cow-free riparian area with ample evidence of beavers. Alder, cottonwood, water birch, and dogwood are found here, while the views across the river to the south are of a diverse larch, pine, and fir forest. As it continues, the trail showcases the diversity of this wilderness—from mixed conifer forests to sparse pine grasslands, and streamside wetlands to wildflower-laden rocky outcrops—as it rolls up and down along the north side of the river canyon, climbing gradually.

Patches of younger forest with a lot of low shrubs, which likely had localized disturbance events, are interspersed along the trail. Look for tall snags indicating there may have been a fire or a localized disease patch. In places, such as at about 1.4 miles, the forest gets quite dense in the flatter areas next to the river. These areas have a closed canopy—large Pacific yews draped in moss and lichen and moisture-loving Engelmann spruce trees with their flaky gray-scaled bark. Several creek-crossings, as well as springs, mean there are patches of wet, muddy areas on the trail.

Where the trail climbs to viewpoints of the river below, look for logjams forming pools as well as other habitat for native fish. From these high points, you can also get good views of the surrounding plateaus and their much more open grassland habitat. At about 2.4 miles, you'll enter a forest with the biggest Douglas-firs and nicest old forest structure yet. This continues as you cross two small ravines, where there are tall snags and old trees with plenty of character.

Pacific yew trees are found in moist streamside areas in the North Fork Umatilla Wilderness.

As you approach Coyote Creek, which you reach at 2.9 miles, a side trail to a campsite is on the right. At the creek-crossing, you'll find some giant (twenty-inch-diameter) Pacific yew trees. The forest here is lovely—draped in lichen with a mixture of spruce, yew, alder, and tall shrubs along the creek. It is a great place to rest before heading back to the trailhead.

If you'd like to continue for a longer, more difficult hike, cross Coyote Creek on logs and continue for another 1.5 miles until the trail makes a sharp turn away from and above the river, climbing up to the top of Cougar Ridge with views of the whole drainage and a high plateau of open grassland and pine.

Wildlife: Shapers of Their Habitat

Many wildlife species depend on certain structures, vegetation, and foods in a forest in order to survive. Bears depend on rotting logs filled with insect larvae for winter sustenance; elk depend on openings in the forest that get more sunlight and grow more of the plants they eat; and bats depend on crevices within or behind bark on slowly rotting snags for roosting during the day.

But just as wildlife species depend on the structures and functions of ancient forest ecosystems, so too are these forests shaped by the wildlife that inhabit them. Some alterations are small scale. Cougars leave their mark by shredding the bark on small trees, shaping them for decades. Woodpeckers hollow out cavities in snags that later serve as nesting sites for any number of critters. Beavers cut streamside trees for their dams and food, creating wetland habitat for shrubs, waterfowl, and fish.

But some of the smallest forest dwellers can play an outsized role in shaping the whole forest. Take the flying squirrel, which lives in moist forests in western Oregon. These nocturnal rodents have a real taste for truffles—the subterranean fruit of mycorrhizal fungi (see "Forest Soil—More Than Dirt" in the Upper Willamette and McKenzie chapter). It digs them up and eats them, and as they pass through their system, the reproductive spores of the fungi end up spread all over the forest. Not only that, a northern spotted owl might eat the squirrel and distribute those spores even farther away, leading to new symbiotic relationships that enhance the growth of the ancient forest the owl also depends on. The food webs of a forest might be complex, but the habitat web can be a real mind-blower.

Beavers shape their environment, gnawing down trees that create habitat for a variety of other plants and animals.

77. BUCK CREEK

DISTANCE: 3 miles round-trip
TRAILHEAD LOCATION: 45.7179°, -118.1860°
STARTING ELEVATION/ELEVATION GAIN:
2440 feet/300 feet
DIFFICULTY: Easy
SEASON: Spring through late fall, access
dependent on snow

FOREST TYPE: Mixed conifer, ponderosa pine
PROTECTIONS: North Fork Umatilla
Wilderness
MANAGEMENT: Umatilla National Forest
NOTES: No restrooms at trailhead; no
parking fee or permit required

GETTING THERE: Follow the directions to the North Fork Umatilla River Trail (Hike 76). Instead of staying left to enter the Umatilla Forks Day-Use Area, continue on Forest Road 32 across the bridge. Pass a campground and go another quarter mile. Just before another bridge, turn left on FR 045 and go a quarter mile to the trailhead and parking at the end of this road.

This second hike in the North Fork Umatilla Wilderness is practically right next door to the North Fork Umatilla River Trail. The Buck Creek Trail follows the other major drainage in the North Fork Umatilla Wilderness, Buck Creek (of course), which flows between Ninemile Ridge to the north and Buck Mountain to the south. It's another marvelous, cow-free streamside trail that truly feels like wilderness.

Large cottonwood trees mark a trail junction near Buck Creek in the North Fork Umatilla Wilderness.

Just after starting on the Buck Creek Trail, you'll come to a trail junction: up and to the left is the Ninemile Ridge Trail, to the right is the Buck Mountain Trail, while the Buck Creek Trail continues straight ahead. The North Fork Umatilla River Trail is on the north side of Ninemile Ridge, but the Ninemile Ridge Trail, unfortunately, does not connect with it—the steep canyon walls simply make this too difficult.

Near this junction, you'll find a small grove of huge cottonwoods, with large ponderosa pines and larch on the slope to the left. Continue ahead on the Buck Creek Trail, which is lined with young fir trees, a variety of shrubs, and scattered large Douglas-fir and ponderosa pines. On the south bank of the creek, the canyon walls are covered in a dense mixed conifer forest

where larches stand out in the autumn. After a half mile, you'll enter a moist forest stand of three-foot-diameter Douglas-firs and big Pacific yews, with a dense canopy and an understory of ferns. As you continue, you'll pass more of these flat, moist areas on the creek side of the trail, with patches of tall pines (living and dead) on the uphill side.

The trail alternately travels along the edge of rocky, open slopes with interesting formations and through drier pine stands. Look for some especially large ponderosa pines with a cluster of fat larch snags at about 1.4 miles. The trail continues 3.5 miles, rolling up and down, to the Lake Creek Trail, but once you've passed the 1.5-mile point, turn around wherever you like to experience the same forest diversity on the way back.

78. DUTCH FLAT CREEK

DISTANCE: 5.8 miles round-trip
TRAILHEAD LOCATION: 44.9625°, -118.1172°
STARTING ELEVATION/ELEVATION GAIN: 4940 feet/650 feet
DIFFICULTY: Moderate
SEASON: Early summer through fall, access dependent on snow

FOREST TYPE: Mixed conifer, ponderosa pine
PROTECTIONS: Inventoried roadless area
MANAGEMENT: Wallowa-Whitman National Forest
NOTES: No restrooms at trailhead; no parking fee or permit required

GETTING THERE: From Baker City, head north on US Highway 30 toward Haines approximately 10 miles. In Haines turn left and follow Anthony Lake Highway for about 14 miles. The road turns into Forest Road 73 at the national forest boundary; just past the 1-mile mark from this point, turn left onto FR 7307 at a sign for Dutch Flat Creek Trail. Follow this road 1.3 miles to its end (which is only rough for the last half mile) in a large turnaround and the trailhead.

The Elkhorn Mountains, a unique granitic mountain range that looms to the west of the Powder River basin and Baker City, contain the headwaters of the Grande Ronde, North Fork John Day, and North Powder Rivers. The western portion of the range is part of the North Fork John Day Wilderness, which was protected in 1984 in four units totaling 121,000 acres. The eastern face of the range with its ancient and high-elevation forests is part of the massive Twin Mountain Roadless Area but does not have permanent protections.

Leading into the heart of the Elkhorn Mountains, the Dutch Flat Creek Trail climbs through a mix of forest types.

The Dutch Flat Creek Trail provides an intimate look at the heart of this special mountain range. "Diverse" is the best word to describe both the landscape and the forest here. The trail follows Dutch Flat Creek, which feeds the North Powder River and has cut a deep valley between Twin Mountain and Van Patten Ridge, to its source at Dutch Flat Lake. Much of the trail is through intermittent streamside groves of old-growth Engelmann spruce and larch and drier ponderosa pine slopes.

The trail begins among tall, fat Douglas-firs, young firs in the understory, and plenty of snags and down wood. Some lodgepole pine mixed in lets you know you're above 5000 feet. The trail climbs over the first half mile or so up a rocky, dusty section of trail, passing grassy slopes with big ponderosa pines and periodic views to the southeast of Twin Mountain and the Elkhorn Ridge. Dutch Flat Creek's deep, eroding channel appears, though sightings of the creek remain elusive for more than a mile.

As you continue, you'll pass through a stand of lodgepole pine where the trail is lined with grouseberry (look for the tiny but delicious berries in the fall) between 0.8 and 1.2 miles and scattered ponderosa pines in the overstory left from when a fire regenerated the area. At this point, a little over a mile into the hike, you'll hear the creek and finally come to a perfect spot to camp or explore at the creek's edge, just off the trail to the left.

The trail continues west, following (but not within view of) the creek. Pockets of Engelmann spruce, larch, and Douglas-fir start to break up the lodgepole, as do some scattered ponderosa in more open patches along the trail.

After 1.5 miles, the forest gets a decidedly older and more mixed feel to it. It is also filled with life—a multitude of birds, deer, and mammalian predators live here. Closer to 2 miles, the trail approaches the stream again, with a patch of alders and other riparian vegetation for contrast. The trail then crests a rise with a view of craggy peaks through some bigger trees.

Between 2.5 and 2.8 miles, big spruce and Douglas-fir grow downhill near the creek and then march up the drainage to the trail. Past this point, the trail climbs up through an opening and rocky area with huge ponderosa pine and some big Douglas-firs before crossing a clear, fast-running creek flowing down from Van Patten Lake far above. Enjoy this cool, moist riparian area with cottonwood, alder, willow, spruce, and wildflowers.

This creek, just before the 3-mile mark, is a great place to turn around on a day hike, but the trail continues another 4.5 miles to Dutch Flat Meadow and another mile beyond that to Dutch Flat Lake. A steep additional mile of switchbacks takes you to Dutch Flat Saddle and the Elkhorn Crest Trail, with magnificent views and access to longer backcountry trips into the North Fork John Day Wilderness and surrounding wildlands.

79. SOUTH FORK DESOLATION CREEK

DISTANCE: 5.4 miles round-trip
TRAILHEAD LOCATION: 44.8094°, -118.6796°
STARTING ELEVATION/ELEVATION GAIN:
5300 feet/600 feet
DIFFICULTY: Moderate
SEASON: Summer and early fall, access dependent on snow

FOREST TYPE: Mixed conifer
PROTECTIONS: Unprotected roadless area; inventoried roadless area; Vinegar Hill–Indian Rock Scenic Area
MANAGEMENT: Umatilla National Forest
NOTES: No restrooms at trailhead; no parking fee or permit required

GETTING THERE: This is one of the most remote hikes in this guide—it is roughly a one-hour drive from US Highway 395.

From Pendleton, take US 395 south about 60 miles. Between Ukiah and Dale, the highway corridor along Camas Creek is lined with beautiful ponderosa pines. Turn left on Texas Bar Road (Forest Road 55) and drive just under a mile to a bridge over the North Fork John Day River. Turn right here near Toll Bridge Campground and follow FR 10 for 21 miles, climbing up through the North Fork John Day canyon along the way. At a sign for FR 45, turn right and proceed 1 mile to the trailhead—with a pullout to the right and a trail sign and wooden fence on the left.

This trail along South Fork Desolation Creek leads south into the twenty-five-thousand-acre Vinegar Hill–Indian Rock Scenic Area and Greenhorn Mountain Roadless Area. This series of wild ridges on the southeast edge of the North Fork John Day Wilderness bridges the divide between the North Fork (to the north) and the Middle Fork John Day Rivers and features amazing wildflowers, wildlife, views, and diverse forests, though few trails (or roads) grant easy access.

Since this trail begins at 5300 feet, it's no surprise that the forest includes a lot of lodgepole pine. I'll admit to not being a big fan of lodgepole forests—and few of them are featured in this book because they never get to be truly ancient. But, in this case, the mixed nature of this forest—and its age and beauty—make this hike a standout. The trail begins in a stand of nearly pure, tall lodgepole, but Engelmann spruce and larch invade this monoculture pretty quickly. These three tree species make up the forest on most of this hike, and the first example of an old-growth spruce grove shows itself at just over a quarter mile along the trail.

At about a half mile, the trail skirts a rock outcrop and you can hear a stream in this riparian area with more spruce and larch. The trail generally follows South Fork Desolation Creek—often out of view even if nearby—to the south. At about 1 mile, the trail ascends a bit into a grove with some big larches—including some snags and true giants (for larches) at over four feet in diameter with fire scars, shelf fungus, and huge upper branches.

At just over 1.3 miles, take note of some large white fir—a few are over three feet in diameter. This species is also scattered among the forest, though they aren't as conspicuous when they are

Lodgepole pines are mixed with giant larch trees along the South Fork Desolation Creek Trail.

small. The trail winds up and down, passing rock outcrops, some small creeks with wildflowers, and patches of denser forest with Douglas- and white fir and a layered effect. At about 1.7 miles there are some nice big larches—an especially interesting one has a lightning scar and multiple tops. Huckleberry lines the trail. Pass an opening at 1.8 miles with bracken fern and elderberry, a bunch of snags, and some large ponderosa pines upslope.

For the next half mile, the diverse and structure-rich forest continues, with occasional views of rocky slopes and ridgetops nearby. Switchback away from the creek into another drainage, descending into the confluence of this and the original creek drainage in a flat area at about 2.5 miles. The drier slope on the left has more Douglas-fir snags and blown-down trees, and at 2.6 miles, it's easy to descend off-trail through the open larch forest toward a rocky outcrop along the creek. This is a good place to check out the creek, which has a lot of down wood, gravel bars, and some short burnt stumps as evidence of the past forest stand. Follow the creek upstream a little ways and loop back to the trail through the forest in the flat area, turning left to head back the way you came.

The trail goes on another 1.5 miles to the abandoned Portland Mine if you are inclined to check it out.

BLUE MOUNTAINS HIKES

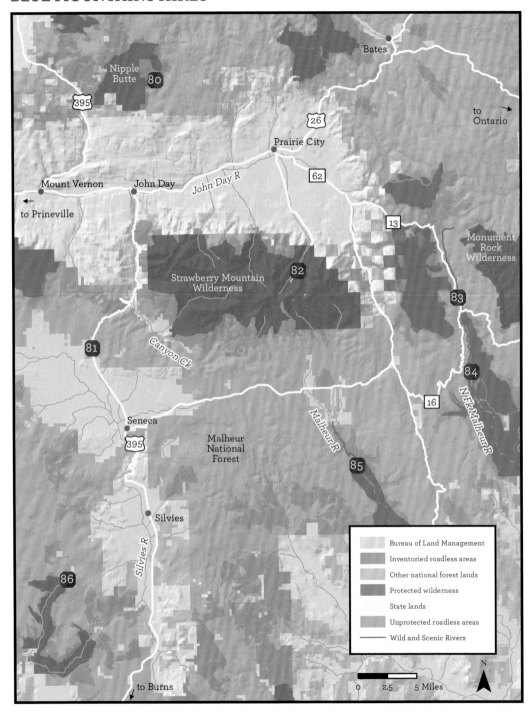

Bates

to
Ontario

Nipple
Butte

80

395

26

Prairie City

62

Mount Vernon

John Day

John Day R

13

to Prineville

Monument
Rock
Wilderness

Strawberry Mountain
Wilderness

82

83

81

Canyon Ck

84

Malheur R

16

Seneca

Malheur
National
Forest

395

N.F. Malheur R

85

Silvies

Silvies R

86

Bureau of Land Management
Inventoried roadless areas
Other national forest lands
Protected wilderness
State lands
Unprotected roadless areas
Wild and Scenic Rivers

N

to Burns

0   2.5   5 Miles

BLUE MOUNTAINS

While the Blue Mountains technically include the mountains throughout central and northeast Oregon, this region focuses on the Malheur National Forest and parts of the Umatilla and Wallowa-Whitman National Forests that are south of the North Fork John Day River and east of the Ochoco National Forest. At this region's heart are the east–west Strawberry Mountains. It also includes the upper Malheur River, the Little Malheur with its headwaters in the Monument Rock Wilderness, the headwaters of the South Fork and mainstem John Day, Canyon Creek flowing from south of the Strawberry Mountains, and the Silvies River, all of which end up in the John Day and flow to the Columbia across a thousand miles of undammed river system. Streams and rivers in this area, typically confined to the canyons they've cut through the plateaus, are fed by springs at the base of these plateaus in marshes and prairies.

The Blue Mountains featured in this region are largely dominated by ponderosa pine forest, but the vegetation ranges significantly based on aspect, slope, soil, elevation, and fire history. Both lower elevations and some plateau tops are dominated by sage and grassland, with scattered junipers and, in places, mountain mahogany. Moister north-facing slopes include a mix of grand fir, Douglas-fir, larch, and Engelmann spruce, while higher elevations have lodgepole pine and subalpine fir. Fire historically played a big role in maintaining the open ponderosa pine forests—burning on average every ten to fifteen years, while fire might only return every one hundred to three hundred years in moister forests.

Ancient ponderosa pines, like this one in the Aldrich Mountain area, are found throughout the Blue Mountains.

There are only two protected wilderness areas in this region—the beautiful and popular Strawberry Mountain Wilderness and the rugged Monument Rock Wilderness. Large unroaded forested areas can be found around Murderers Creek in the South Fork John Day drainage and in the North Fork Malheur River drainage between the Strawberry Mountains and Monument Rock. In between, logging and high grading of forests is evident, but the biggest impacts to the forests in the Blue Mountains are from fire (or a lack of it). Following several large fires since the 1990s, much of this region is in the beginning stages of recovery and regrowth. Unfortunately, natural fires have been complicated here by a history of livestock grazing. In fact, livestock grazing complicates pretty much everything in the area—including hiking in ancient forests.

80. MAGONE LAKE

DISTANCE: 3 miles round-trip (Magone Slide Trail, 1.3 miles round-trip; Magone Lake, 1.7-mile loop)
TRAILHEAD LOCATION: 44.5493°, -118.9130°
STARTING ELEVATION/ELEVATION GAIN: Magone Slide Trail, 5000 feet/650 feet; Magone Lake, 5000 feet/Minimal
DIFFICULTY: Easy

SEASON: Late spring through fall, access dependent on snow
FOREST TYPE: Mixed conifer, ponderosa pine
PROTECTIONS: Partly within unprotected roadless area with no specific protection from logging
MANAGEMENT: Malheur National Forest
NOTES: Restrooms at trailhead; no parking fee or permit required

GETTING THERE: From the town of John Day, go east on US Highway 26 for just over 9 miles, or from Prairie City, travel west on US 26 for 3.5 miles. Turn north on Keeney Forks Road (County Road 18) and follow this paved road for about 10 miles to Forest Road 3620. Turn left, go about a mile, and then turn right on FR 3618 to enter the Magone Lake Day-Use Area. Continue to the lakeshore area to park.

Or, from the town of Mount Vernon west of John Day on US 26, turn north on US 395 and drive 10 miles. Just past the Malheur National Forest sign and milepost 112, turn right on gravel East Beech Creek Lane at a sign for "Magone Lake 10." Follow this washboard-y road through ancient forest and younger managed forests for 10.5 miles, then turn left on FR 3618. In 2 miles, you'll enter the Magone Recreation Area. Continue straight past a gravel road to the left and then turn right to the day-use area and continue down to the lakeshore area to park.

Magone Lake is a popular destination in the summer, with its accessible swimming, fishing, and camping. Scattered park-like groves of big ponderosa pine, Douglas-fir, and larch surround this picturesque, forty-five-acre lake. To the west, eleven thousand acres of unprotected wild forest surround Nipple Butte, with ancient forests in the canyon bottoms. Two short hikes here give a good sense of the area.

Magone Lake is lined with ponderosa and lodgepole pines.

First, from the day-use area, walk back up the road away from the lake to a sign for the Magone Slide Trail. Follow the trail uphill and cross the entry road. The trail then passes open areas with large ponderosa pines and through a denser fir stand that is slated for some logging, which will change the character of this forest but is meant to restore a more natural forest structure after decades of fire suppression.

In just over a half mile, the trail splits in an open area with big pines. To the right, go a short way to view part of the huge landslide that formed Magone Lake in the early 1800s. Mountain mahogany grows on the rocky slopes. Back at the split, continue a short distance to the trail's end at a fenced overlook.

To hike around the lake, start out from the day-use area near the beach and head clockwise on the paved path. Evidence of beaver is common along the lakeshore: look for the pointed tips of chewed lodgepole pine and Engelmann spruce. Just past the campground, pass a wet slough and a boat launch; then walk around the shallow, wide inlet. Around the north side of the lake, ponderosa pines march down the dry slope with juniper and fir mixed in. Down logs float along the lakeshore.

Around the lake on the east side the forest is moister, with Engelmann spruce, firs, lodgepole pine, and larch. Heavily browsed alder sprouts along the shore. On the south end, a jumble of old logs crowds the lake's outlet, where you cross a bridge to finish the loop.

Interpretive signage guides visitors through a stand of ancient ponderosa pines in the Swick Old Growth Grove.

81. SWICK OLD GROWTH GROVE

DISTANCE: 0.7-mile loop
TRAILHEAD LOCATION: 44.2268°, -119.0300°
STARTING ELEVATION/ELEVATION GAIN:
4800 feet/Minimal
DIFFICULTY: Easy
SEASON: Year-round

FOREST TYPE: Ponderosa pine
PROTECTIONS: No specific protection from logging
MANAGEMENT: Malheur National Forest
NOTES: Accessible path; restrooms at trailhead; no parking fee or permit required

GETTING THERE: From the town of John Day on US Highway 26, turn south on US 395 and follow it for about 18 miles. Just north of milepost 18c, at a sign for Swick Old Growth, turn left (east) directly across from County Road 63 (which heads west to Izee/Paulina). The trailhead and parking area are on the right after just 0.1 mile.

This accessible paved path just off the main highway south of John Day offers an easy way to learn about and admire a stand of old-growth ponderosa pine. Though impacted by some logging and fire suppression, it has good examples of natural forest structure.

As you begin this short loop trail near an interpretive sign, tall pines tower overhead and patches of young tree growth populate the understory above the grasses, an illustration of how pine forests can fill in in the absence of regular fire. As you walk, you'll see orange-barked giants—both living and dead—and down logs heavily scattered in the forest. Look and listen for woodpeckers, which find ideal habitat in forests like this. Stumps from past logging of both big and smaller pines is also evident. While interpretive signs along the path address the ecology of pine forests, they unfortunately do not discuss management of the area or possible reasons for the failing health of some of the oldest trees.

82. STRAWBERRY LAKE

DISTANCE: 4 miles round-trip
TRAILHEAD LOCATION: 44.3200°, -118.6726°
STARTING ELEVATION/ELEVATION GAIN:
5750 feet/450 feet
DIFFICULTY: Moderate
SEASON: Early summer through fall, access dependent on snow

FOREST TYPE: Mixed conifer
PROTECTIONS: Strawberry Mountain Wilderness
MANAGEMENT: Malheur National Forest
NOTES: Restrooms at trailhead; no parking fee or permit required

GETTING THERE: From the town of Prairie City on US Highway 26, turn south onto South Main Street. Follow South Main Street for just under a half mile to the junction with Bridge Street at a stop sign next to Depot Park. Turn left and then immediately right onto County Road 60 following signs for Strawberry Campground. CR 60 is paved for 3 miles, then turns to good gravel for another 6 miles before entering the national forest and getting a bit rougher for the last 2 miles. Strawberry Campground and the trailhead are at the end of the road, a total of 11.5 miles from US 26. Look for the trail parking area on the right.

A ridge of the Strawberry Mountains rises above pristine, forest-ringed Strawberry Lake.

The Strawberry Mountains have long been recognized as a special place. Included in the originally designated wilderness areas in 1964, the Strawberry Mountain Wilderness was expanded in 1984 to over 168,000 acres. This east–west range lies south of the John Day valley and dominates the landscape from US 26. A good portion of the wilderness has burned over the last decade, and evidence of past fires and landslides is common. Strawberry Lake, a popular and easily accessible destination, lies in the glacially carved valley on the east slope of Strawberry Mountain's peak, where Strawberry Creek descends on its way north to the John Day River valley.

The beautiful trail climbs gently up through a mixed conifer forest of Engelmann spruce, lodgepole pine, white fir, Douglas-fir, and larch, with huckleberry in the understory. Patches of blowdown and of young regenerating forest are interspersed as the trail gently switchbacks up, with a view through tall snags at the half-mile point. After three-quarters of a mile the trail flattens out in a stand of lodgepole pine and larch. Pass the Slide Basin Trail on the left in just under a mile, then hike through an area strewn with big boulders and huge, ancient larch trees.

When you reach the lake's shore, at about the 1.3-mile mark, turn right to take the loop counterclockwise. Be warned: the views over the lake and the long ridge between the Strawberry and Slide Lakes basin might take your breath away. The forest on the west side of the lake has impressive Douglas-firs, white fir, spruce, and lodgepole,

and big rocks have tumbled down to the lake's shore. Keep an eye out for bald eagles, ospreys, and ducks. Patches of aspen shimmer along the shore, with some alder and mountain mahogany mixed in. At about 1.8 miles, start to cross a series of inlet creeks lined with wildflowers; big spruces grow in the marshy openings along the shore.

As you turn the corner to head up the east side of the lake, the forest changes dramatically. On this side, the slumping hillside is covered with a dense lodgepole pine and larch forest. At 2.2 miles, pass a junction and a sign for Little Strawberry Lake, then pass a series of springs coming out of the hillside. A bit farther on, cross a more substantial stream and follow it down to the lakeshore where a series of campsites are spread out in the open and flat spruce and lodgepole forest, When you're ready, finish the loop and head back to the trailhead.

83. SHEEP CREEK

DISTANCE: 3 miles round-trip
TRAILHEAD LOCATION: 44.2823°, -118.3994°
STARTING ELEVATION/ELEVATION GAIN:
5150 feet/400 feet
DIFFICULTY: Easy
SEASON: Early summer through fall, access dependent on snow

FOREST TYPE: Mixed conifer
PROTECTIONS: Partly within inventoried roadless area
MANAGEMENT: Malheur National Forest
NOTES: No restrooms at trailhead; no parking fee or permit required

GETTING THERE: From Prairie City on US Highway 26, turn south onto South Main Street. Follow South Main Street just under a half mile to the junction with Bridge Street at a stop sign next to Depot Park. Turn left and follow Bridge Street past the local cemetery and as it becomes

No Fire + Cattle Grazing = Unhealthy Forests

Fire historically played a large role in shaping forest ecology, but throughout central and eastern Oregon and especially in the ponderosa pine forest type, natural fire regimes have been altered by human fire suppression and livestock introduction.

Throughout the past century policies to put out natural fires on public lands have largely stopped the low-intensity fires that historically burned every five to fifteen years in dry forest. This approach has allowed small trees that would have been killed by those fires to crowd into open forest areas near old-growth trees, altering the forest structure. Grasses and forest litter accumulated as well. When a fire starts in this altered environment today, it is often much hotter and has more severe impacts because of these added fuels, which can kill trees that historically would have survived.

Compounding the effects of fire suppression, livestock grazing across central and eastern Oregon has had major impacts on natural vegetation on forested public lands. Grazing removes natural vegetation like grasses that historically carried frequent, low-severity fires, making it difficult for this natural fire regime to function. Livestock also have negative impacts on natural streamside vegetation and add unnatural nutrient loads to streams, upsetting the natural system and wildlife habitat, not to mention upsetting trail-users who might not like to step in cow pies.

Restoring a more natural vegetation structure and using prescribed fire to restore a more natural fire cycle would go a long way to address the impacts of human fire suppression. But removing livestock is also essential for the health of these forests as well as for streams, native wildlife, and recreation users.

Domestic cattle have big impacts on native vegetation and stream health in national forests in central and eastern Oregon.

County Road 62. Follow CR 62 for about 8 miles to the junction with Deardorff Road (Forest Road 13). Turn left and follow FR 13 for approximately 12 miles. Watch for the mile markers on the side of the road, and where milepost 15 should be (it is currently missing), pull off to the left at an old gravel road marked 491. Cross the road to find the faint trailhead just north of Sheep Creek.

Glacier Mountain's long eroding ridge lies between the Strawberry Mountains and the Monument Rock Wilderness, and divides the watersheds of the John Day River (to the north) and Malheur River (to the south). The ridge and its forested eastern slope comprise nearly twenty thousand acres of wild, unlogged forest, designated as a roadless area but unprotected as wilderness.

The Sheep Creek Trail follows an old road uphill, with Sheep Creek to the left—which is heard but not seen for most of the hike. The cool, moist ancient forest here is a mix of Engelmann spruce, white fir, Douglas-fir, larch, ponderosa pine, and, as you gain elevation, lodgepole pine. Plenty of snags and down wood, trees hollowed out by rot and woodpecker activity, and a mix of understory

Mixed conifer forests including large Douglas-fir and Engelmann spruce lead into the Glacier Mountain Roadless Area along Sheep Creek.

grasses, wildflowers, and dwarf huckleberry make for a lot to take in as you gradually gain elevation. In a little under a mile, you might notice a logged area to the right through the trees: at this point the trail has yet to enter the designated roadless area.

Pass in and out of wetter and drier forest areas ranging from lichen-draped spruce to open ponderosa pine. At 1.3 miles, an old logging trail crosses the path and you enter an area that was logged in the past but that still has some diversity.

Turn around at the 1.5-mile point and return to the trailhead unless you really want a climb. The trail continues to the top of Lookout Mountain at 5.4 miles, gaining elevation as it transitions to lodgepole pine forest and then into a burned area.

84. NORTH FORK MALHEUR RIVER

DISTANCE: 6 miles round-trip
TRAILHEAD LOCATION: 44.1952°, -118.3810°
STARTING ELEVATION/ELEVATION GAIN:
4500 feet/500 feet
DIFFICULTY: Moderate
SEASON: Early summer through fall, access dependent on snow

FOREST TYPE: Ponderosa pine
PROTECTIONS: Wild and scenic river corridor; inventoried roadless area
MANAGEMENT: Malheur National Forest
NOTES: No restrooms at trailhead, but one at nearby campground; no parking fee or permit required

GETTING THERE: From Prairie City on US Highway 26, turn south onto South Main Street. Follow South Main Street just under a half mile to the junction with Bridge Street at a stop sign next to Depot Park. Turn left and follow Bridge Street past the local cemetery and as it becomes County Road 62. Follow CR 62 for about 8 miles to the junction with Deardorff Road (Forest Road 13). Turn left and follow FR 13 for just over 16 miles to the junction with FR 16. Bear right here and follow FR 16 for 2.3 miles to FR 1675. Turn right on FR 1675 toward North Fork Malheur Campground and take this rough, bumpy road 2.5 miles to a free campground on the river. The trailhead is another mile ahead, in the large clearing at the end of the road.

The North Fork Malheur River begins on the northwest slope of the Monument Rock Wilderness and flows south through a large complex of designated roadless forestlands before emerging from the national forest and meeting the Malheur River. Designated a wild and scenic river for its entire run through national forestlands, the North Fork passes through park-like stands of ponderosa pine and a rimrock canyon. Unfortunately, this designation does not protect the riverside forest from grazing, and evidence of cattle damage to the riparian area is rampant.

The narrow dirt trail crosses the river right away on a log bridge and heads south along the western bank through an open bench with big pines. Watch your step to avoid hard pine cones and soft cow pies. For the first mile the trail isn't very close to the river but eventually alternates being close to the flat floodplain area and on a small ridge above it, rolling in and out of denser lodgepole and more open ponderosa pine stands, with Douglas-fir and white fir mixed in. Views of both sides of the river are of giant ponderosa pines clinging to the slopes.

Ponderosa pines shade the Wild and Scenic North Fork Malheur River.

At about 2.5 miles, larch trees enter the mix, and after you pass through a cattle gate and reach the Crane Creek crossing (at a little under 3 miles), there are even more. Check out the beautiful larch and pine forest along this creek by turning right up this old wagon and jeep road for a quarter mile to a wet meadow. Then head back the way you came.

85. MALHEUR RIVER CANYON

DISTANCE: 4.5 miles round-trip
TRAILHEAD LOCATION: 44.0854°, -118.5779°
STARTING ELEVATION/ELEVATION GAIN:
4750 feet/250 feet
DIFFICULTY: Moderate
SEASON: Late spring through late fall, access dependent on snow

FOREST TYPE: Mixed conifer
PROTECTIONS: Wild and scenic river corridor; inventoried roadless area
MANAGEMENT: Malheur National Forest
NOTES: Restrooms at trailhead; no parking fee or permit required

GETTING THERE: From John Day, head south on US Highway 395 for just under 10 miles and turn left onto County Road 65 (which turns into Forest Road 15) at a sign for Wickiup Campground. Follow this paved road 13.6 miles, then turn left onto FR 16 toward Logan Valley.

From Burns, head north on US 395 to the town of Seneca. Turn right on FR 16. Continue straight at the intersection with FR 15 after 9.5 miles.

A little over 5 miles east of the intersection of FR 15 and 16, just before you get to Logan Valley, turn right just east of milepost 16 onto FR 1643. Follow this wide, flat gravel road for 8.7 miles; then take the left fork onto FR 1651 toward the Malheur River. Cross Dollar Basin and then descend the bumpy road—a total of 1.2 miles—to the trailhead and Malheur Ford. It's a total of 9.9 miles from the FR 16 turnoff.

If you want to start at the other end of the trail and leave a shuttle at the Malheur Ford Trailhead, return to FR 1643, turn left, and drive to Hog Flat, another 6.2 miles. Turn left on FR 142 and cross a sagebrush plateau for 1.3 miles to the road's end and trailhead.

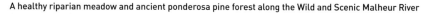

The Malheur River Trail begins about 5.5 miles from the river's headwaters, at the Malheur Ford, and heads downstream past steep canyon walls up to 1000 feet tall. Upstream of the trail, logging and grazing have impacted the forests, but the stretch of designated wild and scenic river downstream of the Malheur Ford really feels wild. The deep river canyon, healthy riparian vegetation, and lack of cows make the hike much more pleasant than some of the other riverside trails in this region.

The forest along the trail is dominated by big lodgepole (by lodgepole standards) and ponderosa pines and Douglas-firs, while also illustrating a lot of age, species, and structural diversity in the understory. After following close by the river for nearly a mile, the trail then gradually climbs to

A healthy riparian meadow and ancient ponderosa pine forest along the Wild and Scenic Malheur River

a bench covered in big ponderosas, many with burn scars at their base. Then you descend again and cross Miller Flat Creek, where larch becomes more dominant. Between 1.3 and 1.5 miles the trail passes through the toe of a lava rock slope, with huge Douglas-firs and a riparian zone dominated by red-twig dogwood and alder.

Then it's a climb to a more rocky and steep section of trail that goes up and down, crosses a few rocky slide areas, and passes a big outcrop with views of the canyon. Finally the trail descends again, crossing another small drainage, and at 2 miles you land in a beautiful stand of ancient larch trees. I recommend walking another quarter mile past the 2-mile mark to enjoy this stand before heading back.

This trail continues another 6 miles to its southern trailhead on top of an arid plateau above the canyon at Hog Flat. If you're able to do a car shuttle, you could start at this southern end (to descend, rather than ascend, the steep drop into the canyon) and hike the whole trail.

86. MYRTLE CREEK

DISTANCE: 5 miles round-trip
TRAILHEAD LOCATION: 43.9565°, -119.0793°
STARTING ELEVATION/ELEVATION GAIN: 5380 feet/700 feet
DIFFICULTY: Moderate
SEASON: Early summer through fall, access dependent on snow

FOREST TYPE: Ponderosa pine
PROTECTIONS: Inventoried roadless area
MANAGEMENT: Malheur National Forest
NOTES: No restrooms at trailhead; no parking fee or permit required

GETTING THERE: From US Highway 20 in Burns, turn north on US 395 and go a little over 15 miles to Forest Road 31 and turn left. Follow FR 31 just over 13 miles and turn left at a sign for Myrtle Creek Trail on FR 226, just before the creek-crossing. The road ends at the trailhead parking area in 0.2 mile.

From John Day, head south on US 395 through the town of Seneca and then 6 more miles. Turn right (west) on FR 37 at a sign for Silvies Valley Ranch. The road is paved for about 7 miles, then continues as a good gravel road along Camp Creek and through grazed meadows. In just under 13 miles, take a hard left to stay on FR 37 when you reach the intersection of FR 37 and FR 31. Stay straight (left) at the next intersection to take paved FR 31 where a sign says "Myrtle Creek, 6 miles." After 5 miles, you'll look down into Myrtle Park Meadows and descend to cross Myrtle Creek. Just after this crossing, turn right onto FR 226 at a sign for Myrtle Creek Trail, which ends at the trailhead parking area in 0.2 mile.

There are nearly twelve thousand acres of wild, forested lands surrounding Myrtle Creek and the Silvies River as it passes south of Burnt Mountain through the Malheur National Forest. The wide river canyons are stretched between tall plateaus that offer a nice scenic backdrop to the pine forests in the bottomlands. Grazing is, unfortunately, everywhere in this part of the national forest—the designated roadless area no exception—and its impacts are keenly felt along the otherwise scenic Myrtle Creek Trail.

Ponderosa pines and willows thrive along Myrtle Creek, at least where cattle are excluded from the streamside.

The trail follows a barbed-wire fence along Myrtle Creek, with an adjacent lodgepole pine forest and a view of a young ponderosa pine forest across the creek. In about 0.3 mile, the trail goes uphill into an older forest with rocky outcrops and big ponderosa pine as Myrtle Creek drops into a deeper ravine. Hike across a bench with a mix of tree species, large pine snags with evidence of beetle and woodpecker activity, and views of the forested slope across the canyon. At 0.8 mile, descend back to the valley bottom, where willows and aspen are thriving, thanks to down logs keeping cows away.

A bit past the 1-mile point, the trail climbs away from the creek again to a bench with many large ponderosa pines, and some young pine thickets, then descends again to a flat meadow beside the creek. Here, at about 1.3 miles, you'll find a gigantic pine measuring four and a half feet in diameter, with impressively thick branches. At 1.5 miles, the trail crosses the creek (if the bridge is out, down logs are fairly easy to cross). Continue across a streamside meadow packed with wildflowers and pass Crane Creek (which is often dry) as the trail closely follows the riparian area.

Just past the 2-mile point, a very faint West Myrtle Trail goes uphill to the right, and you cross West Myrtle Creek on rocks. From here, the canyon walls close in a bit, with crumbling rock piles tumbling down from basalt cliffs. The trail crosses some of these rocky areas, and views up the canyon are wonderful. This point around 2.5 miles is a decent place to turn around, but if the cattle presence isn't too annoying and you'd like to go farther, the trail continues for a total of 8 miles through the canyon and ancient forest.

WALLOWAS HIKES

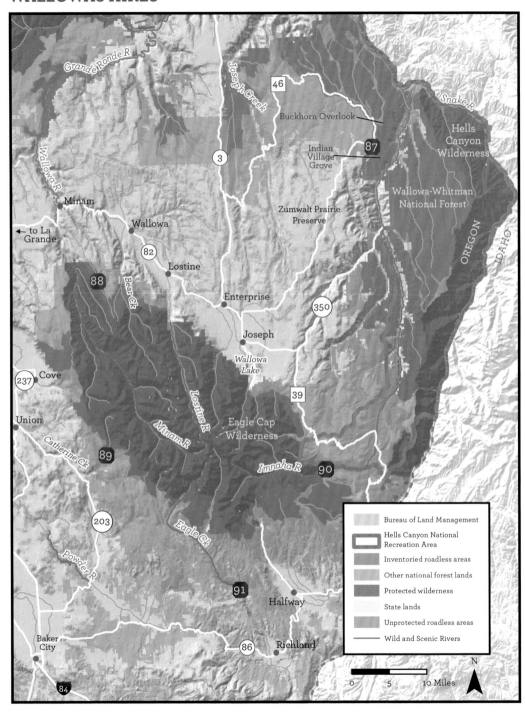

WALLOWAS

The Wallowas region covers the northeastern corner of Oregon, bordering Washington to the north and the Snake River and Hells Canyon to the east, and including the area south of the Wallowa Mountains to the Powder River. Most public lands here are managed by the Wallowa-Whitman National Forest, while the broad Wallowa River valley is privately owned and managed largely for livestock ranching. The expansive Zumwalt Prairie Preserve is managed by the Nature Conservancy for wildlife, native grasslands, and some livestock.

On the north side of the Wallowa Valley, the plateau to the west of Hells Canyon is largely covered in grassland but also has stringers of moist, mixed conifer forest and some spectacular ponderosa pines. Native peoples used this plateau and nearby river crossroads for travel, hunting, and subsistence and left visible signs on the landscape.

South of the Wallowa Valley in the heart of the Wallowa Mountains is Eagle Cap, Oregon's largest designated wilderness, protecting a vast landscape of Oregon's oldest geology with stunning mountain peaks and glacier-carved valleys.

Forests in the Wallowas region and Hells Canyon area often follow moist ravines.

Surrounding Eagle Cap's peaks and isolated ancient trees are beautiful ancient forests along many wild streams that flow from every slope into the Grande Ronde or Snake Rivers—Eagle Creek, Catherine Creek, Bear Creek, and the Lostine, Minam, and Imnaha Rivers.

Depending on the elevation, aspect, slope, moisture, and fire history, the forests found surrounding Eagle Cap might be ancient mixed conifer forests of larch, Engelmann spruce, and white fir; or they might be dominated by ponderosa pine. Streams are lined with a diverse mixture of conifers, cottonwoods, and alders. Higher elevations get into more alpine forest types.

Much of the stunning and rugged scenery of the Wallowas and Hells Canyon area—largely devoid of productive timber-producing forests and beloved by hunters, anglers, boaters, and backpackers—has been protected. However, Eagle Cap and Hells Canyon Wilderness areas have additional surrounding wild forestlands that remain at risk. While most of these are either in designated roadless areas or in wild and scenic river corridors, loopholes and excuses to remove ancient trees from otherwise protected forests, as in the Imnaha River corridor, mean that even some of the state's most beautiful and beloved forests are still threatened.

87. HELLS CANYON NATIONAL RECREATION AREA: CORRAL CREEK

DISTANCE: 3.3 miles round-trip
TRAILHEAD LOCATION: 45.7142°, -116.8554°
STARTING ELEVATION/ELEVATION GAIN: 5200 feet/750 feet
DIFFICULTY: Moderate
SEASON: Early summer through fall, access dependent on snow
FOREST TYPE: Mixed conifer, ponderosa pine

PROTECTIONS: Unprotected and inventoried roadless areas adjacent to Hells Canyon Wilderness
MANAGEMENT: Wallowa-Whitman National Forest
NOTES: No restrooms at trailhead; no parking fee or permit required

GETTING THERE: Follow Oregon Route 82 for 3 miles east of Enterprise and turn left (north) on Crow Creek Road at a sign for Buckhorn Springs. Follow this paved road for 5 miles, then turn right on Zumwalt Road. Follow this road for 2.5 more paved miles, then 22 more on good, well-graded gravel before crossing into the national forest, where you'll start to see stringers of forest. Three miles past the national forest boundary, on what is now Forest Road 46, you'll pass Thomason Meadows, and 2.5 miles past that you'll come to FR 880 on the right. Park on the side of the road at this intersection to find the Corral Creek Trail.

Before or after hiking at Corral Creek, it's worth driving a few miles farther to Buckhorn Overlook, where an amazing view and giant ponderosa pines await. Keep going on FR 46 about 3 miles past FR 880 and turn right on FR 780. Stay right at the first road junction, then keep right at the next two to find Buckhorn Overlook in about a mile.

The drive from the Wallowa Valley to the plateau where the Corral Creek Trail begins isn't exactly forested. For miles and miles, the road crosses the Zumwalt Prairie, an extensive thirty-three thousand acres of native bunchgrass prairie managed by the Nature Conservancy. The trees don't really start until you've entered the national forest, where stringers of forest follow stream drainages, and scattered ponderosa pines populate the plateau and ridges that overlook Hells Canyon.

This trail highlights this landscape type, following Dry Lake Fork to Corral Creek, which flows down off the plateau to the Imnaha River. Part of a complex of designated roadless areas that reach from the ridgetops to the canyon bottom in several places in this corner of the state, these rugged canyons provide ideal habitat for deer, elk, bear, and wolves.

To find the trail, look for cairns—stacks of rocks, some marked with posts—in the meadow southeast of the road junction, and follow them to the east toward dense trees. In a quarter mile, you'll come to a dry riparian area, and the trail begins to follow a small creek drainage. Pacific ninebark, wild rose, and snowberry shrubs line the faint trail. A dry, open slope with scattered ponderosa pines rises to the left, and a dense mixed conifer stand heads downslope to the right.

Pass a mucky stock pond and through a movable fence. The trail, now more obvious, continues to descend gradually through a dense forest of larch, Engelmann spruce, Douglas-fir, and white fir (there's a huge one at about 0.9 mile), while ponderosa pines march down the slope from the left and approach the trail here and there.

At the 1-mile mark, you'll come close to the edge of the moist riparian area, with a good view of the slope uphill, and then come to a spring and an area where multiple trees have blown over or succumbed to disease. In 1.3 miles, the ravine gets steeper and drier before passing through another wetter patch with thimbleberry, elderberry, and a giant four-and-a-half-foot-diameter white fir.

At around 1.4 miles, the forest thins out again, with big ponderosa pines taking over near the trail. A quarter mile farther will bring you to the confluence with Corral Creek, a good turnaround point.

Pines and firs coexist in the stringer forests of the Hells Canyon National Recreation Area as along the Corral Creek Trail.

Indian Village Grove

"Culturally modified" ponderosa pines, peeled by Native people, are found in the Indian Village Grove.

A few miles from the Corral Creek Trailhead is Indian Village. This short loop highlights a fascinating remnant of the way the Nez Perce people used the ancient ponderosa pines in this area: peeling bark to encourage pitch production that was then used for food and medicine. From the parking area for Hike 87, turn right on Forest Road 880 and follow it for 2 miles through lovely pine groves to the trailhead and a sign for Indian Village. Follow the faint trail through the stand to find the few remaining ancient pines.

88. COUGAR RIDGE

DISTANCE: 4.3 miles round-trip
TRAILHEAD LOCATION: 45.4800°, -117.6265°
STARTING ELEVATION/ELEVATION GAIN: 5630 feet/400 feet
DIFFICULTY: Moderate
SEASON: Summer through fall, access dependent on snow
FOREST TYPE: Ponderosa pine, mixed conifer

PROTECTIONS: Inventoried roadless area; Eagle Cap Wilderness
MANAGEMENT: Wallowa-Whitman National Forest
NOTES: No restrooms at trailhead; no parking fee required but self-issued, free wilderness permit required at trailhead

GETTING THERE: This is a lovely hike, but getting here can be rough. Give yourself plenty of time (about an hour from the highway) and drive a high-clearance vehicle that you don't mind getting a bit shaken up. Whether traveling east or west on Oregon Route 82, turn south on Big Canyon Road (Forest Road 8270) just west of milepost 35 and about 1.4 miles east of the turn to Minam River Recreation Area. Follow this rough gravel road. You'll enter the national forest after 9 miles; then, just over 11 miles in, go right to stay on FR 8270. Five miles later (the last 1.5 miles is the worst of the whole route), you'll get to the end of the road at the trailhead and large parking area.

The Cougar Ridge Trail isn't far from the northwestern corner of the Eagle Cap Wilderness, where the Wallowa and Minam Rivers meet in the valley north of the Wallowa Mountains. The first part of the trail is in the Huckleberry Inventoried Roadless Area, which wraps around this northwestern border of the wilderness and offers some protection from the logging that threatens other places just outside the wilderness. The trail then follows Cougar Ridge inside the wilderness boundary, one of a series of north–south ridges that bisects the area, streams flowing in the canyons below.

Ponderosa pines cast shadows on the Cougar Ridge Trail.

The trail starts out at a signboard and wilderness registration station, then continues on an old road that heads uphill through a plantation forest. At a fork about a quarter mile up the road, stay to the right to climb up and around the plantation; then at a trail junction at a half mile, turn right to head northwest and downhill on the Cougar Ridge Trail. The next mile and a quarter of the trail passes through a mixed conifer forest of Douglas-fir, Engelmann spruce, white fir, larch, and ponderosa pine—mostly on the smaller side, but unlogged and developing into a complex, structure-rich forest—with periodic openings, patches of large trees, and a wet seep with more Engelmann spruce.

Between 1.5 and 2 miles, you'll pass some giant ponderosa pines and a large, isolated Douglas-fir before coming out onto the wide-open ridge-top meadow with scattered orange-barked pines, grasses, and wildflowers. The trail gets somewhat faint through the meadow, but the way is obvious.

Views to the west across the Trout Creek canyon are spectacular, but when the ridge begins to peter out at the end of the meadow at just over 2 miles, it's time to turn around unless you plan to make the steep descent to the confluence of Trout Creek and the Minam River. (If you're backpacking, you can make this descent and then hike upstream on the Minam River Trail for more beautiful ponderosa pines in the wild and scenic river canyon.)

On the way back, try walking off-trail up to the top of the ridge in the meadow and then look over to the east. The forest on this east slope of Cougar Ridge, marching down to Cougar Creek, is a dense, moist mixture of conifers—completely different from the dry, open meadow with scattered pines on the ridgetop and western slope.

89. NORTH FORK CATHERINE CREEK

DISTANCE: 8.6 miles round-trip
TRAILHEAD LOCATION: 45.1527°, -117.6172°
STARTING ELEVATION/ELEVATION GAIN: 4200 feet/1450 feet
DIFFICULTY: Difficult
SEASON: Late spring through fall; best wildflowers in July
FOREST TYPE: Mixed conifer

PROTECTIONS: Unprotected roadless area; Eagle Cap Wilderness
MANAGEMENT: Wallowa-Whitman National Forest
NOTES: Restrooms at trailhead; $5 fee or permit required to park; self-issued, free wilderness permit required at trailhead

GETTING THERE: From Interstate 84 in La Grande, take exit 265 and follow Oregon Route 203 south for 14 miles to the town of Union. In Union, turn left on East Beakman Street and follow the signs to continue on Medical Springs Highway (OR 203) for 11 more miles to Catherine Creek Lane, where you'll turn left.

From Baker City, travel north on I-84 to exit 282 for OR 203 toward Medical Springs. After 24 miles, you'll enter the national forest; at 27 miles turn right on gravel Catherine Creek Lane.

Catherine Creek Lane turns into Forest Road 7785 after a half mile. Stay left to stay on FR 7785; about 3 miles later, cross into the national forest (again) and pass a sign for the North Fork Catherine Creek Recreation Area. Travel another 1.8 miles on this rather bumpy road to reach the trailhead. Don't cross the bridge, but park in a big parking area near the restroom.

North Fork Catherine Creek tumbles over boulders through mixed conifers and riparian shrubs.

The campground and trailhead at North Fork Catherine Creek is a popular gateway to the extensive trail system in the southwest part of the Eagle Cap Wilderness. Catherine Creek and its forks flow west and then north into the Grande Ronde. Forests along the North, Middle, and South Forks of Catherine Creek outside of the Eagle Cap Wilderness are not protected, though they are part of roadless wildlands contiguous with the wilderness—they were swapped out of the 1983 wilderness bill protecting Eagle Cap because they had ancient forests the timber industry wanted.

From the trailhead parking area, walk up the road toward the group campground to reach the actual trailhead and wilderness registration—a short eighth of a mile. From there, the trail first climbs up to a bench above the creek, overlooking a lovely canyon with cottonwood, Rocky Mountain maple, Engelmann spruce, and other conifers. Starting at about a third of a mile, you'll cross a series of small creeks and wet areas and then enter a forest of big spruce and white fir, with some lodgepole pine, larch, and Douglas-firs mixed in, with some younger and older areas and a different mix of species in different spots.

At 1.3 miles, climb to a bench above Catherine Creek, pass some rocky outcrops, and take in the view of mountains to the north. As the trail crosses more small creeks along the way, the moist soils of these small drainages support many wildflowers and water-loving shrubs and trees.

At just over 1.5 miles, cross over Catherine Creek on a bridge and climb, with the creek now on the left, up through a denser forest of larch, spruce, ponderosa pine, and fir. Huckleberries line the trail, and you get views across the stream's canyon to the rocky slope on the other side. After 2 miles or so, the trail begins to cross some openings of lava rock dominated by disturbance-loving plants like larch, ceanothus, and fireweed. Less-rocky openings have more wildflowers, with conifer seedlings, alders, and cottonwood along their edges.

Just over 2.6 miles in, you officially enter the Eagle Cap Wilderness, and look down into a long, wet meadow—part of the series leading to the largest meadows farther up the trail. The forest in this stretch is gorgeous, with scattered examples of really huge trees (including a larch that is over four feet in diameter). This mixed conifer forest continues, broken up by the series of meadows, until you reach Catherine Creek Meadows at 4.3 miles—a great place to explore and rest before you head back.

90. IMNAHA RIVER

DISTANCE: 5 miles round-trip
TRAILHEAD LOCATION: 45.1120°, -117.0155°
STARTING ELEVATION/ELEVATION GAIN:
4600 feet/350 feet
DIFFICULTY: Moderate
SEASON: Late spring through fall, access dependent on snow
FOREST TYPE: Ponderosa pine

PROTECTIONS: Wild and scenic river corridor; unprotected roadless area; Eagle Cap Wilderness
MANAGEMENT: Wallowa-Whitman National Forest
NOTES: Restrooms at trailhead; $5 fee or permit required to park; self-issued, free wilderness permit required at trailhead

Forests along the Imnaha River are recovering from the 1994 Twin Lakes Fire.

GETTING THERE: From the town of Joseph, turn north onto Wallowa Street (County Road 350) toward Halfway and Imnaha. Follow this for 8 miles, then turn right on Wallowa Mountain Loop Road (Forest Road 39), also known as Hells Canyon Scenic Byway. This beautiful scenic drive passes through glacier-carved valleys and forests of lodgepole pine, larch, and other conifers. After 28 miles, stay right to follow the river and stay on FR 39. Two miles later, just past Black Horse Campground, turn right on FR 3960 at a sign for Indian Crossing Campground. Drive 9 miles on this paved road; then go a half mile farther on bumpy gravel to the road's end at Indian Crossing Campground. Park in the lot near the restroom before coming to a bridge over the river.

The Wild and Scenic Imnaha River, stretching from the headwaters of its south fork on the eastern side of the Eagle Cap Wilderness to its confluence with the Snake River far to the north, is among the most beautiful river corridors in the state. The ancient ponderosa pines along the last few miles to the trailhead make for a lovely drive, though even in this wild and popular corridor these forests aren't safe: past high grading and recent "fuels reduction" projects have led to the misguided logging of some of the ancient pines that grow here.

The trail heads west from the parking and wilderness registration area through a moist, mixed conifer forest of Douglas-fir, lodgepole and ponderosa pine, and large cottonwoods along the river. Along the first 0.9 mile of trail, the river comes in and out of view, and openings along the way highlight more pure ponderosa pine stands. Stay left at the faint trail split at just over 0.6 mile.

After this, you'll enter part of the vast area that burned in the Twin Lakes Fire in 1994, where shade will start to be at a premium, but scattered living trees and tall, dense shrubs offer some relief at various points along the trail. The fire left patches of living trees but also regenerated the forest—lodgepole and ponderosa seedlings are growing up, snags and down logs add structure and nutrients to the recovering forest, and ceanothus, a nitrogen-fixing shrub, is helping the soil recover. The open vistas across and surrounding the river show the extent of the fire.

Ancient Trees Outside of Ancient Forests

While our focus is on ancient forests—as ecosystems and as dynamic collections of trees—a lot of individual ancient trees are out there too. Forest trees like western redcedar, Douglas-fir, and ponderosa pine can all live to be five to eight hundred or more years old, but many of Oregon's oldest trees aren't found within a forest setting. Instead, whitebark pine, limber pine, curl-leaf mountain mahogany, and other ancient trees might live high in the mountains, scattered among rocky soils with only a few sparse wildflowers or grasses for company. This environment is too harsh to support many trees or to function like a forest, but these tree species can live for a millennium, growing slowly, stunted by snow and wind.

The oldest known living tree in Oregon—estimated to be over fifteen hundred years old—is a limber pine growing in the Wallowas on poor limestone soils. Other species, like western juniper, live across the arid regions of the state, their twisted, ancient forms dotting the landscape.

Some ancient trees use another tactic for long life: clones. Found across eastern Oregon, individual aspen trees may live less than a hundred years, but their root systems can resprout so that a clonal colony can live for centuries. Despite humanity's obsession, trees seem to have the advantage in the quest for immortality.

Ancient whitebark pines grow in harsh conditions at high elevations in the Wallowas and elsewhere. *(Photo by Doug Heiken)*

Enter the Eagle Cap Wilderness at 1.3 miles and continue deeper into the burn through patches of tall live trees and dense, fast-growing pine saplings. Around 1.6 miles, a moister area of tall lodgepole pine, larch, and cottonwood adds interest just before you encounter the rocky debris of an eroding peak to the right. A small stream-crossing at 1.8 miles and meadow just beyond highlight elderberry, ferns, willows, alders, aspen, mountain ash, and wildflowers that thrive in the wetter areas of this landscape. At 2 miles, the trail gets rougher as it follows a wet, rocky streambed uphill.

At a sign for Twin Lakes Trail, follow it to the left and downhill through a stand of larch trees to a flat area by the river. Here you can wade into the icy cold river to cool off and look upstream into the narrow gorge of Blue Hole. Climb up the stairstep rocks to overlook the narrow canyon and peer into the clear blue water below. (If you're lucky, you might even catch sight of spawning salmon as I did in late summer.)

From the top of the rocky area, find the Imnaha River Trail again, turn left, and continue another half mile. The trail ascends between rock walls and past beautiful aspen stands to a stunning view of the wilderness to the west—a good place to turn around, though the trail continues into the wilderness from here.

91. EAGLE CREEK

DISTANCE: 4 miles round-trip
TRAILHEAD LOCATION: 44.8915°, -117.2615°
STARTING ELEVATION/ELEVATION GAIN: 3050 feet/200 feet
DIFFICULTY: Easy
SEASON: Late spring through fall, access dependent on snow

FOREST TYPE: Ponderosa pine
PROTECTIONS: Wild and scenic river corridor
MANAGEMENT: Wallowa-Whitman National Forest
NOTES: Restrooms at nearby campground; no parking fee or permit required

GETTING THERE: From Baker City, head north on Interstate 84 to exit 302 for Oregon Route 86. Drive east on OR 86 to the town of Richland. Turn north at a sign that says "New Bridge 3 miles" at the west end of town. Drive 2.4 miles to New Bridge, and go straight on Eagle Creek Road rather than taking a sharp left in town. Eagle Creek Road is paved for 1 mile but continues on gravel for a total of 7.6 miles from Richland before becoming Little Eagle Road (FR 7735) at a sign that says "Eagle Forks Campground 3 miles." From here, go 2.5 miles and turn left at an intersection with a sign for the campground. Trailhead parking (a few spots) is on the left just before you enter the small creekside campground.

Eagle Creek, designated a wild and scenic river from its headwaters to the national forest boundary just south of the Eagle Forks Campground, flows south from the high peaks of the Eagle Cap Wilderness. The Martin Bridge Trail heads up this scenic stream corridor for several miles starting near the confluence with East Eagle Creek. The forest here is protected in a narrow band by its wild and scenic status, though roadless but unprotected wild forests continue well outside the corridor.

Ponderosa pines line the shore of Eagle Creek, which flows south out of the Eagle Cap Wilderness.

To begin the Martin Bridge Trail, cross a small creek—ironically without a bridge—but it's small enough to hop across. The trail crosses a cattle gate before entering the mixed forest of ponderosa pine, white fir, and Douglas-fir with its rocky and grassy understory. Eagle Creek canyon is lovely, with scattered rock outcrops along the ridges on both sides. The creek itself is clear with large boulders, logjams, deep holes, and fast-flowing riffles—a great example of a mountain stream. The trail, which rolls up and down on the slope beside the creek, offers a nice contrast between the dry slopes with sage, wildflowers, and pines, and the lush streamside shrubs below. You'll cross Holcomb Creek just under a half mile in, then climb back above the creek through some rocky areas.

As the trail passes in and out of the rocky areas, wandering closer to and farther from the creek, signage indicates wildlife habitat—and it sure is: watch out for prairie rattlesnakes in the summer and black bears eating the elderberries near the stream. The ponderosa pines along the trail show the character of older trees but aren't huge, in contrast to the patch of large Douglas-fir trees (mostly snags) at about 1.2 miles.

Just past these, the riparian shrubs—red-twig dogwood, hawthorn, alder, and blue elderberry—get much denser, including in a small tributary's drainage that passes through a wildflower-filled meadow. Past the meadow, the pines get bigger, and the trail becomes a bit narrower on a steeper slope—watch your footing here. At about 2 miles, cross the crumbling base of a large rock outcrop and reach a series of waterfalls that tumble through giant boulders in the creek. This is a great place to take in the views of the pine-filled canyon, have a snack, and head back the way you came.

ACKNOWLEDGMENTS

It takes a village—or a state—to complete a book like this. Many thanks are due to many people in this endeavor, and I'd like to mention some of them here.

First and foremost, this book is dedicated to all those individuals and organizations who helped protect Oregon's forests over the past several decades so there are still ancient forests and hikes to write about. Without the work of pioneering forest advocates who dedicated their lives and careers—or even just a few years—to protecting Oregon's remaining ancient forests, there would be nothing to write about or for any of us to enjoy.

While there are many, many people who deserve this thanks, I'd especially like to honor the legacies of Wendell Wood and Tim Lillebo. Wendell and Tim were two of the longest serving, most dedicated, and most charismatic individuals Oregon's forests and wild places could have asked for. Oregon would have far fewer ancient forests without these tireless forest lovers who dedicated their lives to fighting to protect these places. I am lucky to have had them both as colleagues, mentors, and friends, but Oregon's forests hit the jackpot with these two.

I want to thank the dozens of ancient forest lovers and fans of the original Wendell Wood book who donated funds to support this edition's development, and in particular, Gilian Hearst and Sara Walker for their donations.

Thanks also to those who offered knowledge, information, and opinions about specific places, regions, and the structure and content of the book. I may not have included or heeded everything they offered, but all that advice helped me to craft the final version of this text. Special thanks to Erik Fernandez, Doug Heiken, Andy Kerr, and Sean Stevens.

Thank you to Erik Fernandez for giving me the advice, tutoring, and patience I needed to learn the ins and outs of ArcGIS, and for then doing the bulk of the work and many, many detailed touches needed to produce the maps in this book. Thanks to him, too, for coordinating the work of two stellar volunteers who also spent time developing the maps.

It's hard to bring the forest alive on the page, to capture the lushness and beauty of such wild places—but a host of talented photographers contributed images to this project that did just that. Even if your pictures didn't ultimately appear in the book, thank you for sharing: Mahogany Aulenbach, Brett Cole, Sarah Cuddy, Jim Davis, Jenessa Dragovich, Gary Hale, Doug Heiken, Kurtis Hough, Melissa Hubler, Jonathan Jelen, James Johnston, Katie Kepsel, Brian Kibbons, Tom Kloster, Brizz Meddings, Gary Miller, Steve Miller, Renee Moog, Kelly Morgan, Danielle Nelson, Sue Newman, Shannon Rose, Rick Seymour, Kristian Skyback, John Sparks, Greg Vaughn, and Pamela Winders.

Big thanks to Sarah Cuddy, Erik Fernandez, Melissa Hubler, Jean Jancaitis, Jonathan Jelen, and Jonathan Plummer for their contributions to the trail research and descriptions.

While I explored most of the areas in this book (and many more that were ultimately not included) by myself, I am grateful to the friends, family members, and colleagues who kept me company on some of the hikes. It's nice to not talk only to yourself on the trail, so thanks Eric Anderson, Kate Blazar, Jesse Cary-Hobbs, Erin Chaparro, Marielle

Cowdin, Jason Gonzales, Jeremy Hall, Jean Jancaitis, Jonathan Jelen, Katie Kepsel, Rob Klavins, Heather O'Donnell, Jonathan Plummer, Christine Slaven, Jessica Southwick, the Tribou clan, and Sue Walden (a.k.a. Mom)!

In addition to dozens of campgrounds and the occasional hotel, I also took advantage of the kindness of friends and colleagues for warm, dry places to stay throughout the development of the book. Thanks to Animosa (Kate Blazar), Barking Mad Farm (Rob and Emily Klavins), Marielle Cowdin, Jean Jancaitis and Jonathan Plummer, and Crystal McMahon for your teardrop camper, lawn, or extra room.

Finally, and most importantly, I need to thank my family and dearest friends (yes, *you*) who were so supportive of this endeavor. Knowing that your community of loved ones thinks you're doing something cool, and that you can pull it off, goes a long way. Thank you all for your love, support, questions about how things are going, gentle nudges, and celebratory moments. Special thanks go to my dear Christine and to my husband, Eric Anderson, for their unwavering moral, emotional, and material support for this project. Hopefully you'll all agree that my time away from home and working long hours for many months was worthwhile.

GLOSSARY

ancient forest: A forest that has been in existence for a very long time and that developed naturally after disturbance events without major human influence. Ancient forests typically contain a diversity of tree species and structures including large, old trees, snags and down wood, and a multileveled canopy; provide homes for a diversity of wildlife species in a diversity of habitats; and have healthy soils and streams.

area of critical environmental concern: A designated area that the Bureau of Land Management (BLM) manages with a focus on protecting its important habitat, natural processes, scenic, or other values.

biomass: The amount of living matter in a given area.

canopy: The upper layer of vegetation in a forest, formed by the crowns of trees.

carbon sink: A carbon sink absorbs more carbon from the atmosphere than it emits.

carbon source: A carbon source emits more than it absorbs.

conifer: A type of tree that bears cones and usually has needle-like or scale-like leaves. Conifers are usually evergreen (not losing their leaves all at once each year).

disturbance: An agent that causes change in the vegetation of a forest. A disturbance can be natural—such as a wind or ice storm, disease outbreak, or fire—or human-caused like logging. Disturbances can range in size and impact.

diversity: Biological diversity refers to the combined different forms and types of life in an ecosystem or landscape, as well as the different ecological roles they play in an ecosystem's function and habitats. Generally, more diversity means that an ecosystem is better able to adapt to disturbance.

drinking watershed: A stream or river system and the surrounding lands that drain into it from which people obtain drinking water.

ecosystem: A system of interconnected living things and the physical environment they live within and interact with.

fire regime: The way that fire impacts a certain forest type or area over time, including the fire's severity, intensity, and frequency.

fire suppression: The act or process of putting out or preventing fires from burning.

forest: An ecosystem primarily covered with trees and including other woody vegetation.

forest structure: Components of a forest that result in the distribution of horizontal and vertical layers, including different vegetation layers and sizes, snags, and down wood.

habitat: The natural environment of a living thing; a place where it can survive and thrive, including the physical and biological components of that place.

inventoried roadless area: A large area (usually over five thousand acres) of unroaded, unlogged, and undeveloped national forestland protected from most logging and development under the 2001 Roadless Area Conservation Rule (Roadless Rule).

microclimate: The specific climate of a small area that may be different from that of the general region.

natural forest: A forest, regardless of successional stage, that has grown and developed without significant human interference.

old-growth forest: A mature forest that has reached a structurally complex stage of succession and usually includes large, old trees, snags and down wood, and a multileveled canopy. This complex structure usually develops when the forest is between one and three centuries old. Old-growth trees—large old trees with a complex structure of their own—are one component of an old-growth forest.

plantation: A forest stand that has been planted after logging, often with just one tree species. Also called a managed forest.

prescribed fire: A fire lit and managed by humans for management purposes, to accomplish specific ecosystem or fuel goals.

research natural area (RNA): An area located on national forest or BLM land designated for being a high-quality example of an ecosystem type, habitat, or geologic feature that is managed to allow natural processes to predominate.

riparian: The area on either side of a stream or adjacent to another water body where the soil and vegetation are generally moister than that of the surrounding area.

salvage logging: Cutting and removing dead or dying trees after a fire or other disturbance.

snag: A standing, dead tree.

stringer: A narrow band of forest-covered land usually found in the bottoms of ravines or along stream courses where moisture is harbored in an otherwise arid landscape.

succession: The way that vegetation, structure, and other components of a forest (or other ecosystem) grow and change over time after a disturbance.

understory: The plants—usually younger trees, as well as shrubs, wildflowers, grasses, and ferns—that grow in a forest under the main canopy.

unprotected roadless area: A large area (over one thousand acres) of unroaded, unlogged, and undeveloped national forestland that does not have protection from logging and development under the Roadless Rule or other legal or policy designation.

wild and scenic river: A stream or river corridor designated under the authority of the Wild and Scenic Rivers Act of 1968, usually protecting a quarter-mile buffer on each side of the designated stretch from logging and development.

wilderness: An area designated by Congress under the authority of the Wilderness Act of 1964.

RESOURCES

More information, additional resources, and other content related to this book can be found at www.oregonwild.org /ancientforestsguide.

GOVERNMENT AGENCIES

Federal and state agencies are tasked with the management and enforcement of law on Oregon's public forestlands. These agencies employ experts in forestry, wildlife, botany, cultural resources, recreation, and more.

Additional information about wilderness and wild and scenic river policy and management can be found at www.fs.fed.us/managing-land /wilderness and www.rivers.gov/oregon.php.

BUREAU OF LAND MANAGEMENT

Headquarters for the Oregon-Washington region of the BLM are in Portland. In addition to BLM lands, the BLM also administers the Cascade-Siskiyou National Monument (www.blm.gov/programs/national-conservation -lands/national-monuments/oregon-washington /cascade-siskiyou). Forested BLM areas are found in the following districts (more info at www.blm.gov/oregon-washington):

Oregon-Washington State Office
1220 SW Third Avenue
Portland, OR 97204
503-808-6001

Coos Bay District
1300 Airport Lane
North Bend, OR 97459
541-756-0100

Medford District
3040 Biddle Road
Medford, OR 97504
541-618-2200

Northwest Oregon District
1717 Fabry Road SE
Salem, OR 97306
503-375-5646

Northwest Oregon District, Springfield Interagency Office
3106 Pierce Parkway, Suite E
Springfield, OR 97477
541-683-6600

Roseburg District
777 NW Garden Valley Boulevard
Roseburg, OR 97471
541-440-4930

Vale District
100 Oregon Street
Vale, OR 97918
541-473-3144

NATIONAL PARK SERVICE

Crater Lake National Park
PO Box 7
Crater Lake, OR 97604
541-594-3000
www.nps.gov/crla/index.htm

Oregon Caves National Monument
19000 Caves Highway
Cave Junction, OR 97523
541-592-2100
www.nps.gov/orca/index.htm

OREGON STATE AGENCIES

Oregon Department of Forestry
2600 State Street
Salem, OR 97310
503-945-7200
www.oregon.gov/odf/
For information about state forest and
private forest management

Oregon Parks and Recreation Department
725 Summer Street NE, Suite C
Salem, OR 97301
800-551-6949
http://oregonstateparks.org
For information about Oregon state parks

Travel Oregon
https://traveloregon.com
Oregon's official tourism department

US FOREST SERVICE

Oregon's national forests fall under Region 6
of the US Forest Service. Region 6 headquarters are in Portland. Individual national forests
have more local information—see the relevant
national forest website for links to specific
districts.

Deschutes National Forest
www.fs.usda.gov/deschutes. Headquarters
in Bend, with ranger stations in Crescent and
Sisters

Fremont-Winema National Forest
www.fs.usda.gov/fremont-winema.
Headquarters in Lakeview, with ranger
stations in Bly, Chemist, Chiloquin, Klamath
Falls, Paisley, and Silver Lake

Malheur National Forest
www.fs.usda.gov/malheur. Headquarters in
John Day, with ranger stations in Hines and
Prairie City

Mount Hood National Forest
www.fs.usda.gov/mthood. Headquarters
in Sandy, with ranger stations in Dufur,
Estacada, Hood River, and Zigzag

Ochoco National Forest
www.fs.usda.gov/ochoco. Headquarters in
Prineville

Rogue River–Siskiyou National Forest
www.fs.usda.gov/rogue-siskiyou.
Headquarters in Medford, with ranger
stations in Butte Falls, Cave Junction, Gold
Beach, Grants Pass, Jacksonville, Powers,
and Prospect

Siuslaw National Forest
www.fs.usda.gov/siuslaw. Headquarters in
Corvallis, with ranger stations in Hebo and
Waldport

Umatilla National Forest
www.fs.usda.gov/umatilla. Headquarters in
Pendleton, with ranger stations in Heppner,
Ukiah, and Walla Walla, WA

Umpqua National Forest
www.fs.usda.gov/umpqua. Headquarters in
Roseburg, with ranger stations in Cottage
Grove, Glide, Idleyld Park, and Tiller

Wallowa-Whitman National Forest
www.fs.usda.gov/wallowa-whitman.
Headquarters in Baker City, with ranger
stations in Halfway, Joseph, and La Grande

Willamette National Forest
www.fs.usda.gov/willamette. Headquarters
in Springfield, with ranger stations in Detroit,
McKenzie Bridge, Sweet Home, and Westfir

NATURAL HISTORY GUIDES AND ORGANIZATIONS

Want to learn more about forest ecology as a
whole or any of the individual pieces that make up
a forest? Here are some organizations and other
books that can help you expand your knowledge.

BIRDS AND WILDLIFE

Audubon Society. Find local chapters at
www.audubon.org.

Moskowitz, David. *Wildlife of the Pacific Northwest: Tracking and Identifying Mammals, Birds, Reptiles, Amphibians, and Invertebrates.* Timber Press Field Guide. Portland, Oregon: Timber Press, 2010.

Shewey, John, and Tim Blount. *Birds of the Pacific Northwest.* Timber Press Field Guide. Portland, Oregon: Timber Press, 2017.

EDIBLE PLANTS

Deur, Douglas. *Pacific Northwest Foraging: 120 Wild and Flavorful Edibles from Alaska Blueberries to Wild Hazelnuts.* Portland, Oregon: Timber Press, 2014.

MUSHROOMS

Ammirati, Joe, and Steve Trudell. *Mushrooms of the Pacific Northwest.* Timber Press Field Guide. Portland, Oregon: Timber Press, 2009.

Arora, David. *All that the Rain Promises, and More: A Hip Pocket Guide to Western Mushrooms.* San Francisco: Ten Speed Press, 1991.

Cascade Mycological Society. http://cascademyco.org.

Oregon Mycological Society. www.wildmushrooms.org.

TREES AND PLANTS

Cantor, Cliff. *Trees Pacific NW.* Version 2.0. https://www.treespnw.com/. 2018.

High Country Apps LLC and Oregon State University. *Oregon Wildflowers.* http://www.highcountryapps.com/OregonWildflowers.aspx. 2015.

Jensen, Ed. *Trees to Know in Oregon.* Oregon State University Extension Service. https://oregonstate.edu/trees/index.html. 2010.

Native Plant Society of Oregon. www.npsoregon.org.

Pojar, Jim, and Andy MacKinnon. *Plants of the Pacific Northwest Coast.* Edmonton, Alberta: Lone Pine Publishing, 1994.

Turner, Mark, and Ellen Kulhmann. *Trees and Shrubs of the Pacific Northwest.* Timber Press Field Guide. Portland, Oregon: Timber Press, 2014.

REFERENCES

Cissel, John, and Diane Cissel. *Old-Growth Forest Hikes: Washington and Oregon Cascades.* Seattle: Mountaineers Books, 2003.

Dalton, M. M., K. D. Dello, L. Hawkins, P. W. Mote, and D. E. Rupp. *The Third Oregon Climate Assessment Report*, Oregon Climate Change Research Institute, College of Earth, Ocean and Atmospheric Sciences, Oregon State University, Corvallis, OR. www.occri.net /media/1042/ocar3_final_125_web.pdf. 2017.

Franklin, J. F., et al. *Ecological Characteristics of Old-Growth Douglas-Fir Forests.* USDA Forest Service General Technical Report PNW-118. Portland, Oregon: Pacific Northwest Forest and Range Experiment Station, 1981.

Kelly, David, and Gary Braasch. *Secrets of the Old-Growth Forest.* Layton, Utah: Gibbs Smith Publisher, 1988.

Kerr, Andy. *Oregon Wild: Endangered Forest Wilderness.* Portland, Oregon: Oregon Natural Resources Council, 2004.

Maser, Chris, Andrew W. Claridge, and James M. Trappe. *Trees, Truffles, and Beasts: How Forests Function.* New Brunswick, New Jersey: Rutgers University Press, 2008.

The Oregon Global Warming Commission, Forest Carbon Task Force. www.keeporegoncool.org/home.

Oregon Hikers Forum. www.oregonhikers.org.

Palmer, Tim. *Field Guide to Oregon Rivers.* Corvallis, Oregon: Oregon State University Press, 2014.

Sullivan, William L. *100 Hikes / Travel Guide* series. Eugene, Oregon: Navillus Press. www.oregonhiking.com.

Van Pelt, Robert. *Identifying Mature and Old Forests in Western Washington.* Olympia, Washington: Washington State Department of Natural Resources, 2007.

Van Pelt, Robert. *Identifying Old Trees and Forests in Eastern Washington.* Olympia, Washington: Washington State Department of Natural Resources, 2008.

Wood, Wendell. *A Walking Guide to Oregon's Ancient Forests.* Portland, Oregon: Oregon Natural Resources Council, 1991.

INDEX

ABOUT OREGON WILD

The mission of Oregon Wild is to protect and restore Oregon's wildlands, wildlife, and waters as an enduring legacy for future generations.

Founded in 1974, Oregon Wild is the state's oldest and largest group dedicated to conserving Oregon's public lands and the wildlife that call them home. Across five decades the organization has worked to secure protections for 1.7 million acres of wilderness and almost 1800 miles of wild and scenic rivers. Oregon Wild is the region's leading voice for the protection and restoration of dwindling ancient forests in the Pacific Northwest, Oregon's fragile population of gray wolves, and the wetlands of the Klamath Basin.

OREGON WILD

Oregon Wild keeps Oregon a special place to live, work, and play by harnessing citizen power to protect the public lands and resources upon which we all rely. Using the latest science, a deep knowledge of the Oregon landscape, and expertise in environmental policy and law, the organization strives to ensure that the ecological integrity of Oregon's outdoors is maintained. Through enforcement of federal environmental safeguards and the mobilization of public opinion through media outreach and electronic advocacy, Oregon Wild convinces land and wildlife managers and our elected leaders to protect the place we call home.

Protecting ancient forests is a key part of Oregon Wild history and its future. Starting in the early 1980s, the group—then called the Oregon Natural Resources Council—helped nationalize the ancient forest issue and raised public awareness about the values of old-growth forests. Oregon Wild has advanced protection for millions of acres of old-growth forest habitat through wilderness legislation, the Roadless Rule, the Northwest Forest Plan, and the Eastside Screens. And it has supported campaigns to secure permanent protection of mature and old-growth forests in the Northwest through federal legislation.

Oregon Wild continues to devote significant resources to advocate for the protection and restoration of Oregon's last remaining ancient forests by commenting on logging and other development plans on behalf of its supporters, advancing its commonsense vision for forest management, and holding federal agencies accountable to bedrock environmental laws. The group works to inspire and empower forest lovers through outdoor excursions, advocacy training, and educational programs.

Oregon Wild is supported by more than three thousand donors and twenty thousand activists across the state and nation, relying on donations from individuals to fund the majority of their work. Join in keeping Oregon wild: www.oregonwild.org.

ABOUT THE AUTHOR

GARY HALE

Born and raised among the cornfields and hardwood trees of southeastern Michigan, Chandra LeGue is proud to engage in work protecting and restoring the forests and wildlands of Oregon, her adopted home state.

She earned her BS in biology from Carthage College on the shores of Lake Michigan before moving to Oregon in 1999 to earn her master's degree in environmental studies at the University of Oregon. Eugene has been her home ever since.

Chandra has worked for Oregon Wild since 2003; she promotes policies that protect and restore Oregon's forests. She has led dozens of hikes in the Eugene area for Oregon Wild supporters, and working on this book has given her a great excuse to explore forests farther from home.

In addition to her work at Oregon Wild, Chandra has served on the boards of directors of other nonprofit organizations and tries to give generously to many others. She lives in Eugene with her husband and cats among a yard and gardens that get too little attention but are lovely nonetheless.

MOUNTAINEERS BOOKS is a leading publisher of mountaineering literature and guides—including our flagship title, *Mountaineering: The Freedom of the Hills*—as well as adventure narratives, natural history, and general outdoor recreation. Through our two imprints, Skipstone and Braided River, we also publish titles on sustainability and conservation. We are committed to supporting the environmental and educational goals of our organization by providing expert information on human-powered adventure, sustainable practices at home and on the trail, and preservation of wilderness.

The Mountaineers, founded in 1906, is a 501(c)(3) nonprofit outdoor recreation and conservation organization whose mission is to enrich lives and communities by helping people "explore, conserve, learn about, and enjoy the lands and waters of the Pacific Northwest and beyond." One of the largest such organizations in the United States, it sponsors classes and year-round outdoor activities throughout the Pacific Northwest, including climbing, hiking, backcountry skiing, snowshoeing, camping, kayaking, sailing, and more. The Mountaineers also supports its mission through its publishing division, Mountaineers Books, and promotes environmental education and citizen engagement. For more information, visit The Mountaineers Program Center, 7700 Sand Point Way NE, Seattle, WA 98115-3996; phone 206-521-6001; www.mountaineers.org; or email info@mountaineers.org.

Our publications are made possible through the generosity of donors and through sales of more than 800 titles on outdoor recreation, sustainable lifestyle, and conservation. To donate, purchase books, or learn more, visit us online:

MOUNTAINEERS BOOKS
1001 SW Klickitat Way, Suite 201 • Seattle, WA 98134
800-553-4453 • mbooks@mountaineersbooks.org • www.mountaineersbooks.org

An independent nonprofit publisher since 1960

 Mountaineers Books is proud to support the Leave No Trace Center for Outdoor Ethics, whose mission is to promote and inspire responsible outdoor recreation through education, research, and partnerships. The Leave No Trace program is focused specifically on human-powered (nonmotorized) recreation. For more information, visit www.lnt.org.